AGAINST EMPIRE

THEOPOLITICAL VISIONS

SERIES EDITORS:

Thomas Heilke
D. Stephen Long
and Debra Dean Murphy

Theopolitical Visions seeks to open up new vistas on public life, hosting fresh conversations between theology and political theory. This series assembles writers who wish to revive theopolitical imagination for the sake of our common good.

Theopolitical Visions hopes to re-source modern imaginations with those ancient traditions in which political theorists were often also theologians. Whether it was Jeremiah's prophetic vision of exiles "seeking the peace of the city," Plato's illuminations on piety and the civic virtues in the Republic, St. Paul's call to "a common life worthy of the Gospel," St. Augustine's beatific vision of the City of God, or the gothic heights of medieval political theology, much of Western thought has found it necessary to think theologically about politics, and to think politically about theology. This series is founded in the hope that the renewal of such mutual illumination might make a genuine contribution to the peace of our cities.

FORTHCOMING VOLUMES:

David Deane
The Matter of the Spirit: How Soteriology Shapes the Moral Life

Steven J. Battin
Intercommunal Ecclesiology: The Church, Salvation, and Intergroup Conflict

Michael L. Budde
The Killer Christ: Notes toward a Disarmed Christianity

AGAINST EMPIRE

Ekklesial Resistance and the Politics of Radical Democracy

MATTHEW T. EGGEMEIER

CASCADE *Books* · Eugene, Oregon

AGAINST EMPIRE
Ekklesial Resistance and the Politics of Radical Democracy

Theopolitical Visions 25

Cascade Books
An Imprint of Wipf and Stock Publishers
199 W. 8th Ave., Suite 3
Eugene, OR 97401

www.wipfandstock.com

PAPERBACK ISBN: 978-1-5326-5786-3
HARDCOVER ISBN: 978-1-5326-5787-0
EBOOK ISBN: 978-1-5326-5788-7

Cataloguing-in-Publication data:

Names: Eggemeier, Matthew T., author.

Title: Against empire : ekklesial resistance and the politics of radical democracy / by Matthew T. Eggemeier.

Description: Eugene, OR : Cascade Books, 2020 | Series: Theopolitical Visions 25 | Includes bibliographical references and index.

Identifiers: ISBN 978-1-5326-5786-3 (paperback) | ISBN 978-1-5326-5787-0 (hardcover) | ISBN 978-1-5326-5788-7 (ebook)

Subjects: LCSH: Christianity and politics. | Democracy—Religious aspects—Christianity. | Christianity and politics—United States.

Classification: BR115.P7 E50 2020 (print) | BR115.P7 E50 (ebook)

Manufactured in the U.S.A.   09/03/20

Contents

Acknowledgments

THIS BOOK HAS BEEN in the works for some time and I have acquired many debts along the way. Thanks are due to my colleagues in the Department of Religious Studies at Holy Cross for their enthusiastic support and encouragement: Alan Avery-Peck, Bill Clark, SJ, Caner Dagli, Gary DeAngelis, Peter Fritz, John Gavin, Karen Guth, Mary Hobgood, Caroline Johnson Hodge, Alice Laffey, Mahri Leonard-Fleckman, Todd Lewis, Benny Liew, Joanne Pierce, Mary Roche, Ginny Ryan, and Mathew Schmalz. A special thanks to my colleague and co-author, Peter Fritz, who read and offered suggestions for improving several of these chapters. I'm grateful for the opportunity to collaborate with such a brilliant theologian and dear friend. Thanks also to Tom Landy, the Director of the McFarland Center for Religion, Ethics, and Culture, for his friendship and ongoing support of my teaching and scholarship at Holy Cross.

Thanks to my colleagues in the Class Dean's office who with tireless support and good humor created the space for me to work on this project while welcoming the class of 2023 to Holy Cross: John Anderson, Robert Bellin, Loren Cass, Tina Chen, Francisco Gago-Jover, Lynn Levesque, Pat Kramer, Shawn Maurer, Patricia Ring, and Stanzi Royden. Thanks as well to the administration of the College of the Holy Cross, especially Philip L. Boroughs, president, and Margaret N. Freije, provost and dean, for granting me a sabbatical during the 2017-2018 academic year and a Batchelor-Ford summer fellowship in 2017 to work on the manuscript. Thanks also are due to the Committee on Faculty Scholarship for funds that paid for professional indexing.

Thanks to Charlie Collier, editor of theology and ethics at Wipf and Stock Publishers, for his enthusiasm for this project; to Jacob Martin for his keen editorial eye; to Matthew Wimer, Calvin Jaffarian, Mike Surber, and Zechariah Mickel for all the work they did to bring this manuscript to press;

and to Thomas Heilke, D. Stephen Long, and Debra Murphy for welcoming this book into the Theopolitical Visions Series.

I'd like to express gratitude to my family for their interest in my scholarship, their steadfast support, and for the ways both large and small that they bring joy to my life: my parents, Tom and Judy Eggemeier, my brothers and their families, Tom, Katie, Libby, and Will Eggemeier and Chris, Sara, Jonah, and Bea Eggemeier. Finally, my deepest appreciation and most heartfelt thanks go to Alice Cheng. Along with our beloved four-legged friend, Libby, Alice has accompanied me with extraordinary patience and boundless compassion as I juggled the demands of being a class dean with several long-term scholarly projects. For this and the countless other graces she bestows upon me daily I am forever grateful.

Introduction

DISILLUSIONMENT WITH LIBERAL DEMOCRACY is widespread throughout the North Atlantic world. What began as a series of upheavals at the grassroots level (the Tea Party and Occupy Wall Street, the alt-right and Black Lives Matter) has captured electoral politics in the United States (Donald Trump and Bernie Sanders) and Europe (Nigel Farage/Boris Johnson and Jeremy Corbyn, Marine Le Pen and Jean-Luc Mélenchon) and has generated a right-wing populist wave around the world (Narendra Modi, Recep Tayyip Erdoğan, Rodrigo Duterte, and Jair Bolsonaro). The dream of a triumphal liberal democratic order, prophesied by Francis Fukuyama in 1989, is faltering, dealt a series of devastating blows by the events of the past several years.[1] It is not only that the end of history has not arrived, but that we are experiencing a near-universal breakdown of stable political consensus with little sense of what lies ahead. The most fitting way to characterize our political situation is to invoke Antonio Gramsci's notion of an "interregnum," which describes a scene in which an old order is dying but a new one has yet to be born.[2]

In view of this scene of generalized crisis, several pressing questions emerge. What has caused this political and cultural upheaval? Does this fatigue with liberal democracy portend the emergence of populist authoritarianism as a dominant political form? Do there exist plausible alternatives to both democracy in its liberal form as well as authoritarian populism?

In the United States, this crisis was generated by the confluence of a set of mutually amplifying forces. The autopsies given in response to the rise of Trumpism have converged around two interpretative positions that offer competing analyses of its genesis.

1. Fukuyama, "End of History," 114.

2. Streeck, "Returned of the Repressed," 165–66; Fraser, "From Progressive Neoliberalism to Trump—and Beyond"; and Fraser, *The Old Is Dying*.

1

The first interpretation posits that the recent ascendancy of authoritarian populism in the United States was driven by economic anxiety created by a series of economic convulsions and neoliberal reforms since the late 1970s. As Thomas Piketty argued in *Capital in the Twenty-First Century*, the brief period of relative postwar equality—itself an aberration in the history of capitalism—has dissolved over the past forty years and given way to an era of extreme inequality.[3] The dual processes of deindustrialization and globalization produced a new relation between capital and labor, deregulation led to the financialization of capitalism, and austerity measures restricted the state's welfare functions. These overlapping economic-political transformations empowered capital, dispossessed the poor, and created a pervasive sense of insecurity among the working class in the United States. Trump appealed to these insecurities at a rhetorical level—and it appears exclusively at a rhetorical level—by promising his voters economic protection through the rejection of new trade deals (TPP) or the renegotiation of old ones (NAFTA), the restoration of economic security by bringing back jobs lost to globalization (coal and steel), and by building a wall at the US-Mexico border to protect (white) Americans from those who threaten their economic security (Mexicans/Latinxs).[4] The data suggests that Trump's populist pitch was effective at appealing to those communities most devastated by neoliberal restructuring over the past forty years. For example, where in 2016 Hillary Clinton won only 472 counties, Trump won 2,584 counties. However, while Clinton's counties accounted for 64 percent of the aggregate share of the United States' GDP, Trump's counties accounted for only 36 percent of the GDP.[5]

The second interpretation, often offered as an alternative to "economic anxiety" as an explanation for emergent forms of authoritarian populism in the United States, points to racism as the primary motivation. Trump, of course, is not unique in his political appeal to racial resentments. Politicians employed the dog-whistle racism of the Southern strategy after the civil rights movement as a means of appealing to disaffected whites.[6] Trump intensified the strategies of Nixon, Reagan, Bush 41, and Clinton by running an amplified dog-whistle—a virtual foghorn—campaign that assembled racial resentments around a renewed focus on "law and order" and the attendant call to imprison, expel, or eliminate those populations

3. Piketty, *Capital in the Twenty-First Century*.

4. Heer, "The Populist Realignment That Never Came."

5. Muro and Liu, "Another Clinton-Trump Divide."

6. López, *Dog Whistle Politics: How Coded Racial Appeals Have Reinvented Racism & Wrecked the Middle Class*.

that pose security threats to the United States. Trump described the cause of Americans' insecurity in racialized terms by invoking fear about Muslim, Latinx, and African-American populations and offered public policies to discipline these populations: a ban on citizens of certain countries from entering the United States (the "Muslim ban"), increased activity around mass deportations and the restriction of funding to sanctuary cities, and a renewed effort to combat "urban crime."[7] Trump's bold appeal to racialized resentments was stunningly successful. Eighty percent of Trump's support was white, and several studies have established a strong correlation between racial resentment toward minoritized populations and support for Trump in 2016.[8]

The narratives about "economic anxiety" and "racial resentment" both possess an explanatory power, but neither is convincing on its own. The loss of economic power and the loss of cultural status do not function as two separate stories, but rather as two parts of the same story in which some Americans feel that the America into which they were born is being replaced with another America.[9] This explains the rhetorical power of Trump's slogan, "Make America Great Again," which simultaneously invokes the restoration of economic security *and* cultural power to white Americans. And while there is also some evidence that fatigue over the war on terror was a contributing factor in the United States, ultimately, as with European populism, economic anxiety and racial resentment serve as the primary drivers.[10]

In the face of this type of emergent political formation, what is to be done? Is the task of the left to defend the norms of liberal democracy and the dominant political order against its authoritarian critics? Or should the left view this crisis as an opportunity to push democracy beyond its liberal frame toward more radical futures? The center-left and center-right have argued that the best that can be done is to hold the center. A wave of analyses has been produced that suggest that the most urgent task is to uphold the norms of liberal democracy (despite its historical entanglement with predatory capitalism, militarism, colonialism, and racial and gendered hierarchies). Those who embrace this strategy argue that

---

7. Coates, "My President Was Black."

8. Lopez, "Trump Won Because of Racial Resentment," and McElwee and McDaniel, "Economic Anxiety Didn't Make People Vote Trump, Racism Did."

9. Roberts, "Are Trump Supporters Driven by Economic Anxiety or Racial Resentment? Yes."

10. Kriner and Shen, "Battlefield Causalities and Ballot Box Defeat."

authoritarian populism is too dangerous a political threat to do anything other than to preserve the liberal political order.[11]

In his work on the rise of "authoritarian populism" under Thatcher and Reagan, Stuart Hall suggests that we draw an entirely different lesson from political crises of this sort. Not dissimilar from our situation, the late 1970s and early 1980s were a period of upheaval in which an old order was unraveling but a new political hegemony had yet to take hold. Similar to Trump, Thatcher and Reagan utilized race, immigration, and crime as "ideological conductor[s]" to generate a "conservative backlash" against the democratic socialist/New Deal political orders. They assembled a new hegemony by stitching together racialized discourses about crime and security threats, nationalism, and neoliberal assaults on the welfare state to reconstruct the political field. The response on the left was reactive and failed to develop a political vision responsive to shifting cultural and political dynamics. The left assumed that the working class would naturally see their interests reflected in the Labour platform and did little to contest the new political formation on the right or to build a new coalition in response to it. Thatcher's observation that her greatest achievement was Tony Blair and New Labour demonstrates the scope of the hegemony established by the right during this period. Clinton and Blair made the judgment that working within the neoliberal-neoconservative hegemony established by Thatcher and Reagan was the only winning strategy during that time. As a result, the left was reduced to airing moralistic critiques of Thatcher (e.g., "Isn't she a cow?"[12]) instead of engaging in the difficult work of comprehending the cultural and political dynamics that made her brand of authoritarian populism possible. We find a similar pattern in response to Trump in which criticism often focuses on his public persona—his impulsiveness, political incorrectness, and crude bigotry—rather than the underlying structural dynamics that make his style of authoritarian populism attractive to many Americans.

As in Hall's time, one of the central questions in our time is whether the left will continue to react to the provocations of Trump or if it will generate a substantive analysis of the dynamics of the hegemony on the right and offer an alternative to it. This task has been taken up by a variety of thinkers on the left for whom the present political task cannot be defined exclusively by the attempt to uphold the norms of the established political order. In different ways, Nancy Fraser, Wendy Brown, Chantal Mouffe, and William Connolly maintain that the left's embrace of centrism and its attempt to

---

11. Mounk, *The People vs. Democracy*; Levitsky and Ziblatt, *How Democracies Die*; and Luce, *The Retreat of Western Liberalism*.

12. Hall, *Hard Road to Renewal*, 273.

manage the neoliberal-neoconservative hegemony more progressively created the conditions that led to our current political crisis.[13] Accordingly, they contend that the constructive political task is to offer a radical approach to democracy that presents a real alternative to both neoliberal-neoconservative hegemony as well as the mutation of this hegemony into new forms of authoritarian populism.

Radical democracy is inclusive of a number of different theoretical and political orientations that range from deliberative (Jürgen Habermas), anarchist (Jacques Rancière), agonistic (Chantal Mouffe, Ernesto Laclau), autonomist (Michael Hardt and Antonio Negri), and decolonial (Enrique Dussel) to fugitive (Sheldon Wolin), feminist (Nancy Fraser), pluralist (William Connolly), and grassroots (Romand Coles and Jeffrey Stout). These diverse trajectories in radical democratic theory differ in important respects but share a common set of political commitments organized around an ethos of radicalization. The "radical" in radical democracy signifies the attempt to return democracy to its "roots" (*radix*) and to a politics that returns power or rule (*kratos*) to the people (*demos*).

This formal ethos of radicalization is rooted in a set of overlapping concerns. First, radical democratic theorists view dominant forms of democracy in the North Atlantic world as significantly weakened by representative and constitutional systems that delimit the power of the people and disincentivize their political engagement. They respond to this situation by advocating for more egalitarian approaches to power-sharing through horizontal forms of democratic participation (Hardt and Negri), localism (Wolin), or community-based organizations (Stout, Coles).[14] Second, proponents of radical democracy criticize the proximity that exists both ideologically and historically between capitalism and liberal democracy. Neoliberals defend this proximity and argue that the economic freedom guaranteed by capitalism is the prerequisite for the political freedom of democracy. For instance, for Milton Friedman, the free market represents an ideal form of democracy insofar as it represents the synthesis of the individual free choice of all participants. Against neoliberalism, radical democratic theorists argue that an inverse relationship exists between capitalism and democracy, and so it follows that economic democracy is needed to support

13. Fraser, "The End of Progressive Neoliberalism"; Fraser, "From Progressive Neoliberalism to Trump—and Beyond"; Brown, "Apocalyptic Populism"; Mouffe, "America in Populist Times: An Interview with Chantal Mouffe"; Mouffe, *For a Left Populism*; Connolly, "Trump, the Working Class, and Fascist Rhetoric"; and Connolly, *Aspirational Fascism*.

14. Wolin, *Democracy Incorporated*, 2.

the political project of democracy.[15] Finally, radical democratic theory is committed to pluralism in two respects. For radical democratic theorists, democracy constitutes an open, unfinished project for which there exists no specific or predetermined political form. Ernesto Laclau has argued that radical democracy supports a "plurality of ways of radicalization" and so when "*radical* democracy" is invoked it "cannot be attached to any a priori fixed institutional formula."[16] A second area where radical democratic theorists focus on the importance of pluralism is in relation to the project of coalition building. In contrast to reductionistic forms of leftist politics that view class struggle as the exclusive site of resistance and organization, radical democratic theorists affirm the need for a plurality of sites, forms, and coalitions of resistance to the dominant social order.[17]

Even though a deep commitment to pluralism is a fundamental mark of radical democracy, the significance of religion for political struggle often has been dismissed by radical democratic theorists. For instance, Michael Hardt and Antonio Negri observe without argumentation that "today there is not even the illusion of a transcendent God" and that "every metaphysical tradition is now completely worn out."[18] Hardt and Negri flatly reject transcendence and claim that the "multitude" has "dissolved" transcendence and "recuperated its power."[19] For them, immanent struggle among diverse constituencies represents the sole basis for an authentic contemporary politics. Accordingly, they evaluate religious belief as a backward remnant from the past that blocks the path to an emancipatory politics of immanence.[20] Chantal Mouffe offers a slightly different approach to the relation between radical politics and religion but similarly marginalizes religion from participation in radical democratic projects. Mouffe observes,

> Far from being an irreversible event, the democratic revolution may come under threat and has to be defended. The rise of various forms of religious fundamentalism of Christian origin in the USA and the resurgence of Catholic integrism in France indicate that the danger does not come solely from outside but

15. Friedman, *Capitalism and Freedom*, 8.

16. Laclau, "Future of Radical Democracy," 261, and Laclau, "Glimpsing the Future," 295. Emphasis original.

17. Laclau, "Structure, History, and the Political," 203.

18. Hardt and Negri, *Empire*, 157 and 368. See Connolly's critique of this in *Pluralism*, 150.

19. Hardt and Negri, *Empire*, 157.

20. There has been significant work in theology that has engaged Hardt and Negri's framework and demonstrated how it might serve as a guide for radical Christian politics. See, for instance, Rieger and Pui-lan, *Occupy Religion*.

also from our tradition. The relegation of religion to the private sphere, which we now have to make Muslims accept, was only imposed with great difficulty upon the Christian Church and is still not completely accomplished.[21]

Mouffe expresses legitimate fears about how religious extremism threatens democracy, but her approach is worrisome insofar as she groups all religious identities together and then proceeds to relegate these identities to the private realm. In this regard, the foundational commitment to pluralism and difference is extended everywhere but to the religious realm. Within Mouffe's framework, religious persons are invited to participate in radical democratic politics only if they leave their religious commitments at the door.[22]

Of course, nonreligious radical democratic theorists like Jürgen Habermas, William Connolly, Romand Coles, and Jeffrey Stout have made something of a postsecular turn by contesting the secularist commitments of the left.[23] In his recent work, Habermas has argued that democracy relies on pre-political and often religious sources for its vitality and that if these sources are eliminated from civil society or hijacked by dogmatic and exclusionary voices it will lead to disastrous results. He maintains that the Judeo-Christian tradition in the West is the wellspring from which the commitment to morality, solidarity, human rights, and democracy emerged and "up to this day there is no alternative to it."[24] He thus calls for a renewed engagement with religious traditions precisely because these traditions offer critical sources of moral and political formation not readily available elsewhere in civil society.

If there has been something of a turn to religion by several radical democratic theorists, there has been an analogous turn in contemporary Christian political theology to radical democracy. Stanley Hauerwas's turn to radical democratic theory has occupied a central role in these debates. In his response to Jeffrey Stout's criticisms in *Democracy and Tradition*, in which Stout argued that Hauerwas's theology had been corrosive to American politics and fueled resentment toward public life among Christians, Hauerwas invoked the radical democratic politics of Sheldon Wolin and Romand

21. Mouffe, *Return of the Political*, 132.

22. See Jones, "Liberation Theology and 'Democratic Futures,'" 281ff. Mouffe seems to have softened her position recently in "Religion, Liberal Democracy, and Citizenship."

23. Connolly, *Why I Am Not a Secularist*; Ratzinger and Habermas, *Dialectics of Secularization*; Habermas, *Between Naturalism and Religion*; Coles, *Beyond Gated Politics*; Hauerwas and Coles, *Christianity, Democracy, and the Radical Ordinary*; Stout, *Blessed Are the Organized*; and Stout, *Democracy and Tradition*.

24. See Habermas, *Religion and Rationality*, 149.

Coles as models for political engagement.[25] Hauerwas's engagement with radical democratic theory has received a great deal of attention in recent debates, in part, because this engagement appears to represent a significant departure from his perceived aversion to non-ekklesial politics. However, it is important to note here that Elisabeth Schüssler Fiorenza and Cornel West advocated for the alignment of Christianity with radical democratic politics long before Hauerwas's engagement with the work of Wolin and Coles. Furthermore, Schüssler Fiorenza and West's engagement with radical democratic theory emerges out of other trajectories in American political theology, offering a very different understanding of the relationship between Christian theology and radical democracy. Specifically, where Hauerwas views American forms of radical democratic theory as well suited to support a peaceable politics of ekklesial witness, Schüssler Fiorenza and West view radical democracy as a means for Christians to witness to an intersectional approach to justice for the oppressed and marginalized.

In *Against Empire*, we examine the relationship between radical democracy and political theology by analyzing four approaches to ekklesial politics. The approach to ekklesia adopted here is rooted in a retrieval of the original political meaning of the Greek word *ekklesia* as a political assembly.[26] The political theologians analyzed in this work describe plural forms of ekklesia as radical democratic spaces of resistance to multiple forms of oppression that include racism, sexism, poverty, and political violence: the black church (Cornel West), the ekklesia of wo/men (Elisabeth Schüssler Fiorenza), the church of the poor (Ignacio Ellacuría and Jon Sobrino), and the peaceable church (Stanley Hauerwas).[27]

---

25. Hauerwas has offered several responses to Stout's criticisms, first in "Postscript: A Response to Jeff Stout's *Democracy and Tradition*" (*Performing the Faith*, 215–42), then in his explicit engagement with the radical democratic theory of Wolin in "Democratic Time: Lessons Learned from Yoder and Wolin" (*State of the University*, 147–64), and finally in the essays in *Christianity, Democracy, and the Radical Ordinary*.

26. Elisabeth Schüssler Fiorenza observes, "The Greek word *ekklesia* is usually translated as 'church,' although the English word church derives from the Greek word *kyriake*—belonging to the lord/master/father/husband. Accordingly, the translation of *ekklesia* as 'church' is misleading. *Ekklesia* is best rendered as 'democratic assembly/congress of full citizens.'" Schüssler Fiorenza, *Sharing Her Word*, 112; see also *But She Said*, 128. John Howard Yoder makes a similar point in *Revolutionary Christian Citizenship*.

27. This book does not directly engage political Augustinians who often identify with some form of radical democratic politics. Luke Bretherton's work in *Resurrecting Democracy* is a prominent example of this type of Augustinian engagement with radical democratic politics. The primary reason that we do not examine Bretherton's work is that the focus of his ethnographic work is England and *Against Empire* focuses on the work of political theologians in North America.

In distinctive ways, West, Schüssler Fiorenza, Ellacuría/Sobrino, and Hauerwas call for the mobilization of ekklesial communities toward a politics of resistance to empire. However, because their work remains largely disconnected, a theoretical task of this work is to examine the links that exist between these diverse forms of ekklesial resistance. The work of coalition building is a central area of focus in radical democratic theory. The question of how to link diverse ideological movements—from feminists, antiracists, and environmentalists to antiwar activists and critics of capitalism—is central to the attempt to theorize a radical politics that moves beyond the class-based politics of Marxism. Ernesto Laclau and Chantal Mouffe refer to this project of coalition building as establishing chains of equivalence among different social movements. They maintain that the goal of radical politics is to establish areas of commonality among diverse groups so that no single struggle takes precedence over another and each group retains its distinctive focus and autonomy. Equivalence does not eliminate difference but rather establishes connections between movements that occupy a similar position of subordination in society.[28] Radical democratic theorists establish equivalence between these diverse movements by producing a common "antagonist" that generates a "we" or coalition of resistance to the dominant social order. For instance, Mouffe contends that within the contemporary economic-political configuration this "we" should take form as radical democratic citizenship.[29]

Against Empire argues that a chain of equivalence exists between black prophetic thought, feminist theology, Latin American liberation theology, and peaceable theology. These political theologies differ in their specific focus but share common resistance to neoliberalism, nationalism, and militarism as networks of power that intersect with racism, sexism, and neo-colonialism to form what they refer to as "empire." In Laclau and Mouffe's terminology, "empire" represents the common antagonist for these political theologies. The "we," or the positive link between black prophetic thought, feminist theology, Latin American liberation theology, and peaceable theology, is established through their commitment to "radical democracy."

This book offers an intervention in contemporary debates in political theology in three ways. First, on the face of it, it seems that there is more that divides West, Schüssler Fiorenza, Ellacuría/Sobrino, and Hauerwas than unites them. Schüssler Fiorenza famously criticized Latin American liberation theology for its blindness to patriarchy, West has publicly aired his disagreement with Hauerwas on the nature of prophetic Christianity,

28. Mouffe, *Chantal Mouffe*, 140.
29. Mouffe, *Chantal Mouffe*, 140.

and if pressed Hauerwas would likely view the projects of Schüssler Fiorenza, Ellacuría/Sobrino, and West as subtle forms of "neo-neo-neo-Con-
stantianism" that relinquish the distinctiveness of Christian witness for the
sake of political relevance. Despite these tensions, *Against Empire* performs
the task of drawing together these Christian thinkers as a diverse theo-
political assemblage that prioritizes critical resistance to empire alongside
a constructive commitment to the politics of radical democracy. In this
regard, it fulfills the pluralist mandate of radical democracy by bringing
together diverse voices based on shared opposition to oppressive political formations. Thus, while the standard narrative would suggest that the
peaceable theology of Hauerwas has little to do with the feminist theology of Schüssler Fiorenza, I demonstrate that they share overlapping and
strategic concerns, even as they differ over specific theological and political
questions. There exist various ways of stating this point, but the argument
made in this book is that ekklesia should aspire to be a site of radical democratic pluralism that affirms difference and seeks to generate commonalities
amid these differences. Second, the postsecular turn has been dominated
by nonreligious philosophers reflecting on the role of religion in the public sphere. *Against Empire* focuses on how religious thinkers, specifically
political theologians, describe the contribution that Christianity makes to
a radical democratic politics. Because of the central role that the Moral
Majority and the religious right have played in conservative politics in the
United States, it is commonplace to view religion as the exclusive province
of the right. However, this judgment is entirely inaccurate, particularly
when viewed within the long stretch of American history, in which the
religious left played a central role in the abolitionist, suffragist, labor, and
civil rights movements. The political theologians examined in subsequent
chapters attempt to revive this tradition by occupying the contested ground
between secular leftists and the religious right by challenging both those
who wish to purge religion from the public sphere and Christians who use
the gospel to support the politics of empire.

Finally, this work contributes to the postsecular conversation between
political theologians and radical democratic theorists by exploring the distinctively Christian forms of radical democratic politics generated through
this engagement. The political theologians examined in this work creatively
refigure their approaches to politics based on their dialogue with radical
democratic theory. But a productive postsecular dialogue should result in
mutual transformation. Accordingly, it is essential to attend to the process
by which theologians challenge and reconfigure radical democracy based
on their retrieval of the radical politics of the Christian tradition. For example, radical democratic theorists have tended to focus on the economic

dimension of empire and have deemphasized or, at the very least, failed to foreground concerns about structural racism and militarism. In relation to these issues, political theologians challenge and supplement secular forms of radical democratic theory. Cornel West develops a distinctive approach to radical democratic politics by challenging secular radical democratic theory based on his extensive retrieval of the antiracist politics of black Christianity and the black prophetic tradition. Similarly, Hauerwas's retrieval of the peaceable politics of the Christian church serves as a corrective to radical democratic theorists' failure to confront adequately the political violence of the nation-state. Constructively, each political theologian examined produces a distinctive approach to radical democracy drawn from the resources of the Christian tradition: prophetic-pragmatist (West), feminist-transnational (Schüssler Fiorenza), liberative-populist (Ellacuría, Sobrino), and peaceable-postliberal (Hauerwas).

The argument of *Against Empire* unfolds in six chapters. The first chapter analyzes two political formations—neoliberalism and neoconservatism. In the introductory comments, we emphasized the unique challenges posed to democracy by the ascendency of authoritarian populism, but it is important to emphasize that the emergence of this political formation was made possible by the antidemocratic effects of the neoliberal-neoconservative hegemony. This chapter aims to analyze the underlying logic of neoliberalism and neoconservatism, to describe the complicated relationship between them, and to trace the mutation of neoliberal-neoconservative hegemony into new forms of populist authoritarianism.

The second chapter provides an overview of significant trajectories in contemporary radical democratic theory by charting how radical democratic theorists have conceptualized their approach to politics. We focus on two dominant approaches in radical democratic theory: an institutional-reformist approach that calls for the need to radicalize existing democratic institutions (Ernesto Laclau, Chantal Mouffe, and Jeffrey Stout) and a withdrawal-radicalist approach that advocates for the need to create political movements and communities that exist outside of traditional democratic structures and institutions (Michael Hardt, Antonio Negri, and Sheldon Wolin). The chapter serves two important purposes within the overall argument of *Against Empire*. First, it offers an introduction to the radical democratic theorists that influence the political theologians examined in subsequent chapters. Wolin is by far the most significant conversation partner for these theologians, but Hardt and Negri, Laclau and Mouffe, Stout, and Coles also influence their approaches to Christian politics. Because the tendency in North American political theology has been to reduce radical democracy to Wolin's criticisms of liberalism, it is important to broaden our understanding of the politics of radical democracy and the diverse ways in which it has shaped Christian political engagement. This chapter, then, seeks to provide a thicker description than is often offered in theological commentary by contextualizing important currents in contemporary radical democratic theory.

In addition, chapter 2 focuses on the withdrawal-engagement debate in radical democratic theory and traces how it plays out in post-Marxist and postliberal discourse. A central debate in radical democratic theory is whether politics should emerge in civil society at a distance from liberal democratic structures that have been captured by neoliberalism and neoconservatism, or if it should attempt to reform these democratic structures and push them beyond their liberal frame toward a more radical space. This withdrawal-engagement debate plays out among political theologians as well, with some locating their politics at a distance from traditional institutional forms (Latin American liberation theology, feminist theology, peaceable theology) and others advocating for a more direct, but no less critical, engagement with existing political institutions (black prophetic thought).

We organize the next four chapters into two subgroups. The third and fourth chapters examine the relationship between political theology and radical democracy as a pluralist form of coalition building. Black prophetic thought and feminist theology approach ekklesial politics by examining the interconnection between racism, sexism, capitalism, and militarism. Cornel West and Elisabeth Schüssler Fiorenza adopt a pragmatic and praxis-oriented approach to the relation between Christianity and radical democracy that focuses on the retrieval of radical resources in the Christian tradition as a means of cultivating a broad-based, pluralist form of political resistance to empire that includes Christians, members of other religious traditions, as well as nonreligious persons.[30]

The fifth and sixth chapters examine the more focused confrontation with capitalism and political violence in the work of Latin American liberation and peaceable theologians. Although the primary object of criticism differs, Latin American liberation theology and peaceable theology share the common diagnosis that capitalism (Latin American liberation theology) and political violence (peaceable theology) represent forms of idolatry that demand the sacrifice of victims to subsist. In contrast to the work of West and Schüssler Fiorenza, Ellacuría, Sobrino, and Hauerwas approach radical democratic politics by way of a robust set of christological and ecclesiological commitments rooted in the defense of the poor (Ellacuría/Sobrino) and

---

30. Importantly, both Schüssler Fiorenza and West maintain that democracy is an internal norm of Christianity. See Schüssler Fiorenza, *Power of the Word*, 7, and West, *Prophesy Deliverance!*, 18ff. and 91ff.

the witness to peace in a violent world (Hauerwas). Furthermore, Ellacuría, Sobrino, and Hauerwas only reservedly approach democratic politics, so that where Ellacuría and Sobrino offer unrelenting criticisms of Western democracy's entanglement with imperialism and capitalism, Hauerwas evinces a staunch opposition to liberal democracy due to its association with secularism and political violence. Despite this opposition to imperialist (Ellacuría/Sobrino) and liberal (Hauerwas) forms of democracy, Ellacuría, Sobrino, and Hauerwas provide openings for an *ad hoc* Christian engagement with radical democracy to the extent that this alliance serves their more basic Christian commitment to the option for the poor (Ellacuría/Sobrino) and peaceable witness (Hauerwas).

The conclusion reflects on the future, specifically on the possibility of a radical democratic future in the face of political formations that not only block the expansion of democracy (neoliberal-neoconservative hegemony) but also attempt to retrench its achievements (authoritarian populism). It is argued that in response to each of these political formations Christians should enter the field of political struggle by engaging in a radical democratic politics of resistance to empire.

CHAPTER 1

Empire[1]

OURS IS A PERIOD of profound social upheaval. A prominent symptom of this upheaval is the collapse of public confidence in the normative institutions of liberal democracy. This crisis has been gestating for many years, but two events crystallize the contradictions of our cultural moment: the political and military debacles in Afghanistan (2001) and Iraq (2003) and the financial crisis of 2007–2008. Combined with the exploitation of long-simmering racial resentments for political gain, the fundamental crises of the military and financial institutions of the liberal order created an opening for the emergence of the right-wing populist movements now ascendant.

As discussed in the introduction, these political formations have attempted to undermine features of democracy that block the expansion of plutocratic and racist policies. In the United States, the dominant response among critics to the ascendancy of Trump's authoritarian populism has been to diagnose it as an aberration and to argue that if he is defeated in 2020 order will be restored to the American political system. This interpretation is either extraordinarily naïve about American history or a disingenuous attempt to pathologize an individual rather than criticize an entire system. In either scenario, the result is to inoculate the American public from a confrontation with the economic, political, and cultural contradictions that have generated the politics of exclusion now on the rise in the United States.

1. We use the term "empire" here in a manner consistent with its use by the Christian thinkers examined in chapters 3–6. While they differ with regard to particulars, West, Schüssler Fiorenza, Ellacuría/Sobrino, and Hauerwas all approach empire as the exercise of American power as figured by neoliberal globalization, US militarism, and a conservative cultural politics. The broader literature on "empire" and "imperialism" is extensive. Generally, there exist four streams of analysis of empire: the New Left, cultural, Marxist, and postcolonial. For historiographical overviews of these trajectories, see Kramer, "Power and Connection"; Wolfe, "History and Imperialism"; and Cooper, "Decolonizing Situations."

In this chapter, we examine these conditions by criticizing the neoliberal-neoconservative hegemony that preceded this authoritarian populist formation and prepared the ground for its ascendency. We first analyze neoliberalism as the dominant economic-political formation in our world today that serves to economize both the political and cultural realm and that has generated a widespread sense of nihilism among certain demographics in the United States. Second, we examine neoconservatism as an ideological and policy orientation that plays a critical role in the maintenance of a neoliberal order via both its cultural politics as well as foreign policy commitments. We conclude the chapter by examining the alliance of neoliberalism and neoconservatism with religious conservativism as well as its mutation into an authoritarian populist and white nationalist politics under Trump.

While Trump and Trumpism will be invoked throughout this chapter, it should be emphasized that the object of critique remains a broader set of political formations: the neoliberal-neoconservative hegemony and its mutation into a new form of authoritarian populism on the right. Trump is a vulgar carrier and a weak representative of this political orientation. As a result, he might very well be defeated in 2020. If he is defeated this will not represent the end of the brand of authoritarian populism ascendant on the right. There will be successors to the movement, and these successors will be far more disciplined and effective than Trump at practicing the revanchist politics that deliver plutocratic victories to economic elites and racialized grievance politics to the base.[2] It is important, therefore, to grapple with authoritarian populism as not just the politics of an individual (Trump) but as a broader and more durable political movement that seeks to undermine egalitarian aspirations in society.

Neoliberalism

Neoliberalism is notoriously difficult to define, even to the point that some scholars claim that it is merely a label for "whatever I do not like." It is true that the particular term "neoliberalism" is generally used by its critics from the left side of the political spectrum. Also, given that in the United States, "liberalism" tends to be associated with "leftist," social welfare policies, it is difficult to figure how neoliberalism was originally a product of the political right. Even worse, those who espouse the political-economic ethos that others call neoliberalism refuse to use that name. But when properly defined

2. See, for instance, Barkan, "The Fascism to Come."

neoliberalism offers an important lens through which to analyze the dominant political and cultural formation in our world today.[3]

The history of neoliberalism is remarkable. In dramatic fashion, neoliberalism emerged from an obscure economic ideology debated among members of the Mont Pelerin Society in the 1940s and 1950s to the common-sense understanding of much of the world in the twenty-first century.[4] Neoliberalism has spread in distinctive ways in response to the concrete demands of diverse political and economic situations. In the global South, neoliberalism spread through the use of military/political force (foreign interventions, juntas, and the disciplining of populations by the police/military) and economic coercion (structural adjustment policies).[5] In the late 1970s and early 1980s the method in the North Atlantic world was ideological and pursued by equating freedom with free markets, by disseminating best practices in nonprofit sectors, and by subtly transforming law, the state, and the human subject to accord with market dictates.[6] A bipartisan consensus—one that counts among its advocates Thatcher and Blair, Reagan and Clinton, Bush and Obama—has supported this project.

In academic literature, neoliberalism is often depicted as an approach to political economy that favors market reform through privatization, deregulation, free trade, cuts to spending, and tax cuts. This is an accurate characterization of some features of neoliberal policy but fails to describe its revolutionary force as a project that aspires to transform the state, the human person, as well as common sense in society. A number of different frameworks have been offered to interpret the meaning of neoliberalism for democracy and society, but two recommend themselves for our purposes: Marxist and Foucauldian.[7]

The standard Marxist interpretation, exemplified in the work of David Harvey, interprets neoliberalism as a modification of classical economic liberalism and as the latest phase in the history of capitalism. In *A Brief History*

3. Some of this discussion of neoliberalism is taken from my book on the topic, coauthored by Peter Fritz, titled *Send Lazarus*.

4. Mirowski, *Never Let a Serious Crisis Go to Waste*.

5. Brown, *Undoing the Demos*, 151.

6. As Wendy Brown describes the process, "Law was mobilized to privatize state industries, seduce foreign ownership and investment, secure profit retention, and reduce trade restrictions. On the other hand, popular assemblies and Left parties were outlawed, strikes were criminalized, unions banned." One exception is the way in which neoliberalism spread in response to natural and human-made disasters. See Klein, *The Shock Doctrine*.

7. The autonomist Marxism of Michael Hardt and Antonio Negri—which will be examined below—is a third approach that combines Marxism with features of Foucault's and Deleuze's work.

of Neoliberalism, Harvey argues that we can "interpret neoliberalization either as a utopian project to realize a theoretical design for the reorganization of international capitalism or as a political project to re-establish the conditions for capital accumulation and to restore the power of economic elites." He maintains that the political project of restoring wealth and power has dominated in practice, while the utopian project of reorganizing capitalism has worked "as a system of justification or legitimation."[8] When the theoretical principles of the utopian project have conflicted with concrete policies that would restore class power, the utopian principles have been abandoned. At its core, Harvey maintains, neoliberalism is a political-economic project motivated by class warfare, even as it is legitimated as a utopian project designed to enhance human flourishing "by liberating individual entrepreneurial freedoms and skills within an institutional framework characterized by strong private property rights, free markets, and free trade."[9]

For Harvey, neoliberalism represents a new formation of capitalism or a new stage of economic liberalism that attacks any structures that delimit the power of capital. Neoliberalism came to prominence as a project to turn back the Keynesian tide—a regulatory state, progressive taxation, labor controls, and the redistribution of wealth by a welfare state—and restore power to the capital class. And while neoliberalism developed in distinctive ways in response to political and economic pressures in different parts of the world, all of these manifestations held one feature in common: they were a response to the capital accumulation crisis of the 1970s which threatened the economic and political power of the ruling class. In response to this crisis, economic and political elites orchestrated a multifaceted assault on domestic and international structures that restricted the power of capital and obstructed the process of accumulation. Harvey observes that "the ruling class wasn't omniscient but they recognized that there were a number of fronts on which they had to struggle: the ideological front, the political front, and above all they had struggle to curb the power of labor by whatever means possible. Out of this merged a political project which I would call neoliberalism."[10] The result of these efforts was dramatic: the rapid ascendancy of neoliberalism, which gained state power throughout the North Atlantic world in the 1980s and achieved global hegemony in the 1990s through a variety of means, but most importantly, the efforts of international economic bodies—the IMF, World Bank, and WTO.

8. Harvey, *Brief History of Neoliberalism*, 19.
9. Harvey, *Brief History of Neoliberalism*, 2.
10. Harvey, "Neoliberalism Is a Political Project."

In the North Atlantic world—particularly England and the United States—the fundamental strategy for dissemination has been ideological. Neoliberals recognized that because it would be impossible to convince the general public to consent to a political-economic project whose aim was to restore class power it would be necessary to cultivate consent by appealing to deeply held convictions and values "of regional or national traditions."[11] Neoliberals chose well when they seized on individual freedom as the ideal to sell neoliberal reforms to a popular base. Freedom not only represents a core value of Western civilization but also served as an ideological bulwark against twentieth-century totalitarian regimes: fascism, socialism, and communism. And while individual freedom served as the ideological rallying cry, neoliberals labored to draw the link between individual freedom and private property rights, free markets, and free trade. And because the regulatory and distributive power of the state was cast as a threat to these institutional arrangements, neoliberalism emerged "as the exclusive guarantor of freedom."[12]

Harvey highlights the role that the ideological struggle played in the ascendancy of neoliberalism, noting that Hayek recognized that the battle of ideas would be critical, and it would take some time to defeat all forms of political-economic organization opposed to the neoliberal vision of economic freedom (communism, socialism, Keynesianism).[13] Neoliberals used corporations, the media, and institutions of civil society (schools, churches, and professional associations) to wage this battle. The Business Roundtable was created, and alongside the Chamber of Commerce of the United States, it served as the lobbying arm of the neoliberal movement. Additionally, Harvey contends that because neoliberals viewed universities as inhospitable terrain for the cultivation and dissemination of their ideas, they funded a series of think tanks that could serve as neoliberal laboratories: the Manhattan Institute, the Heritage Foundation, and the American Enterprise Institute. These think tanks were given the task of producing "serious technical and empirical studies and political-philosophical arguments broadly in support of neoliberal policies."[14]

All of these efforts—lobbying efforts, think tanks, and media—contributed to neoliberalism's ideological success, but Harvey maintains that the political victories of Thatcher and Reagan proved decisive. He observes, "Once the state apparatus made the neoliberal turn it could use its powers

11. Harvey, *Brief History of Neoliberalism*, 39.
12. Harvey, *Brief History of Neoliberalism*, 40.
13. Harvey, *Brief History of Neoliberalism*, 21.
14. Harvey, *Brief History of Neoliberalism*, 44.

of persuasion, co-optation, bribery, and threat to maintain the climate of consent necessary to perpetuate its power. This was Thatcher's and Reagan's particular forte."[15] Reagan and Thatcher utilized political power to discipline and transform the population through neoliberal policies and offered reforms that emerged out of the same playbook: attack and dismantle unions (coal mining with Thatcher and air traffic control with Reagan), reduce taxes, privatize and deregulate industries, and cut the welfare state. These policies had a twofold effect. First, they served the interest of their corporate donors and supporters and created enormous wealth for the capital class. Second, these policies disciplined the population and began to remake social relations and reform expectations about the function of government. In this, Thatcher and Reagan made decisive progress toward the neoliberal goal of producing new subjects. As Thatcher famously quipped, "Economics are the method . . . but the object is to change the soul."[16]

The cultivation of democratic consent to these policies tells only a part of the story, even if it represents the dominant piece of it in the North Atlantic world. Harvey argues that the creation or manipulation of crises—natural disasters, coups, wars, and financial crises—were often the central means by which neoliberal policies were imposed on society.[17] In the United States and Europe financial crises have led to austerity measures that further facilitated the neoliberal reorganization of society. It was in the global South, however, that the creation, management, and manipulation of crises served as the primary method for neoliberalization. Harvey points to Chile in 1973 and Iraq in 2003 as bookends of the process through which military intervention served as a precursor to neoliberalization. He observes of Chile and Argentina in the 1970s that the imposition of neoliberalism "was swift, brutal, and sure: a military coup backed by the traditional upper class (as well as by the US government), followed by the fierce repression of all solidarities created within the labour and urban social movements which had so threatened their power."[18] Harvey describes Iraq in similar terms, observing that after the "Shock and Awe" campaign in 2003 the United States went about the business of establishing a "capitalist dream" in the Middle East.[19] Paul Bremer, the head of the Coalition Provisional Authority in Iraq, dictated orders to reorganize the economy of Iraq, which included the privatization

15. Harvey, *Brief History of Neoliberalism*, 40.

16. Quoted in Harvey, *Brief History of Neoliberalism*, 23.

17. This is the central thesis of Naomi Klein's *Shock Doctrine: The Rise of Disaster Capitalism*. See also Loewenstein, *Disaster Capitalism: Making a Killing Out of Catastrophe*.

18. Harvey, *Brief History of Neoliberalism*, 39.

19. Harvey, *Brief History of Neoliberalism*, 7.

of public enterprises, the elimination of trade barriers, the disciplining of the labor market, a regressive "flat tax," the full repatriation of foreign profits, and full ownership of Iraqi businesses by foreign firms.[20] This represented a wish list for neoliberals insofar as these orders secured economic "freedoms" for Iraqis "that reflect[ed] the interests of private property owners, businesses, multinational corporations, and financial capital."[21]

As evidenced by Chile and Iraq, military force represented a dominant means of establishing neoliberalism internationally. But the more common practice was to employ the power of the IMF and the World Bank to impose neoliberal policies on countries in the global South.[22] This tactic was created in response to the economic crisis in Mexico when Mexico defaulted on its debt in the early 1980s. The Reagan administration pushed the US Treasury and the IMF to roll over the debt, but to do so only on the condition that Mexico would undertake neoliberal reforms. This policy served to protect New York bankers from Mexico's debt default and to disseminate neoliberal policies in the developing world. These so-called structural adjustment policies, which were created in response to the crisis in Mexico, soon became the standard practice of the IMF and World Bank (which, by the mid-1980s, had purged itself of any "Keynesian influence"). In return for debt rescheduling, structural adjustment policies required indebted countries to cut welfare, disband unions, and privatize public industries.[23] Thus, while debt represents a very different type of crisis than military intervention, it nevertheless served as a potent means for imposing neoliberal policy on less developed countries.

This brief narrative gives a sense of how neoliberalism spread globally over the past forty years. Once installed, the neoliberal approach to statecraft followed a fairly standard set of policies: privatization, deregulation, the reduction or elimination of social spending (welfare, health care, education, pensions), liberalization of trade, tax cuts, and the eradication of unions as well as other organized forms of solidarity.[24] For Harvey, the end result of these policies—across geographical and sociopolitical diversity—has been to restore class power for global elites.

20. Harvey, *Brief History of Neoliberalism*, 6.

21. Harvey, *Brief History of Neoliberalism*, 7.

22. Overall, Harvey observes, "Almost all states, from those newly minted after the collapse of the Soviet Union to old-style social democracies and welfare states such as New Zealand and Sweden, have embraced, sometimes voluntarily and sometimes in response to coercive pressures, some version of neoliberal theory" (*Brief History of Neoliberalism*, 3).

23. Harvey, *Brief History of Neoliberalism*, 29.

24. Harvey, *Brief History of Neoliberalism*, 65.

With this characterization of neoliberalism, we return to the tension between the utopian and political dimensions of the neoliberal project. According to Harvey, the utopian interpretation posits that the freedom of the market—of businesses, corporations, and individual entrepreneurial initiative—is critical to wealth creation, which eventually increases the living standards and well-being of everyone. As Harvey puts it, "Under the assumption that 'a rising tide lifts all boats,' or of 'trickle down,' neoliberal theory holds that the elimination of poverty (both domestically and worldwide) can best be secured through free markets and free trade." But while neoliberalism presents itself as a utopian political-economic project that institutes policies that will benefit everyone, "the main substantive achievement of neoliberalization . . . has been to redistribute, rather than to generate, wealth and income."[25] Harvey rejects the utopian justification of neoliberalism as an ideological facade and claims that on the basis of its material effects neoliberalism is a class warfare project and not a poverty alleviation program or a set of political-economic reforms oriented toward enhancing human life. For Harvey, the situation is clear: neoliberalism is an intensified capitalist assault on the values of equality and justice, the commons, the environment, and democracy.

The second approach to neoliberalism follows Foucault's 1979 lectures, *The Birth of Biopolitics*, and theorizes it as a modification of political liberalism. This framework differs with the Marxist interpretation in that it approaches neoliberalism not as an intensification of economic liberalism but instead as a new form of liberal governmentality. According to Foucault, where classical liberalism protected the market from government in order to allow society to benefit from market exchange, neoliberalism advocates for an interventionist state that introduces market principles into every sphere of life. Following Foucault, Wendy Brown argues that neoliberalism serves as a reality principle for our world: "Neoliberalism governs as sophisticated common sense, a reality principle remaking institutions and human beings everywhere it settles, nestles, and gains affirmation."[26] The ontological valence of this description of neoliberalism should be emphasized, because it points to the fact that neoliberalism is not simply an economic theory or a set of public policies but more deeply a way of structuring all of reality as market competition—or what, following Foucault, Brown terms a pervasive "political rationality."[27]

25. Harvey, *Brief History of Neoliberalism*, 159.

26. Brown, *Undoing the Demos*, 35.

27. Brown, "Sacrificial Citizenship," 12.

In *Undoing the Demos* Brown turns to Barack Obama's presidency to demonstrate the powerful hold that neoliberalism has on political common sense in the United States. At the beginning of Obama's second term, in a matter of weeks he delivered two major policy speeches, "We the People" and the State of the Union, in which he focused on those "left out of the American dream by virtue of class, race, sexuality, gender, disability, or immigration status."[28] While Obama's first term was characterized by a series of compromises with Republicans and centrist Democrats, these speeches appeared to announce a return to his progressive roots. Obama called for the protection of Medicare, immigration reform, progressive tax reform, the development of clean energy, and the elimination of sexual discrimination and domestic violence.[29] These policies represented the agenda many on the left expected from Obama when he was elected in 2008. But just beneath the surface Brown detects a tension in Obama's renewed progressive rhetoric. Obama justified these policies not on the basis of their moral rectitude or because they comported with the egalitarian aspirations of American democracy. Instead, he pitched these policies to the American public on the basis of their capacity to make the United States economically competitive. According to Brown, Obama is essentially arguing that "clean energy would keep us competitive—'as long as countries like China keep going all-in on clean energy, so must we' . . . Immigration reform will 'harness the talents and ingenuity of striving, hopeful immigrants' and attract 'the highly skilled entrepreneurs and engineers that will help create jobs and grow our economy.' Economic growth would also result 'when our wives, mothers and daughters can live their lives free from discrimination . . . and . . . fear of domestic violence.'"[30] At the level of Obama's rhetoric, the fight for equality and justice is not an end itself, but rather a means to achieve the end of economic growth and competitiveness.

For Brown, this episode summarizes the core truth of neoliberalism as it relates to the state: "Economic growth has become the end and legitimation of government."[31] The state now functions like a firm and shares with it similar priorities: competitive positioning and a healthy credit rating. Brown observes, "Other ends—from sustainable production practices to worker justice—are pursued insofar as they contribute to this end."[32] Many firms view it as an effective business decision or as a strategic marketing

28. Brown, *Undoing the Demos*, 24.
29. Brown, *Undoing the Demos*, 24–25.
30. Brown, *Undoing the Demos*, 25–26.
31. Brown, *Undoing the Demos*, 26.
32. Brown, *Undoing the Demos*, 27.

exercise to engage in fair trade and green business practices not because
of their concern for the rights of global workers or the threat of climate
change but because they see an opportunity to appeal to a niche market
and increase profit and shareholder value. Obama's speeches depart only
minimally from the strategies of modern business firms in this regard. Both
the state and the firm are committed to justice and sustainability, but not
as "ends in themselves."[33] These commitments are valuable to the extent
that they create economic growth and stock/credit rating health. Brown
concludes that Obama's speeches indicate the degree to which political discourse has become so marinated in neoliberal reason that the "goals of the
world's oldest democracy led by a justice-minded president in the twenty-
first century" have been reduced to "attracting investors and developing an
adequately remunerated skilled workforce."[34]

If Obama's speeches disclose the manner in which progressive ideals
are often couched in and motivated by the neoliberal values of economic
growth and competitive advantage, the presidency of Trump depicts a scene
of the near wholesale co-optation of democracy and the state by neoliberalism. The election of a businessman with no political experience and little
knowledge of the US Constitution, democratic norms and procedures, and
judicial principles reveals the extent to which neoliberalism has captured
the political rationality of citizens and recast the function of the state in
primarily economic terms.

Trump's presidency represents the most thoroughgoing economization
of the state to date, as evidenced by a few examples. First, Trump's constant
refrain that previous politicians have made "bad deals"—NAFTA, the Paris
climate accord, the Iran nuclear deal, and so on—and that as a businessper-
son he is uniquely qualified to replace these deals with better deals betrays
the extent to which he and many Americans view democracy as little more
than business conduct. This approach extends to his tendency to punish critics as those on the losing side of the deal. Business conduct mandates that
there are winners and losers and as a "good CEO, he will reward supporters and punish detractors or competitors, whether these are cities or states,
groups or individuals, nations or international organizations."[35]

Second, Trump's presidency reveals the degree to which neoliberalism has successfully recast the political realm as an unhelpful and un-
necessary intrusion into the market. An approach to politics rooted in a
commitment to equality, fairness, and social justice is at best viewed as

33. Brown, *Undoing the Demos*, 27.
34. Brown, *Undoing the Demos*, 25.
35. Brown, "Apocalyptic Populism."

hostile to competition and unfettered market logic and at worst as lead-ing to "tyrannical social justice programs and totalitarianism." Politics is viewed by neoliberals as a hindrance or obstacle to market rule. In this sense, Trump's call to "drain the swamp" was not a demand to restrain Wall Street or restrict the influence of monied interests on politics. Instead, it was a call to purge Washington of politicians, to "get politics and politi-cians out of politics." Politics now recast in market terms is best left to businesspeople, who need not be bothered by democratic procedures and norms as they focus exclusively on generating economic growth. As Brown suggests, this is an anti-political posture and not an anti-state posture that opposes a view of politics in which the state regulates commerce, provides labor protections, redistributes wealth, and so on. Neoliberalism is often presented as anti-state tout court, opposed to it because it disrupts the sov-ereign logic of the market. But this is inaccurate, because it fails to present the entire picture. Neoliberalism approves of a state that intervenes on be-half of markets.[36] Trump, as a quintessential neoliberal, is perfectly happy to employ the power of the state to eliminate those things that present a barrier to a friendly business climate: "regulations, procedures, checks and balances, separation of powers, internal opposition or disloyalty, demands for transparency, an independent press."[37]

These two examples describe the ways that the election of Trump points to the economization of politics through which the fundamental commitments of democracy (freedom, equality, popular sovereignty) are transposed into market terms (economic freedom, inequality, market sov-ereignty). But in addition to this assault on the fundamentals of democracy, the Trump administration has implemented what amounts to an undiluted neoliberal policy package: elimination of labor protections, deregulation, cuts to public funding for education, health care, and the arts, removal of the United States from climate treaties, and enormous tax cuts for the af-fluent.[38] Trump, as a businessman, is the embodiment of a neoliberalization of politics just as his policies serve to deepen and solidify the processes of neoliberalization that led to his presidency.

The examples of Obama and Trump raise a number of important points about the relation between neoliberalism and the state. First, as noted above, the neoliberalization of the state is a bipartisan affair. The foundational neoliberal commitment to economic growth represents the

36. Jamie Peck calls this feature of neoliberalism "a self-contradictory form of regulation-in-denial." Peck, *Constructions of Neoliberal Reason*, xiii.

37. Brown, "Apocalyptic Populism."

38. Bessner and Sparke, "Don't Let His Trade Policy Fool You."

normative basis for consensus in American politics. Democrats and Republicans inflect their neoliberalism differently, with Democrats offering what Nancy Fraser describes as a "progressive" form by blending a politics of cultural emancipation (feminism, multiculturalism, and LGBTQ rights) with financialization and neoliberal economic policies, and Republicans increasingly offering ethno-racial, reactionary, and punitive forms.[39] But they converge in their view of the state as a firm that is responsive to the market above all else. This reality lies beneath the oft-voiced sentiment that while there exist two political parties in the United States, both pledge their most basic allegiance to the party of Wall Street. Related to this point, neoliberalism transforms the scope of the state's responsibilities from a political to an economic register. As Brown notes, the state is now viewed as a firm and so its strategic focus is to facilitate economic growth and attract investors. Traditional concerns about equality, justice, and the well-being of citizens are now demoted, viewed as marginal to the primary responsibility of government, and useful only as instruments that can be deployed to sell neoliberal economic policies to the public.[40]

Despite their different approaches to neoliberalism, Harvey and Brown converge in their assessment that neoliberalism represents a frontal attack on democracy.[41] Harvey claims that the antidemocratic consequences of neoliberalism are most evident in its attempt to unleash the power of capital from the countervailing forces of the state, labor, and other structures of accountability and control. The liberation of capital from these limiting forces not only deepens inequality in society but also intensifies the coordination between financial elites and political representatives.[42] Brown also criticizes neoliberalism for intensifying inequality in society and creating conditions for democracy to devolve into plutocracy.[43] However, Brown argues that neoliberalism's challenge to democracy is both deeper and broader than the consolidation of political and economic power by elites. Neoliberalism's effects are not limited to the corporate takeover of liberal democratic institutions; its influence has spilled over into the spheres of education, culture, and everyday life. Thus, even if it were possible to roll back neoliberal public policies, the effects of neoliberalism would continue to undo democracy because of its presence in diverse social fields, from business and law to

39. See Fraser, "The End of Progressive Neoliberalism."

40. Brown, *Undoing the Demos*, 40.

41. MacLean, *Democracy in Chains*, and Slobodian, *Globalists*.

42. Harvey concludes that it is the "profoundly anti-democratic nature of neoliberalism backed by the authoritarianism of the neoconservatives that should surely be the main focus of political struggle" (*Brief History of Neoliberalism*, 205).

43. Brown, *Undoing the Demos*, 17.

education and cultural life.[44] This is why Brown refers to neoliberalism as a reality principle: "With neoliberalism, the market becomes *the*, rather than *a* site of veridiction *and* becomes so for every arena and type of human activity."[45] Because "the market is itself true" it "represents the true form of all activity." It follows that insofar as persons are rational they "accept these truths" and thereby accept "reality." To refuse to act in accordance with economic rationality in every domain of existence is to refuse reality. As a result, any proposal to organize the political order or even one's life according to principles that differ from economic rationality is quite simply unintelligible within the neoliberal imaginary.[46]

Establishing the market as truth, furthermore, provides cover for a set of actions that sacrifice the needs of citizens, those expelled from the neoliberal order, and the natural world itself. As Brown details in *Undoing the Demos* and a subsequent essay, "Sacrificial Citizenship," neoliberalism's austerity policies require the shared sacrifice of citizens in order to ensure the national economy's competitiveness, the health of its credit rating, and continued economic growth.[47] However, in contrast to Reagan's discourse on trickle-down economics, which made the promise to citizens that economic growth would benefit everyone, neoliberalism dispenses entirely with this pretense and instead demands insecurity, austerity, and sacrifice as the price for economic growth.[48] In addition to the elimination of job security, pensions, and public benefits in the name of economic competitiveness, globally neoliberalism authorizes the sacrifice of the environment, refugees, and the global poor. These represent the "collateral casualties" whose destruction and stunted lives are viewed as the price paid for development and progress.[49]

Neoliberalism, as a pervasive reality principle, deepens these interconnected crises in three ways. First, the public policy commitments of neoliberalism—deregulation, privatization, cuts to social spending—intensify the destruction of the natural world and exacerbate the social suffering of those judged as expendable within the neoliberal order. Second, neoliberalism largely has succeeded in reducing the human person to human capital whose sole responsibility is to compete with other human capital over scarce

44. Brown, *Undoing the Demos*, 201–2.

45. Brown, *Undoing the Demos*, 67. Emphasis original.

46. Brown, *Undoing the Demos*, 68.

47. Brown, *Undoing the Demos*, 213.

48. Brown, *Undoing the Demos*, 83, and Brown, "Sacrificial Citizenship," 9.

49. Slavoj Žižek, for instance, argues that slum-dwellers constitute the "systematically generated 'living dead' of global capitalism." Žižek, *Parallax View*, 425. See also Žižek, *Living in the End Times*, 456.

resources, the effect of which is that inequality now becomes "legitimate, even normative, in every sphere."[50] Life, now viewed as competition without remainder, inevitably generates winners and losers, and the losers deserve the punishment they receive. Furthermore, because one's status in a neoliberal order is always precarious, threatened by downgrades, unemployment, and even expulsion, individuals are pressured constantly to pursue their individual self-interest in every activity. Because it is too great a risk to one's future to pursue those activities that do not directly enhance one's own value, individuals find it almost impossible to do anything other than passively deliver their lives over to the sovereignty of the market. Third, because neoliberalism constitutes a wholesale attack on the social—the common good, social solidarity, social welfare—it undermines many of the protections and securities necessary for a stable social order.[51] In the absence of economic protections, many Americans have become increasingly attracted to authoritarian and antidemocratic leaders who promise protection from economic insecurity and racialized threats by castigating globalization, immigration, and multiculturalism.[52] A felt sense of despair or nihilism lurks just beneath the surface of much of the populist anger on the right, which threatens to enact revenge on the perceived causes of its own insecurity and impotence. Wendy Brown has described the convergence between the experience of precarity generated by neoliberal reforms and the intensification of racist and misogynist impulses among those disempowered by these reforms as a form of apocalyptic populism. This strain of populism is apocalyptic because it would rather destroy the entire political and social order than experience further disempowerment.[53] In this regard, Trump's chaotic approach to politics serves as a fitting expression of the mood of a significant segment in the American electorate.

50. Brown, *Undoing the Demos*, 64 and 38.

51. This argument is developed at length by Wendy Brown in *In the Ruins of Neoliberalism*.

52. Brown, "Interview: Where the Fires Are." As we noted above, a number of authors have explored the link between neoliberalism and political commitments that are antidemocratic (MacLean, *Democracy in Chains*; Slobodian, *Globalists*). Additionally, there have been a number of important studies published on the relationship between neoliberalism and neofascism—see Connolly, *Aspirational Fascism*; Brown, "Apocalyptic Populism"; Brown, "Neoliberalism's Frankenstein"; and Brown, *In the Ruins of Neoliberalism*.

53. Brown, "Apocalyptic Populism."

NEOCONSERVATISM

Following the American military interventions in Afghanistan and Iraq a public debate emerged concerning the question of whether these actions represented a new form of imperialism. Discussion of American imperialism, often dismissed as a "rhetorical excess" of the left, became a focal point of the critical conversation in the 2000s.[54] Those who defended the exercise of American power either celebrated the reemergence of American empire (Niall Ferguson) or employed the euphemism "hegemony" to defend the actions of the United States (Robert Kagan).[55] Critics on both the right (Andrew Bacevich) and the left (Noam Chomsky) argued that the neoconservative policy orientation of the Bush administration in the Middle East had merely intensified the imperialist orientation of American foreign policy.[56] American history is replete with violent foreign interventions, from settler colonialism and the transatlantic slave trade to the Monroe Doctrine and Cold War interventionism in Asia and Latin America. But from the 1980s to the present the neoconservative movement has served as the primary ideological system of legitimation of American interventionism abroad. And while the politics of American empire should not be viewed as coterminous with it, neoconservatism has represented the most bellicose carrier of the militarist features of American foreign policy over the past forty years.

As a distinctive approach to domestic and foreign policy neoconservatism has been a central fixture of the political hegemony on the right since Reagan and, much like neoliberalism, has influenced the policy commitments of politicians on both the left and the right. In what follows we will analyze neoconservatism as a potent manifestation of the politics of American empire that entails both domestic and foreign policy commitments.

As an ideological orientation, neoconservatism is notoriously difficult to define because it lacks ideological uniformity and has shifted over time from a movement on the left with a domestic focus in the 1960s to a movement on the right with a foreign policy focus in the 2000s.[57] In broad terms, neoconservatism proposes a vision for the state in which the state sets a moral orientation for the world by utilizing political persuasion, legal enforcement, and military force to achieve its strategic aims.[58] Neoconservatism emerged in the 1960s as a reaction to the New Left—the civil rights

54. Rosen, *Empire and Dissent*, 1.

55. Ferguson, *Colossus*, and Kagan, *Of Paradise and Power*.

56. Bacevich, *American Empire*, and Chomsky, *Hegemony or Survival*.

57. Vaïsse, *Neoconservatism*, 4.

58. See Brown, "American Nightmare."

movement, the feminist movement, and the antiwar movement—and evaluated this new political formation as fundamentally anti-American.[59] Jeane Kirkpatrick, the secretary of state during the Reagan administration, summarized this view when she argued that the New Left represented a frontal attack on American exceptionalism by claiming that "the United States was immoral—a 'sick society' guilty of racism, materialism, imperialism, and murder of Third World people in Vietnam."[60] Representative of the broader neoconservative response, Norman Podhoretz's response to the New Left called for a "new nationalism" rooted in the fierce embrace of the moral purpose of the nation, a renewed effort to patrol cultural and national borders, a defense of the traditional family, and a celebration the values of Judeo-Christian civilization.[61] While neoconservative opposition to multiculturalism and feminism is not distinctive in relation to the broader conservative movement, these commitments represent a critical piece of the broader neoconservative vision (a vision that often overlaps with the aims of neoliberalism).[62]

As an ideological orientation, neoconservatism became a flashpoint in the 2000s because of its foreign policy commitments, but the neoconservative response to the New Left in the 1970s and 1980s represents an important episode in its history and demonstrates that for neoconservatives the relationship between domestic and foreign policy is linked inextricably. Neoconservatives argue that absent the cultivation of healthy nationalism and patriotism at home it is impossible to sustain the project of American global hegemony abroad. In this regard, the left's demand for deeper racial and gender equality and its criticisms of American militarism posed a unique threat to the neoconservative vision for America.

The foreign policy vision of neoconservatism is rooted in several convictions about the American political experiment. First, and most importantly, neoconservatism proposes a distinctive understanding of the American state and its democratic form as exceptional in relation to other forms of political organization. Second, as a result of this commitment to American exceptionalism, neoconservatives maintain that the United States has been commissioned with the task of disseminating American values—particularly liberal democracy and capitalism—around the world. Neoconservatives describe a stark situation in which either the United States imposes its "universality" on the rest of the world or the world faces "global

59. Drolet, *American Neoconservatism*, 3.

60. Kirkpatrick, "Neoconservatism as a Response to the Counter-Culture," 239.

61. Podhoretz, *Present Danger*, 86–89.

62. On this, see Cooper, *Family Values*.

barbarism."[63] Third, neoconservatives link this messianic project of democratizing the world to a patriotic civil religion that views the role of the state in
moral or even theological terms. At a foreign-policy level, neoconservative
ideology organizes all of reality in terms of those committed to freedom,
human rights, and democracy (the United States and its allies) and those
who oppose these ideals (communists/socialists, terrorists, and other dissidents). Fourth, neoconservatism combines an idealist's moralism about the
significance of democracy in the world with a realist's commitment to the exercise of power. Thus, neoconservatism prefers military solutions to peaceful
negotiations and posits that the only way to provide security for Americans is
by using both indirect (in Latin America in the 1970s and 1980s) and direct
force (in the Middle East from the 1980s to the present).[64]

As noted above, the sequence of events between 9/11 and the war on
terror reignited the debate surrounding the politics of American empire.
Much of the criticism focused on the problematic character of the neoconservative response to the attacks of 9/11. But to focus on neoconservatism
as an aberration from an otherwise democratizing American foreign policy only obscures the continuities that exist between neoconservatism and
the imperialist aims of the mainstream of US foreign policy. Greg Grandin, for instance, has argued that neoconservatism "is just the highly self-
conscious core of a broader consensus that reaches out well beyond the Republican Party to capture ideologue and pragmatist alike."[65] Robert Kagan,
a prominent neoconservative, makes a similar point in "Neocon Nation:
Neoconservatism, c. 1776," when he observes that the basic orientation of
neoconservatism is consistent with the foreign policy ideals of the broad
sweep of the American tradition.[66] According to Kagan, neoconservative
ideology is committed to "a potent moralism and idealism in world affairs,
a belief in America's exceptional role as a promoter of the principles of liberty and democracy, a belief in the preservation of American primacy and
in the exercise of power, including military power, as a tool for defending
and advancing moralistic and idealistic causes." For Kagan, this orientation is consistent with the mainstream of American foreign policy from
its founding in 1776. Of course, it is true that important differences exist
between realists, liberal internationalists, and neoconservatives in terms

63. MacDonald, *Overreach*, 101.

64. Bacevich, *New American Militarism*, 73–79.

65. Grandin, *Kissinger's Shadow*, 191. Others, like Tony Smith and Samuel Moyn,
maintain that liberal internationalism veers dangerously close to the imperialism
of neoconservatism. See Smith, *A Pact with the Devil*, and Moyn, "Beyond Liberal
Internationalism."

66. Kagan, "Neocon Nation: Neoconservatism, c. 1776."

of their willingness to intervene in foreign countries and to use military force. But the fact remains that a bipartisan consensus—which stretches from Kissinger's realism and Albright's liberal internationalism to the neoconservatism of the Bush administration and the liberal realism of the Obama administration—has supported a model of the state rooted in the defense of American exceptionalism and the commitment to the project of American hegemony. This bipartisan consensus is animated by what Andrew Bacevich describes as the foundational commitment of post–World War II American foreign policy to expand the "American imperium" and to create "an open and integrated international order on the principles of democratic capitalism, with the United States as the ultimate guarantor of order and enforcer of norms."[67] According to the Congressional Research Service, more than 80 percent of the United States' interventions abroad since 1946 have taken place after 1989. This means that American interventionism abroad reached its peak during the period in which neoconservatism dominated American foreign policy.[68]

As with neoliberalism, neoconservatism is rooted in a reality principle that offers a vision of world affairs and America's role within it. Henry Kissinger described the reality principle of American empire in 1963, and this same principle would be echoed by an official in the George W. Bush administration in 2004. Kissinger observed, "In the decades ahead, the West will have to lift its sights to encompass a more embracing concept of reality . . . There are two kinds of realists: those who manipulate facts and those who create them. The West requires nothing so much as men able to create their own reality." This statement about the power of a state to create reality is eerily bookmarked by a comment made by a Bush administration official, presumably Karl Rove, about the status of the United States as a global hegemon. The official observed that the United States is an "empire now . . . we create our own reality. And while you're studying that reality—judiciously, as you will—we'll act again, creating other new realities, which you can study too, and that's how things will sort out. We're history's actors."[69]

American foreign policy from Kissinger to Bush and Obama has viewed its task as remaking reality in its own image and likeness.[70] The

67. Bacevich, *American Empire*, 3.

68. Moyn and Wertheim, "The Infinity War."

69. Grandin, *Kissinger's Shadow*, 15.

70. Jon Sobrino characterizes this feature of American foreign policy as a metaphysical commitment, observing of the United States, "The empire decides where and when time is something real, what dates should be recognized as benchmarks in human history. It says: 'Time is real when we say it is.' And the reason for this is ultimately metaphysical: 'Reality is us.'" Sobrino, *Where Is God?*, xi. See also Sobrino, *No Salvation*, 18.

principle that animates this approach to the world is American exceptionalism, which claims that the United States is a nation providentially ordained by God to spread freedom and democracy around the world. Madeline Albright, the secretary of state during the Clinton administration, summarized the logic of this position when she argued that "if we have to use force, it is because we are America; we are the indispensable nation. We stand tall and we see further than other countries into the future."[71] This view serves to legitimate the United States' exercise of power and its use of military force and, as the historical record demonstrates, often blinds the United States to the real motivations that drive its foreign policy.[72]

In view of this ideological distortion of America's motivations, it is unsurprising that democracy is a central area of contradiction within neoconservative ideology and practice. The purported aim of neoconservatism is to defend democracy against its domestic detractors and foreign enemies, but the effects of its cultural politics and military interventions have served to undermine democracy.

In the domestic realm, the assessment of democracy published by Samuel Huntington and his coauthors in 1975 is representative of the contradictions of this approach to democracy. In *The Crisis of Democracy* Huntington responded to civil rights and feminist movements of the 1960s and 1970s by arguing that these movements threatened democracy by demanding too much democratization. He warned that the emergence of a "democratic surge" in the 1960s had made the United States "ungovernable" by allowing democracy to spill over from a system of governance monitored by elites into the cultural life of the United States.[73] Huntington argued that the proper response to the "excess of democracy" demanded by labor, feminism, and African-Americans was to advocate for "a greater degree of moderation in democracy." Huntington's evaluation of grassroots democratic movements is representative of a broader conservative attempt to undermine feminism, civil rights, affirmative action, and the LGBTQ movement in the name of the traditional family, a commitment to nationalism, and the

---

71. Quoted in the preface to Bacevich, *American Empire*.

72. In the name of democratization neoconservatives have invoked states of "exception" that override democratic protections and procedures and have created both "spaces of exception" geographically (Guantanamo Bay; Iraq) as well as "practices of exception" (coercive interrogation, torture, and now drones). More broadly on this contradiction in American foreign policy, see Niebuhr, *The Irony of American History*, and Bacevich, *The Limits of Power*. Both Drolet and Maria Ryan make this argument: neoconservatism employs an idealist cover to legitimate its desire for American hegemony in a unipolar world. See Drolet, *American Neoconservatism*, and Ryan, *Neoconservatism and the New American Century*.

73. Crozier, Huntington, and Watanuki, *The Crisis of Democracy*.

cultivation of a patriotic culture. For neoconservatives, democracy should be affirmed if it serves to defend established hierarchies and to reanimate "aristocratic and traditional values" in society, while those forms of democratic action that upend established orders should be viewed as "excessive" and perceived as a threat to a stable democratic order.

Similarly, while the putative aim of neoconservatism in foreign policy is democratization, neoconservatives evaluate only certain forms of democracy as legitimate. Those forms of democracy not responsive to the political and economic interests of the United States have been dismissed as illegitimate by the architects of neoconservative foreign policy. Furthermore, these architects have supported diverse methods for ousting democracies not responsive to American interests. It is true, of course, that this project of political delegitimization predates neoconservatism and represented a central plank of American foreign policy during the Cold War, as evidenced in the clandestine coup d'états orchestrated by the United States to oust democratically elected leaders in Iran (1953), Guatemala (1954), and Chile (1973).[74] Henry Kissinger summarized the antidemocratic orientation of US foreign policy when he argued that supporting the Chilean coup in 1973 was necessary because "the issues" at stake "are much too important for the Chilean voters to be left to decide for themselves."[75] The Reagan administration intensified this policy in Latin America in the 1980s, and the Bush administration pursued this policy in the Middle East in the 2000s.[76]

Trump has breathed new life into elements of neoconservatism after its collapse in the aftermath of the wars in Afghanistan and Iraq. He has subtly rehabilitated its foreign policy commitments by rejecting the "old rationale of liberal world-ordering" and reanimating it by "tap[ping] existing reserves of cultural chauvinism and nationalist animus."[77] Where neoconservatives advocate for a muscular and interventionist foreign policy rooted in the ideological commitment to freedom and democracy, Trump has little interest in democratic norms or democracy promotion abroad. Trump instead draws close to the nativist, Jacksonian tradition of American foreign policy in which self-interest serves as the motivation and rationale for American foreign policy.[78] Trump justifies the use of military power to assert American

74. This is not to mention the countless other military interventions, covert operations, and clandestine coup d'états—Nicaragua, El Salvador, Haiti, and now the broader Middle East. On this point, see Kinzer, *Overthrow*.

75. Quoted in Williams, *Understanding U.S.-Latin America Relations*, 222.

76. Grandin, *Empire's Workshop*.

77. Wertheim, "Return of the Neocons."

78. Mead, "The Jacksonian Revolt: American Populism and the Liberal Order"; Mead, "Donald Trump's Jacksonian Revolt"; Clarke and Ricketts, "Donald Trump and American Foreign Policy."

dominance around the world in order to take things from other countries. The façade of exceptionalism as the ideological framework that legitimates US militarism has been eliminated, and so what remains is a commitment to the use of brute military force to intimidate and subdue foreign (and domestic) enemies. To this end, Trump has increased the American military budget in 2019 to $750 billion (a record level in the past seventy years). Additionally, even as neoconservatives have distanced themselves from the vulgar racism and xenophobia of Trumpism, subtle forms of "dog whistle" xenophobia and Islamophobia have long served as central features of neoconservative rhetoric. Trump draws from the xenophobic cultural climate cultivated by neoconservatives after 9/11 even as his appeal to belligerent nationalism has become more overt in its Islamophobic rhetoric.[79]

Overall, Trump has reframed the rhetoric of neoconservatism and reset its foreign policy vision while retaining the neoconservative hostility to (racialized) foreign threats and its commitment to American military hegemony.

POLITICAL ASSEMBLAGES

The relationship between neoliberalism and neoconservatism is complicated insofar as neoliberals celebrate open markets and free trade and so have little patience for the nationalistic preoccupation with borders and territorial boundaries of proponents of neoconservatism. Furthermore, where neoliberalism severs bonds of mutuality and solidarity by placing the logic of competitive individualism at the center of society, neoconservatism constructs an order of values rooted in a commitment to the traditional family and nationalism. Remarkably, despite these differences, advocates of neoliberalism and neoconservatism have entered into a strategic alliance over the past forty years to form a durable political coalition on the right.

In view of these tensions, the question that remains is how these ideologies converge to form a political bloc on the right. A number of theorists (Stuart Hall, Sheldon Wolin, David Harvey, and Wendy Brown) have offered an interpretation of this relation that suggests, in effect, that what neoliberalism tears apart with its commitment to competitive individualism, neoconservatism restores with its focus on family, tradition, and nation.[80]

79. Heilbrunn, "Neocons Paved the Way for Trump."

80. Wendy Brown has expressed two different views of the relationship in her writings. First, in "American Nightmare," Brown offered a version of the approach proposed by Hall, Harvey, and Wolin by arguing that neoliberalism and neoconservatism serve as two distinct political rationalities that converge as a politics of de-democratization. But, more recently, in *In the Ruins of Neoliberalism*, Brown endorses Cooper's analysis by

A second approach has been offered by Melinda Cooper in *Family Values: Between Neoliberalism and the New Social Conservatism*, in which she argues that neoliberals entered into a strategic alliance with neoconservatives in defense of the traditional family as a means of offering a moral critique of the welfare state.[81] On this reading, social conservatives emphasized the importance of a small, limited government because it allowed them to preserve the white patriarchal family structure and its gendered and racial hierarchies. Neoliberals, like Gary Becker and Milton Friedman, valued the family for different reasons, viewing it as a means to justify small, limited government (at least with respect to taxation, redistribution, and welfare). Neoliberals did not share the specific moral critique of welfare offered by neoconservatives, but they viewed the alliance with the neoconservatives as an opportunity to replace the welfare state with the private sector. The defense of the family thus emerged as a practical means of extending the broader project of privatization. Third, as noted above, historically, neoconservatism has provided neoliberalism with the ideological framework needed to justify the use of military power to open up new markets around the world. While American military intervention on behalf of capitalism precedes the neoconservative-neoliberal connection (for example, with the coups in Iran in 1953 and Guatemala in 1954), scholars point to Chile in 1973 and Iraq in 2003 as the bookends of the military imposition of neoliberalism on foreign countries.[82]

William Connolly offers a position that converges with these three previous accounts. But he supplements them by analyzing the assemblage on the right through the lens of affect theory.[83] Connolly maintains that the most effective means to comprehend the political assemblage on the right is to shift from a discursive mode of analysis to a description of how these ideologies operate at a visceral level. He argues that political commitments interact as a set of affective sensibilities that resonate together and which have produced an assemblage on the right comprised of neoliberals, neoconservatives/militarists, and religious/social conservatives.

According to Connolly, an assemblage allows groups with divergent beliefs to build a coalition around a set of resonating "spiritual dispositions"

---

analyzing Hayek's assault on social justice and the regulatory and distributive functions of the state as linked to his defense of traditional morality. More broadly, see Harvey, *Spaces of Global Capitalism*, 58. See also Wolin, *Democracy Incorporated*.

81. Cooper, *Family Values*.

82. Harvey, *Brief History of Neoliberalism*, 7.

83. Connolly, *Christianity and Capitalism*; Connolly, *Aspirational Fascism*; and Connolly, "Trump, the Working Class, and Fascist Rhetoric," 34n1.

that operate at an affective register.[84] He observes, "When one part of the assemblage pushes beliefs with which you do not identify, you minimize or ignore the difference because they too exude the existential resentment with which your military dogma, economic creed or religious faith is infused."[85] The connective tissue that stitches these ideologies together is an affective ethos of existential resentment directed toward those groups perceived to be enemies of the free market, American exceptionalism, and Christian exclusivism. Connolly observes, "Today resentment against cultural diversity, economic egalitarianism, and the future whirl together in the same resonance machine. That is why its participants identify similar targets of hatred and marginalization, such as gay marriage; women who seek equal status in work, family and business; secularists, those of Islamic faith, and atheists; and African American residents of the inner city who do not appreciate the abstract beauty of cowboy capitalism."[86] Thus, while neoliberals, proponents of American military hegemony, and religious conservatives have different creedal commitments that generate different targets of resentment, they coalesce to form a "resonance machine" that assembles the right on the basis of overlapping grievances.

Melinda Cooper's analysis provides one example of this phenomenon through which divergent movements align to dismantle welfare. Another example is the way in which the Christian belief in the providence of God and the neoliberal belief in the sovereignty of the market resonate at an affective level despite their divergence at a discursive level. This resonance plays out in terms of how these ideologies approach the future. Evangelical Christians interpret history apocalyptically and insist that the time that remains for the earth is brief. It follows that political and economic projects devoted to environmental protection and sustainability are viewed as a waste of time. Neoliberals adopt a contemporocentric view of the world in which the enhancement of immediate market value is the central imperative of their economic activity. Accordingly, the sacrifice of the planet for short-term financial gains is a rational course of action. In this example, each bloc rejects responsibility for the future for a different reason, but their overlapping commitments resonate in such a way that they create a larger and more powerful political assemblage than would be possible on the basis of the particular interests of each individual bloc. Connolly observes,

84. Connolly, "Ethos of Democratization," 168–69, and Connolly, *Christianity and Capitalism*, 8.

85. Connolly, "Wolin, Superpower, and Christianity."

86. Connolly, "Evangelical-Capitalist Resonance Machine," 879.

The bellicosity and corresponding sense of extreme entitlement of those consumed by economic greed *reverberates* with the transcendental resentment of those visualizing the righteous violence of Christ. Across these modest differentiations, the two parties are bound by similar orientations to the future. One party discounts its responsibilities to the future of the earth to vindicate extreme economic entitlement now, while the other does so to prepare for the day of judgment against nonbelievers. These electrical charges resonate back and forth, generating a political machine much more potent than the aggregation of its parts.[87]

This resonance machine also includes nationalists, neoconservatives, and militarists who align with the evangelical-capitalist political assemblage to enact revenge on the nonbelievers of their respective religions: those who fail to believe in Jesus Christ (secular persons, Muslims, etc.), those who fail to believe in the sovereignty of the market (socialists, leftists, etc.), and those who resist the hegemony of American power (terrorists, dissidents, etc.).

Of course, authoritarian populism has reset the basic contours of this resonance machine by reorienting its evangelical-capitalist elements in a more overtly authoritarian and explicitly white nationalist direction. Trump's 2016 coalition included the traditional elements of a Republican coalition, but the white working-class constituency without a college degree proved decisive in elevating him to the presidency. Just as religious conservatives (particularly, white evangelicals) served as the populist base for the neoliberal-neoconservative hegemony, these same voters (Trump received 81 percent of the white evangelical vote in 2016) as well as other disaffected white working-class voters now serve as the base for the reconfiguration of the evangelical-capitalist resonance machine under Trump (an astonishing 57 percent of Trump's overall vote in 2016 came from whites without a college degree).[88] Trump's capacity to draw overwhelming support from the evangelical Christian base is one of the most remarkable features of this assemblage insofar as Trump seems to embody the very antithesis of the commitment to moral rectitude and family values that Christian evangelicals promote.[89]

As noted in the introduction, Trump has assembled this constituency on the basis of economic and status anxieties. Neoliberal policy has eroded the economic fortunes of significant segments of the working class in the

87. Connolly, *Christianity and Capitalism*, 48–49.

88. McGill, "The Trump Bloc," and Kriner and Shen, "Battlefield Causalities and Ballot Box Defeat."

89. Brown, *In the Ruins of Neoliberalism*, 10. See also Brown, "Neoliberalism's Frankenstein," 75.

United States (and, more broadly, this same population throughout the Euro-Atlantic world). Branko Milanovic's analysis of the distribution of wealth generated by globalization from 1988 to 2008 provides a clear representation of this reality. He observes that while there was relative growth among the poor in Africa and South Asia (up to 50 percent growth), the emerging middle class in China, India, and Brazil (up to 80 percent growth), and an explosion of wealth among the top 1 percent globally, the middle class in the developed world has grown a grand total of 1 percent over the past thirty years. Virtually every segment of the global population has benefited from globalization.[90] Concretely, from 1935 to 1960 the average income in the United States doubled, and from 1960 to 1985 it doubled again.[91] Since the 1980s income growth has been flat for the middle class, while the emerging middle class in the global South and the global 1 percent have experienced extraordinary gains. While this is a direct result of globalization (free trade policies), the situation has been amplified by other neoliberal policies: privatization and financialization (the repeal of Glass-Steagall), tax cuts, cuts to social spending, and attacks on redistribution and unionization.

At least two responses are possible to this situation. As we shall see, the response on the left is to demand a political confrontation between the working class and economic elites and to push for more extensive redistribution of wealth, greater economic protections for the working class (e.g., labor unions), and the expansion of educational opportunities for working-class constituencies. Authoritarian populism offers an alternative by advocating for economic nationalism ("America first") and the creation of antagonisms between the white working class and workers in emerging economies (Mexico, China, etc.). Trump's specific style of populism has transformed the rhetoric of neoliberalism by arguing that the state should use its power to serve the needs of the working class (renegotiating free-trade agreements and restoring manufacturing in the United States). During the first three years of his presidency, his signature legislative achievement was a tax reform bill that delivered a tax cut that almost exclusively benefited the top 1 percent. And while Trump has escalated trade wars with China and other countries by imposing tariffs on a variety of goods, there is little evidence that his other policy priorities have uplifted the working-class populations who have been devastated by more than forty years of deindustrialization, globalization, and neoliberal policies.

In lieu of transformative economic policies, Trump offered charged white nationalist rhetoric coupled with the promise of violence toward racialized domestic and foreign enemies. Wendy Brown observes that this is

90. Milanovic, *Global Inequality*.
91. Mounk, *People vs. Democracy*, 154.

how contemporary forms of authoritarian populism function: "Right-wing and plutocratic politicians can get away with doing nothing substantive for their constituencies as long as they verbally anoint their wounds with anti-immigrant, anti-Black, and anti-globalization rhetoric."[92] Trump's politics are rooted in the dog-whistle racism of the Southern strategy but take form as a more overtly racist, sexist, anti-immigrant, and Islamophobic set of attacks on vulnerable populations. This is evident in terms of the pivotal role that Trump played in amplifying the birther controversy (which raised questions about Obama's birthplace and thereby suggested that he is "foreign" and "unfit" for the presidency); his campaign announcement in 2015 in which he proclaimed that Mexicans were rapists and criminals and as such represented a grave threat to (white) Americans; his claim that he is entitled to grab women by "the pussy"; and the deployment of white male grievance politics in response to the accusation of sexual assault by Brett Kavanaugh (for example, Trump proclaimed that "it's a very scary time for young men in America" in response to the accusation of sexual assault made by Christine Blasey Ford).

The policy objectives he offered on the campaign trail follow directly from this overt use of racism to assemble a white base of supporters, from the call to "build a wall" to enacting a "Muslim ban" to prevent citizens from seven countries in the Middle East from visiting the United States. Trump's ethnonational, anti-immigrant, and transactional form of Christian identity politics draws the white working class, Christian evangelicals, and Southern and rural Americans into a political assemblage driven by resentment toward elites and racialized "others" and the promise of overt violence toward the proclaimed enemies of this identity. As Connolly observes of Trump, "His style is not designed first and foremost to articulate a policy agenda. It draws energy from the anger of its audience as it channels it. It draws into a collage dispersed anxieties and resentments about deindustrialization, race, border issues, immigration, working-class insecurities, trade policies, pluralizing drives, the new place of the United States in the global economy, and tacit uncertainty about the shaky place of neoliberal culture on this planet."[93] This form of politics on the right is performed at the visceral register of cultural life in which various economic, status anxieties, and resentments are assembled into a resonance machine that promises to enact retributive violence on the privileged

92. Nancy Fraser argues the same point, observing that "having abandoned the populist politics of distribution, Trump proceeded to double down on the reactionary politics of recognition, hugely intensified and ever more vicious." Fraser, "From Progressive Neoliberalism to Trump—and Beyond."

93. Connolly, *Aspirational Fascism*, 12.

targets of white male rage: immigrants, Muslims, persons of color in urban centers, feminists, and the LGBTQ+ community.

Again, it is important to emphasize here that while Trumpism represents a vulgar form of right-wing resentment politics, the ground was prepared for the ascendency of this politics by sustained economic disempowerment of the working class (neoliberalism), xenophobic (specifically Islamophobic) militarism (neoconservatism), the dog-whistle politics of the Southern strategy, and misogynistic assaults on women.[94] For Connolly, these structural dynamics, which have been perpetuated by successive political assemblages on the right (from the evangelical-capitalist machine with Reagan, George H. W. Bush, and George W. Bush to the authoritarian machine with Trump), represent the most grave threat to American democracy.[95] He argues that the most effective means to confront the multifaceted attack on democracy from the right is to create a counter-political assemblage on the left.[96] Just as the right cultivates and directs the sensibilities of neoliberals, militarists, evangelical Christians, and white nationalists toward particular political ends, the left must cultivate the sensibilities of a diverse coalition toward democratic ends. He observes, "A new movement on the democratic left, if it emerges, will be organized across religious, class, gender, ethnic, and generational lines without trying to pretend that citizens can leave their faiths entirely behind them when they enter public life."[97] Connolly imagines this assemblage as pluralist and comprised of persons from a diverse range of experiences, social locations, and commitments.[98] Some might join the movement out of "desperate need" or "economic self-interest," while others participate "because of religious or nontheistic ethical commitments that inspire them to extend beyond their constituency needs, interests, and identities."[99] Each component of the assemblage would con-

94. Connolly identifies the common drive of much of the politics on the right as a form of Nietzschean *ressentiment* that directs its frustrated desires at its own impotence toward others. Often *ressentiment* is cultivated among constituencies with a sense of entitlement who experience a series of rapid changes that threaten their privilege and social standing. Connolly maintains that "the feelings of *ressentiment* are likely to be aimed at those constituencies and forces who have injured you most and/or opened a wound in your creed. Carriers of *ressentiment* typically look for vulnerable constituencies to castigate, punish, or attack" ("World of Becoming," 228).

95. Connolly, "Wolin, Superpower, and Christianity."

96. Connolly, *Christianity and Capitalism*, 15.

97. Connolly, *Christianity and Capitalism*, x.

98. Connolly, "Ethos of Democratization," 167.

99. Connolly's political assemblage is similar to Mouffe and Laclau's "chain of equivalence," Enrique Dussel's "analogical hegemon," and Romand Coles's "a politics of countershock." See Laclau and Mouffe, *Hegemony and Socialist Strategy*; Dussel, *Twenty Theses on Politics*, 72; and Coles, *Visionary Pragmatism*.

test the dominant political alliances and institutional structures that oppose the values of inclusion, egalitarianism, and rule by the people. Although this opposition would emerge from different subject positions, Connolly maintains that it is necessary for this pluralism to coalesce into a larger assemblage. He argues, "Hegemony thus can be *resisted* by a variety of tactics; but it can be overcome only if it is countered by an opposing coalition establishing a degree of hegemony through alternative articulations of identity, interests, freedom, equality, and the human relation to the earth."[100] The history of the left in the twentieth century offers a cautionary tale about the failure of various identity groups—labor, environmentalists, feminists, civil rights advocates, anticapitalists, LGBTQ advocates, antiwar activists—to form an organized bloc of power.

Connolly specifically highlights the need for the left to attract a significant segment of the white working class away from the right's new authoritarianism. Where both the right and the left have failed to offer economic policies that ameliorate the social suffering of this population, the right has appealed to the cultural and religious sensibilities of this constituency in order to draw it into the assemblage on the right.[101] Some members of this constituency have embraced the authoritarianism of the populism on the right and, in all likelihood, cannot be convinced to join other political assemblages. Others in this constituency could abandon the populist turn on the right if they come to see that Trump has not delivered on his economic agenda and if they hear from other political blocs that speak convincingly to their grievances.[102] Connolly concludes that "a social democratic agenda is now an essential preliminary to any more transformative practices because the Left can go nowhere until the pluralizing Left and the working class have been drawn closer together. Had such programs been actively pursued earlier there would have been no turn to the radical right by a large section of the white working class."[103] As with other thinkers on the left (Stuart Hall, Chantal Mouffe, Nancy Fraser, Wendy Brown), Connolly rejects any attempt to dichotomize struggles for recognition and efforts to build a more egalitarian economic order. The divide between those on the left who prioritize various recognition claims (race, gender, sexual orientation, etc.) and those focused on pursuing a class-based strategy should be eliminated so that the left can push forward with a pluralist project that draws links between distinctive social movements. Connolly observes, "The idea is to call out

---

100. Connolly, *Identity/Difference*, 214.

101. Connolly, "Trump, the Working Class, and Fascist Rhetoric," 32.

102. Connolly, "Trump, the Working Class, and Fascist Rhetoric," 33.

103. Connolly, "Trump, the Working Class, and Fascist Rhetoric," 33.

expressions of racism, militarism, climate denialism, and misogyny whenever you encounter them as you simultaneously support positive responses to real working-class grievances and point out how reasonable solutions to them are compatible with a pluralizing, more egalitarian culture."[104]

This chapter has argued that in order to comprehend the emergent political assemblage on the right, it is necessary to examine the political formation that preceded it: the neoliberal-neoconservative hegemony. We have explored how this hegemony has undermined democracy and amplified political projects of economic disempowerment and belligerent nationalism. We also have examined its link to cultural politics of dog-whistle racism, an anti-feminist gender politics, and Christian conservatism. The emergent political formation on the right departs in subtle ways from the standard neoliberal-neoconservative hegemony while pushing forward its plutocratic and militarist elements and its cultural politics of overt xenophobia, racism, and misogyny. In conclusion, we described the broad contours of a politics that serves as a radical democratic alternative both to neoliberal-neoconservative hegemony and its mutation into authoritarian populism. In the next chapter we explore this alternative in greater detail.

104. "Trump, the Working Class, and Fascist Rhetoric," 33.

CHAPTER 2

Radical Democracy

THE POLITICAL IMAGINARY ON both the left and the right largely has been captured by neoliberal and neoconservative policy commitments over the past forty years. As a result, the left has been ensnared in a binary in which it either has embraced the politics of centrism and the inevitability of liberal democratic capitalism (Bill Clinton, Barack Obama, and Hilary Clinton) or indulged in a "Left melancholy" that attached itself to missed revolutionary opportunities.[1] This nostalgic attachment to the past is perhaps most evident in the contemporary call on the left for the revitalization of communism as the horizon for radical politics (Slavoj Žižek, Alain Badiou, and Jodi Dean).

The result of this situation is a double bind in which the left affirms the status quo either by failing to offer an alternative to the dominant social order and pursuing a politics of centrism or by arguing that the revitalization of communism or anarchism is the only alternative to capitalist democracy. Contemporary communist and anarchist critics on the left contend that because democracy in its liberal form is little more than a political cover for militarism (empire) and class warfare (neoliberalism) the task of radical politics is to resist not only neoliberalism and empire but also democracy itself insofar as it serves to legitimate these political formations.[2]

By way of contrast, radical democratic theorists maintain that rather than abandoning democracy as a cover for imperialism and capitalist domination, the task is to defend democratic values and struggle over the future meaning of democracy. Thus, while the debate on the radical edges of the left seems to limit the political alternatives to democracy to either communism or anarchism, radical democracy represents a third possibility that aims to

1. Brown, "Resisting Left Melancholy," 25.
2. See, for instance, Dean, *The Communist Horizon*, and Newman, *Postanarchism*.

deepen, broaden, and radicalize the capacity of people to rule themselves and to build a more inclusive and egalitarian social order.

The purpose of this chapter is to offer an overview of radical democratic theory in order to provide a framework for analyzing the distinctive ways in which North American political theologians engage radical democratic theory in subsequent chapters. As a means of developing this framework, we will focus on the question of whether radical politics should pursue a strategy of withdrawal (Michael Hardt, Antonio Negri, Sheldon Wolin) or engagement (Ernesto Laclau, Chantal Mouffe, and Jeffrey Stout) in relation to the politics of the state. While the task of this chapter is not to defend or advocate for a specific position, it should be noted that William Connolly's approach is most consistent with the aim of this book in its advocacy for a radical politics that operates at multiple levels (local, state, national, transnational), that is expressed in diverse ways, and that adopts a postsecular position that seeks to build a political assemblage that includes those with secular as well as faith commitments.

RADICAL DEMOCRACY

Radical democracy is a pluralist tradition inclusive of several different theoretical orientations and political commitments. The most effective way to approach this movement is by distinguishing between the European and American variants of radical democratic theory.

European radical democratic theory emerges in response to Marxist politics. And while the engagement with the Marxist tradition takes different forms in the works of Ernesto Laclau, Chantal Mouffe, Antonio Negri, and Jacques Rancière, these theorists all maintain that radical democracy differs from Marxist politics in a number of ways. First, radical democracy moves beyond the restrictive focus on class as the exclusive site of political resistance in Marxist theory. Radical democratic theorists point to the fact that new social movements have generated opposition to the dominant social order from different subject positions. Thus, opposition to patriarchy, colonialism, environmental degradation, racism, heteronormativity, and political violence represent sites of resistance that are equal to class-based resistance. Second, this shift to the pluralism of social movements in a post-Marxist context requires that the agent of social transformation be reimagined. Several possibilities have been proposed to replace the proletariat of Marxist theory, ranging from the multitude (Negri) and the people (Laclau) to the radical democratic citizen (Mouffe) and the uncounted (Rancière). Finally, European radical democratic theorists reject the Marxist approach to Revolution (with a capital *R*) in which Revolution represents the ultimate antidote to societal problems. With the possible exception of Hardt and Negri's approach to the global revolution of the multitude, European theorists approach democracy as an incomplete project that requires constant, ongoing contestation.[3]

The American approach to radical democratic theory (Sheldon Wolin, Wendy Brown, William Connolly, and Romand Coles) emerges not as a critical engagement with Marxist theory, but rather as a confrontation with the failures of liberal democracy.[4] American radical democratic theorists maintain that because liberal democracy has prioritized individual freedom (liberalism) over rule by the people (democracy) it often serves to legitimate authoritarian, hierarchical, and anti-egalitarian politics. Thus, while liberal democracy has established the formal elements of a democratic order through its commitment to individual rights, elections, parliamentary procedures, and separation of powers, it has failed to deliver on its promise of rule by the people and substantive equality. In particular, the alignment of liberal democracy with the antidemocratic commitments of military empire and neoliberal capitalism has undermined even its most basic egalitarian commitments. As Wendy Brown observes, "To the extent that liberalism has monopolized the meaning of democracy (and worse, to the extent that capitalism has monopolized the meaning of democracy), it is important to be able to articulate the virtues of democracy apart from its liberal-democratic form. Radical democracy marks this distinction; it takes democracy back from its hijacking by liberalism and capitalism. Radical democracy doesn't entail any particular governance form but emphasizes power sharing among the demos."[5] American radical democratic theorists respond to political liberalism's attenuation of democracy by reimagining democracy beyond liberalism as a "ruling in common for the common" (Brown), as a commitment to the proposition that "democracy is democratization" (Coles), by viewing democracy as a culture and "an enduring collection of social practices" (Stout), or by approaching democracy as an event that is "destined to be a moment rather than a form" (Wolin).[6]

This distinction between European (post-Marxist) and American (postliberal) forms of radical democracy represents one way to map different trajectories in radical democratic theory. The distinction that is

3. See Laclau and Mouffe, *Hegemony and Socialist Strategy*, 2, for a criticism of the viability of revolution with a capital *R*.

4. Stears, *Demanding Democracy*.

5. Brown, "Learning to Love Again," 30.

6. Brown, "We're All Democrats Now," 46; Coles, *Beyond Gated Politics*, xi; Stout, *Democracy and Tradition*, 28; and Wolin, "Fugitive Democracy," 108.

drawn by Chantal Mouffe in a text titled "The Importance of Engaging the State" offers another approach for mapping the contours of the contemporary debate.[7] She observes that there exist two dominant approaches in contemporary radical political theory: a politics that withdraws from institutions and the state and a politics that engages institutions and the state. The withdrawal approach avoids engagement with existing institutions and attempts to generate a politics beyond the bounds of the state. By way of contrast, the engagement approach aims to reform and to radicalize existing democratic institutions.

In the analysis that follows Hardt, Negri, and Wolin occupy the withdrawal axis of radical democratic theory. They share the view that radical democratic politics exist only outside of the dominant structures in society, even as they ultimately differ concerning the site they propose as the alternative. Where Hardt and Negri advocate for a spontaneous, transnational politics created by the multitude, Wolin describes the localism of fugitive democracy as the site of democratic resistance. Laclau, Mouffe, and Stout occupy the institutional axis and support a radical democratic politics focused on reform of existing structures, electoral politics, and the cultivation of grassroots democratic organizations. In this chapter, we will take two passes through this withdrawal/engagement framework, first by examining the post-Marxist debate between Hardt and Negri and Laclau and Mouffe, and then by analyzing the postliberal debate between Wolin and Stout.

POST-MARXIST RADICAL DEMOCRACY

In their trilogy of *Empire* (2001), *Multitude* (2004), and *Commonwealth* (2007), Michael Hardt and Antonio Negri have attempted to reanimate features of Marxist politics by refiguring the antagonism between capital and labor in a postmodern context as an antagonism between Empire and the multitude. In these works, they argue that Empire has little to do with the modern imperialisms of the nation-state, which exercised power by policing specific territorial boundaries. The territorial sovereignty of modern imperialism has been replaced by the deterritorializing force of capital, which is comprised of a network of nation-states, supranational institutions, and corporations that upend and overturn previous social arrangements by remaking the world in the image of the market.

In this regard, Empire represents an entirely new form of spatial and political rule by which the logic of a postindustrial economy dominates the global population, not so much as a system of production but as a

7. Mouffe, "The Importance of Engaging the State."

system of socialization through which capitalist subjectivities are created.[8] The transition from modern capitalism (Fordism) to Empire (post-Fordism) involves a shift from industrial labor to immaterial labor in which capitalism produces not just commodities but knowledge, information, desire, and forms of life. Hardt and Negri observe, "The great industrial and fanatical powers produce not only commodities but also subjectivities," so that capitalism is increasingly involved in "the production of social life itself, in which the economy, the political, and the cultural increasingly overlap and invest one another."[9] Accordingly, exploitation is no longer limited to the field of industrial production (as it was during the period of industrial capitalism) but extends to all areas of life that have been captured by the rule of capital. In an era of immaterial labor, the disciplining of all individual and collective powers toward the end of generating surplus value is the dominant form of capitalist exploitation.[10] Hardt and Negri observe rather starkly in this regard that "there is nothing, no 'naked life,' no external standpoint, that can be posed outside this field permeated by money; nothing escapes money."[11]

Because capital now rules the world by socializing everyone into capitalist forms of life, resistance to Empire has become more possible than ever before. Indeed, as the first truly global order, Empire has produced a global people for the first time in history.[12] Hardt and Negri name this people "the multitude" and describe them as all of those persons who "labor under the rule of capital," the almost infinite number of different groups and identities that are "based not only on economic differences but also on those of race, ethnicity, geography, gender, sexuality, and other factors."[13] This means that because all social relations are affected by the rule of capital, it is possible both for the rule of capital to be overthrown and to reimagine sociality based on an alternative logic—cooperation, solidarity, or the commons.

The multitude is not organized in a traditional way by which a transcendent agent (an overarching idea, party, or institution) assembles the people. Accordingly, the class-based politics associated with Marx's proletariat is rejected, and in its place Hardt and Negri propose a pluralist coalition of singularities that work in common cause without a transcendent

8. Hardt and Negri, *Empire*, 146 and xii–xiv.

9. Hardt and Negri, *Empire*, xii. See also Hardt and Negri, *Assembly*, xv.

10. For a discussion of this, see Lemke, *Biopolitics*, 67ff.

11. Hardt and Negri, *Empire*, 32.

12. They observe, "The creative forces of the multitude that sustain Empire are also capable of autonomously constructing a counter-Empire, an alternative political organization of global flows and exchanges." Hardt and Negri, *Empire*, xv.

13. Hardt and Negri, *Multitude*, 103.

principle of unity.[14] An example of the multitude is the 1999 Seattle protests against the World Trade Organization (WTO). The protesters were "trade unionists and environmentalists, church groups and anarchists" who "acted together without any central, unifying structure that subordinates or sets aside their differences."[15] "The real importance of Seattle," Hardt and Negri observe, "was to provide a 'convergence center' for all of the grievances against a global system. Old oppositions between protest groups seemed suddenly to melt away. During the protests, for example, the two most prominent groups were environmentalists and the trade unions, and, to the surprise of most commentators, these two groups, which were thought to have contradictory interests, actually supported each other."[16] In addition to the Seattle protests, Hardt and Negri describe the power of the multitude in a number of resistance movements, from the First Palestinian Intifada (1987) and the Chinese democracy movement (1989) to the Zapatista uprising (1994), Occupy Wall Street (2011), the Arab Spring (2011), and the protests at Ferguson (2014). The structure of these movements was initially nomadic insofar as the antiglobalization movement followed the meetings of the IMF, WTO, and the World Bank from Seattle (1999) to Genoa (2001) in order to protest capitalist globalization. More recently, there has been a shift to an encampment and occupation style of resistance, as with the Occupy Wall Street and Tahrir Square protests. According to Hardt and Negri, these spontaneous forms of local resistance serve as concrete nodes of struggle that communicate with other nodes without a "center of intelligence" or organizing principle. Because each form of struggle "remains singular and tied to its local conditions," it is difficult to discern how these movements of rebellion connect.[17] Hardt and Negri postulate that local instances "leap immediately to the global level and attack the imperial constitution."[18] Multiple, uncoordinated attacks at different sites can have

---

14. Hardt and Negri, *Empire*, 103. Hardt and Negri maintain that revolutionary change is possible, but they resist any attempt to theorize revolution or offer a blueprint for how the multitude will eliminate Empire. They suggest instead the need for concrete forms of "practical experimentation" to open new political spaces of resistance and democratization that involve "micropolitical" practices of resistance, collective instances of revolt, and the attempt to imagine radical alternatives to the present order (what they refer to as "constituent power"). Hardt and Negri, *Empire*, 411. See also Hardt and Negri, "Globalization and Democracy," 118.

15. Hardt and Negri, *Multitude*, 217.

16. Hardt and Negri, *Multitude*, 288–89. Hardt and Negri, furthermore, argue that Occupy Wall Street represents an example of the multitude. See Hardt and Negri, "'Real Democracy' at the Heart of Occupy Wall Street."

17. Hardt and Negri, *Multitude*, 217.

18. Hardt and Negri, *Empire*, 56.

an unforeseen cumulative effect on Empire precisely because it is a diffuse form of power. Or, as Hardt and Negri put it, because Empire is everywhere "the virtual center of Empire can be attacked from any point."[19]

In their most recent work, Hardt and Negri continue to insist that Empire represents the dominant social and political form in our world, but they recognize that Empire has mutated into a new phase and form with the proliferation of right-wing movements around the world. In *Assembly* (2017) Hardt and Negri maintain that what stands at the core of contemporary right-wing movements is the attempt to retain or restore the identity of a people over against foreigners and racialized others.[20] The ideological conductors utilized by proponents of these right-wing movements are race, religion, and national identity, which are invoked as a means of promising the restoration of power to groups that have experienced loss of social standing or prestige: "white men in the United States, white working-class Europeans, or oligarchies in Latin America." In the United States, the specific form that this approach to politics takes is the attempt to "restore an imagined national identity that is primarily white, Christian, and heterosexual."[21] Hardt and Negri note that while these movements appeal to the mass of citizens by invoking images and symbols of restoration, they usually serve to reinforce elite power over the masses.[22] This is evident in the United States, in which, from a policy perspective, Trump's most prominent legislative achievement has been a massive tax cut for economic elites. Beyond this, Trump has largely delivered only symbolic gestures and a scorched-earth politics of resentment toward minoritized communities.

In response to this political formation, Hardt and Negri maintain that the left must offer not only protest and resistance movements but also durable alternatives to these movements on the right. In the trilogy of *Empire*, *Multitude*, and *Commonwealth*, Hardt and Negri rejected standard forms of political organization in favor of spontaneity, eschewed any specific strategy situated within the framework of hierarchical leadership models, and advocated for a revolutionary approach to social change that dismissed reformist approaches. However, with the publication of *Assembly* they acknowledge that a new approach is demanded by the failures of the left and by the new dynamics of the current political situation. In *Assembly*

19. Hardt and Negri, *Empire*, 59. They contend, "These struggles are at once economic, political, and cultural—and hence they are biopolitical struggles, struggles over the form of life. They are constituent struggles, creating new public spaces and new forms of community" (*Empire*, 56).

20. Hardt and Negri, *Assembly*, 49.

21. Hardt and Negri, *Assembly*, 50.

22. Hardt and Negri, *Assembly*, 51.

they retain a focus on the significance of grassroots protest movements but maintain that "without losing sight of the urgency of protest, we need to be thinking with an equal sense of urgency about ways to transform those visions into reality."[23] And in a departure from their call for withdrawal from dominant political institutions in *Empire*, Hardt and Negri now maintain that it is necessary to "take power, but differently." Specifically, Hardt and Negri advocate for a dialectical approach to politics that moves beyond the binaries established in their earlier work, so that they now promote an "all of the above" strategy that moves between spontaneity and organization, horizontalism and leadership, revolution and reform.

In the midst of these important strategic shifts in their politics what remains constant is their view that democracy serves as the alternative to Empire.[24] In contrast to the regnant forms of democracy that legitimate hierarchical and centralized forms of political organization, Hardt and Negri advocate for an approach to democracy that is committed to the "radical, absolute proposition that requires the rule of everyone by everyone."[25] They maintain that democracy is possible when the multitude rules itself rather than submitting to the rule of oligarchs, plutocrats, or the anonymous forces of the market.[26] This call for radical democracy entails two broad commitments: (1) the abolition of private property and the restoration of the commons, and (2) the cultivation of a transnational form of democracy as an alternative to Empire.

First, the democratic politics of the multitude is anticapitalist and, as such, resists any alliance between neoliberalism and democracy.[27] As a result, Hardt and Negri envisage the shift beyond private property (capitalism) and the rule of public property (socialism) as a critical feature of radical democratic politics. The task is to create a new form of political life based on the public commons. This vision necessitates a micropolitical shift away from the desire for private accumulation and toward the desire for a society in which

23. Hardt, "Managing Up."

24. They observe, "Democracy on a global scale is becoming an increasingly widespread demand, sometimes explicit but often implicit in the innumerable grievances and resistances expressed against the current global order. The common currency that runs throughout so many struggles and movements for liberation across the world today—at local, regional, and global levels—is the desire for democracy." Hardt and Negri, *Multitude*, xvi.

25. Hardt and Negri, *Multitude*, 307. On "pure" and "real" democracy see *Multitude*, 244 and 306.

26. Hardt and Negri argue that "when the multitude is finally able to rule itself, democracy becomes possible" (*Multitude*, 340).

27. Purcell, *Recapturing Democracy*, 61.

the "basic means of life" are secured for all.[28] In *Assembly*, Hardt and Negri maintain that offering an alternative vision of fulfillment to that of capitalism represents a critical feature of this work. They observe, "The crucial point is that the affirmation of poverty and the critique of property are not conceived as deprivation or austerity but rather as abundance."[29] Hardt and Negri invoke the historic witness of the Franciscans' commitment to *usus pauper* as the call for the restricted or limited use of goods as an example of both the need "to subvert private property" and to build a social order in which a lack of property is viewed as plentitude and not deprivation.

At a macropolitical level, the goal is to extend democratic rights beyond life, liberty, and the pursuit of happiness to include "free access to the common, equality in the distribution of wealth, and the sustainability of the common."[30] The politics of the commons is rooted in the conviction that it is possible to move beyond both private as well as public control of social wealth by building a social order in which the people rather than elites (capitalists or representative politicians) manage it. In terms of specific proposals, they gesture toward a guaranteed basic income as a "money of the commons."[31] A guaranteed basic income would serve the material aim of mitigating the effects of extreme poverty and inequality as well as the democratic aim of providing individuals and communities with the resources and the time needed to participate in political deliberation. Additionally, they point to the need to develop a politics of the commons in which decisions made about the future of the earth are not limited to capitalist elites who run the fossil fuel industry or the politicians controlled by these elites. Only a radical politics of the commons, which entails the abolition of private and public property, is capable of offering a political vision in which those affected by the destruction of the earth make decisions about its future.[32]

In addition to this abolitionist approach to property and radical democratic approach to the commons, Hardt and Negri maintain that the politics of the multitude should take form as a non-statist, transnational form of democracy.[33] As noted above, because so many of the social crises that humanity faces (e.g., inequality, ecological destruction, and political violence)

28. Hardt and Negri, *Commonwealth*, 380.

29. Hardt and Negri, *Assembly*, 58.

30. Hardt and Negri, *Declaration*, 51.

31. Hardt and Negri, *Assembly*, 294; see also 281–82.

32. Hardt and Negri, *Assembly*, 98.

33. Hardt and Negri, *Multitude*, 93. Hardt and Negri claim that "the autonomy of the multitude and its capacities for economic, political and social self-organization take away any role for sovereignty . . . When the multitude is finally able to rule itself, democracy becomes possible" (*Multitude*, 340).

are global in character, a transnational or truly global form of democracy alone can remedy the situation. And while the anti-statist character of their politics has led some to suggest that Hardt and Negri propose anarchism as an alternative to Empire, they reject this label and insist that they are "communists" who wish to move beyond liberal and socialist visions for society in favor a radical democratic life in common that is "managed by the multitude, organized by the multitude, directed by the multitude."[34]

In their trilogy of *Empire*, *Multitude*, and *Commonwealth* (as well as their more recent reflections in *Declaration* and *Assembly*) Hardt and Negri offer a bold approach to radical politics by describing the emergence of a transnational, pluralist assemblage capable of generating a radical democratic alternative to Empire. Despite the innovative character of their proposals, critics have questioned whether the anti-statist and revolutionary form of politics presented by Hardt and Negri offers a realistic political strategy. Ernesto Laclau and Chantal Mouffe, in particular, have objected sharply to Hardt and Negri's vision by characterizing the hope that democracy will emerge spontaneously in civil society as naïve and unrealistic.[35] Mouffe avers that their position is that "we basically don't have to do anything, just wait for the moment in which the contradiction of Empire will bring about the reign of the multitude."[36] In this regard, Mouffe maintains that this approach represents a postmodern repetition of Marx's thesis that capitalism produces its own gravediggers. Laclau and Mouffe maintain that the current social order and the emergence of any alternative to it is neither inevitable nor necessary, but rather the result of a specific exercise of power. It follows that the future direction of society will depend on concrete political strategies that either succeed or fail to replace the current neoliberal hegemony. Laclau and Mouffe pursue an agonistic politics of hegemonic struggle in which they view the primary challenge for the left as transforming "itself into a *political* movement putting forward concrete alternative proposals."[37]

34. Hardt and Negri, *Empire*, 410. They observe, "No, we are not anarchists but communists who have seen how much repression and destruction of humanity have been wrought by liberal and socialist big governments." Hardt and Negri, *Commonwealth*, vi.

35. Hardt and Negri, *Multitude*, 311, and Mouffe, "Democracy Revisited," 110.

36. Mouffe, "Democracy Revisited," 112; Laclau, *On Populist Reason*, 242. Or, as Laclau frames the point, "Multitudes are never spontaneously multitudinarious; they can only become so through political action." Laclau, "Can Immanence Explain Social Struggles?," 10.

37. Mouffe, *On the Political*, 112. Emphasis original. See also Laclau, *On Populist Reason*, 243. Hardt and Negri have drawn closer to this vision with *Assembly*, and Mouffe acknowledges this in her most recent work, *For a Left Populism*, but retains

The first move of hegemonic struggle is to make explicit the contingency of dominant constellations of power in order to break with an essentialist understanding of society. For Laclau and Mouffe, the configuration of power at any given moment is not the expression of the natural order of things but the result of contingent practices that have established a specific mode of organizing society.[38] For instance, neoliberalism is the direct result of hegemonic moves on the right that successfully transformed the common sense of society concerning the proper relationship between government and capitalism.[39] In the 1940s and 1950s the ideas of neoliberals like Hayek and Friedman stood at the margins of discussions concerning political economy because the dominant hegemony at the time was democratic socialist. The neoliberal response to this hegemony was to organize, build think tanks, and attempt to refigure the public commitment to freedom, the market, and governance along neoliberal lines. The efforts of Hayek, Friedman, and others prepared the discursive space for the electoral victories of Ronald Reagan and Margaret Thatcher. These political victories effected a dramatic transformation that shifted the debate from a focus on economic equality (democratic socialist) to economic liberty (neoliberal).

After Reagan installed the neoliberal hegemony, the left capitulated to it by offering a slightly modified form of neoliberalism that managed the neoliberal order in a more humane way through more extensive redistribution.[40] The third-way politics of the 1990s, exemplified in the presidency of Bill Clinton and the premiership of Tony Blair, announced the end of the stalemate between big government and the market, left and right, equality and liberty. In place of these oppositional political struggles, proponents of the third way strategically implemented conservative economic and criminal justice policies (tax cuts, welfare reform, law-and-order approaches to crime and drug use) and liberal social policies (women's rights and the environment) as a means of building a political coalition that cut across partisan political affiliations.[41] The dominance of third-way politics created

---

similar criticisms of their work. The specific point of contention is that Hardt and Negri continue to claim that "the Multitude could auto-organize itself." See Mouffe, *For a Left Populism*, 53–55.

38. Mouffe observes that "things could always have been otherwise and every order is predicated on the exclusion of other possibilities . . . what is at a given moment considered as the 'natural' order—jointly with the 'common sense' which accompanies it—is the result of sedimented hegemonic practices." Mouffe, *On the Political*, 18.

39. Laclau and Mouffe, *Hegemony and Socialist Strategy*, xvi.

40. Laclau and Mouffe, *Hegemony and Socialist Strategy*, xvi–xvii, and Errejón and Mouffe, *Podemos*, 23.

41. Mouffe, *Chantal Mouffe*, 158.

what Mouffe describes as a "post-political" constellation in which only two forms of neoliberalism have been offered as political options: a reactionary neoliberalism of the right and a progressive neoliberalism of the left.[42] This rapprochement between the left and the right created a political landscape that made possible the emergence of right-wing populism as the only viable political alternative to the neoliberal establishment. Mouffe contends that the left during this period failed to offer a populist alternative because its politics was animated by the anti-institutional politics of the alter-globalization movement and Occupy Wall Street (and the proposals of Hardt and Negri dominated leftist theory). By advocating for a politics of withdrawal, these movements refused to articulate a practical political strategy that could transform existing institutions. Accordingly, Mouffe maintains that the most urgent task for the left is to build an *institutional* alternative to both third-way politics and populism on the right. Specifically, she suggests that the left should develop its own form of populism that builds a pluralist coalition between different groups marginalized by the neoliberal social order. From the perspective of left-wing populism, this involves two strategic tasks: (1) generating a chain of equivalence between different groups and thereby establishing a "people," and (2) engaging in the radical reform of existing liberal democracies.

Laclau and Mouffe theorize political struggle in terms of the need to draw links between demands made by plural constituencies as a means of forming a hegemonic bloc capable of contesting the dominant hegemony. The demands of distinct groups (e.g., Black Lives Matter, #metoo, and those who advocate for the rights of the undocumented) remain differentiated, but it is possible to create links between these groups based on their equivalent experience of subordination. Within this framework, no single struggle takes precedence over others and any attempt to construct a hierarchy of struggles is rejected.[43] Because these groups struggle against plural forms of subordination but do not naturally share a common set of *a priori* goals, links between these groups must be produced through explicit acts of conscious mobilization and political construction. For Mouffe, struggles against sexism and racism and in defense of the environment and the working class should

---

42. Mouffe, *On the Political*, 64ff.

43. Slavoj Žižek disagrees with this move: "My point of contention with Laclau here is that I do not accept that all elements which enter into hegemonic struggle are in principle equal: in the series of struggles (economic, political, feminist, ecological, ethnic, etc.) there is always one which, while it is part of the chain, secretly overdetermines its very horizon." For Žižek, this overdetermined horizon is class struggle. See Žižek, "Holding the Place," 320.

be part of a left-wing hegemonic project.[44] These struggles can be assembled or linked by constructing an antagonistic frontier between these movements and another identity (or an antagonist), such as "the establishment" or "the oligarchy." Establishing a common antagonist is central to the construction of links along a chain of equivalence between different social movements because it serves to provide commonality among diverse struggles. For Laclau and Mouffe, a politics that establishes an "us" (or a people) versus "them" produces a collective left-wing identity amid pluralism.

At a certain level, the approach described by Laclau and Mouffe is similar to Hardt and Negri's description of the multitude in that both focus on the positive significance of pluralism within social movements.[45] However, they differ from Hardt and Negri because they reject the view that the multitude will emerge spontaneously without active construction.[46] For Laclau and Mouffe, the oppressed generate resistance by mobilizing diverse groups toward common democratic ends. Ultimately, "people struggle for equality, not because of some ontological postulate, but because subjects have been constructed in a democratic tradition that puts those values at the center of social life."[47] Furthermore, because the field of conflict has widened in a neoliberal era, it is critical that the work of activation and construction draws voters not traditionally aligned with the left into a coalition opposed to oligarchy.[48]

In addition to this work of pluralist coalition building, Laclau and Mouffe contend that radical politics should focus on reform rather than on a total break with the current political order: "The aim is not to create a completely different kind of society, but to use the symbolic resources of the liberal democratic tradition to struggle against relations of subordination not only in the economy but also those linked to gender, race, or sexual orientation, for example."[49] The problem for radical democrats is not that the ideals of existing democracies are deficient—on the contrary,

44. Laclau and Mouffe, *Hegemony and Socialist Strategy*, xviii. When *Hegemony and Socialist Strategy* was written, the task was to integrate the new social movements against sexism, racism, and in defense of the environment within the framework of a working-class politics. In *For a Left Populism*, Mouffe observes that the situation has changed, and now it is "working-class" demands that have been neglected on the left.

45. Hardt and Negri note this similarity in *Assembly*, 328.

46. Laclau, for instance, argues, "*Either* we assert the possibility of a universality that is not politically constructed and mediated *or* we assert that all universality is precarious and depends on a historical construction out of heterogeneous elements." Laclau, "Can Immanence Explain Social Struggles?," 5. Emphasis original.

47. Mouffe, *Chantal Mouffe*, 52.

48. Mouffe, *For a Left Populism*, 60.

49. Mouffe, "Radical Democracy or Liberal Democracy?," 20.

liberty and justice for all represent *radical* political ideals; the problem is that these ideals have not been realized. Thus, the task is not to reject these values as a mere ideological cover for capitalist forms of domination but to struggle for their "effective implementation."[50] Concretely, this means that the left should discursively resist the right's attempt to reduce the commitment to equality to the equal right to compete and the commitment to freedom to individual consumer choice.[51] Similarly, where the right restricts its understanding of "people" to citizens of a particular nation-state, the task of the left is to expand the meaning of "people" in a cosmopolitan direction that extends political status to refugees and immigrants excluded by existing models of citizenship.[52]

Moreover, because it is impossible to articulate a predetermined hegemonic formation to replace the neoliberal hegemony, it is necessary to generate context-dependent counter-hegemonic formations. Thus, the demand to deepen democracy might take form as "'democratic socialism,' 'eco-socialism,' 'associative democracy' or 'participatory democracy'; everything depends on the contexts and national traditions."[53] This approach follows both from pluralist commitments as well as the pragmatic judgment that left-wing politics must move forward by simultaneously opening up new radical horizons and focusing on what can be realized practically.

While Laclau and Mouffe criticize the politics of Hardt and Negri and offer an alternative to it, the pragmatic orientation of Laclau and Mouffe's approach has been scrutinized by critics as well. Laclau and Mouffe view the central task of leftist politics as a reform of liberal democracy rather than a form of revolution that would eliminate liberal democracy. They reject the Marxist vision of Revolution (with a capital *R*) and maintain that, as a result of restrictive contemporary political conditions, the task for leftists is to work toward the achievable goal of radicalizing existing democracies. For Slavoj Žižek, the problem with this paradigm is straightforward: there is nothing radical in it, insofar as it fails to challenge the hegemony of the "liberal-capitalist regime." It merely accepts the liberal democratic capitalist framework and then offers "palliative measures" that attempt to limit "the damaging effects of the inevitable."[54] Where Žižek criticizes

50. Mouffe, *On the Political*, 32.

51. Laclau and Mouffe, *Hegemony and Socialist Strategy*, 184.

52. On this point, see also Butler, *Notes Toward a Performative Theory of Assembly*, 5ff.

53. Mouffe, *For a Left Populism*, 51.

54. Žižek, "Holding the Place," 321. Wendy Brown similarly criticizes Laclau and Mouffe's approach to radical democracy as a form of politics that has moved increasingly toward a "liberal welfare-statism that is reconciled to both capitalism and liberalism" ("Learning to Love Again," 30). See also Brown, *States of Injury*, 11.

Laclau and Mouffe's radical democratic theory due to its excessive toler-
ance for liberalism and capitalism, Hardt and Negri criticize Laclau and
Mouffe for their appropriation of the Marxist tradition, particularly the
work of Antonio Gramsci. They observe, "Poor Gramsci, communist and
militant before all else, tortured and killed by fascism and ultimately by the
bosses who financed fascism—poor Gramsci was given the gift of being
considered the founder of a strange notion of hegemony that leaves no
place for a Marxian politics . . . We have to defend ourselves from such
generous gifts!" For Hardt and Negri, Laclau and Mouffe transform the
Marxist commitments of Gramsci into liberal-reformist principles and, in
the process, eliminate the radicalism from Gramsci's politics by utilizing
his ideas to support the relatively centrist political-economic forms of liberal democracy and state-regulated capitalism.[55] Furthermore, in *Assembly* Hardt and Negri critique the populist orientation of Laclau's politics
by maintaining that despite similarities between their projects, they differ
with Laclau over the question of how to organize the multitude. Hardt and
Negri maintain that "our primary objection is that the multitude of social
subjectivities should not (and ultimately today cannot) be organized as a
united subject from above, by a hegemonic power; we maintain, instead,
that social subjectivities have the potential to organize themselves as a
multitude (not a people) and create lasting institutions."[56]

In response to these criticisms, Laclau and Mouffe have emphasized
the fact that their approach is radical within the bounds of what is possible.
The politics of Žižek, Hardt, and Negri are more radical than Laclau and
Mouffe's in their demand for a total break with the current political order.
The price paid for this radicalism, however, is that their politics exist only as
an imagined possibility. Laclau, for instance, argues that the anticapitalism
of Žižek is "mere empty talk" because he possesses no concrete political
strategy to challenge capitalism. By way of contrast, Laclau and Mouffe's
agonistic politics offers a concrete strategy for resisting the "prevalent neoliberal economic model" through "state regulation" and "democratic control" of the economy.[57]

POSTLIBERAL RADICAL DEMOCRACY

Even as they diverge with respect to traditions of Marxism that they engage,
the debate between Hardt/Negri and Laclau/Mouffe takes place within the

55. Hardt and Negri, *Empire*, 451n26.
56. Hardt and Negri, *Assembly*, 328.
57. Laclau, "Structure, History and the Political," 206.

ideological framework of the post-Marxist turn in contemporary political theory. Where Hardt and Negri draw from Italian Marxists and Deleuze, Laclau and Mouffe engage Gramsci and poststructuralist thought. A similar debate has transpired in American political theory but has emerged in response to liberalism and its restriction of democracy as a political form and practice. As with the post-Marxist debate, this conversation plays out in terms of the withdrawal-engagement debate in which Sheldon Wolin occupies the withdrawal space and Jeffrey Stout advocates for greater engagement with existing political structures and institutions.

As Wendy Brown points out in her essay "Democracy and Bad Dreams," Wolin adopts a distinctive posture in relation to liberalism. He does not oppose it because it serves as a cover for capitalist domination (Marx) or because of its contempt for "bare life" (Arendt) but rather because it is parasitic on democracy and drains it of its egalitarian commitments.[58] Because Wolin views liberalism as corrosive to democracy, the goal of his mature political theory is to open a space between liberalism and democracy by describing democracy as an anti-institutional moment of resistance "inclined toward anarchy" and "identified with revolution." This definition, of course, contrasts with liberal approaches to democracy that entail a minimal commitment to formal ideals (individual liberty and equality before the law) and a set of institutional procedures and norms (voting rights, political bodies of deliberation—Congress, Parliament, etc.—and constitutional norms).[59] In Mouffe's schematization, Wolin's approach fits within the paradigm of withdrawal insofar as it views democracy not as a set of institutional structures or governing procedures, but rather as periodic moments of resistance to hierarchical and elitist social structures.[60]

In his most famous work, *Politics and Vision*, Wolin offers a description of the twofold task of the political theorist as (1) "posting warnings" or providing citizens with the tools to discern dangerous paths, and (2) describing possibilities for the future that avert paths that lead to disaster.[61] Wolin's thought follows this pattern and so, in our analysis of his approach to radical democracy, we will first attend to his diagnosis of the threats implicit in the liberal political order, which he describes as constitutionalism and capitalism, and then explore the resources available to ward off these threats.

58. Brown, "Democracy and Bad Dreams."

59. Brown makes this point forcefully in "Democracy and Bad Dreams." Wolin claims that democratic theorists have made a "category mistake" when they have evaluated the authenticity of democracy in terms of its institutional forms and procedures. Wolin, *Democracy Incorporated*, 61.

60. Wolin, *Politics and Vision*, 603.

61. Wolin, *Politics and Vision*, 14.

Contrary to the hagiographical accounts of the founding of the United States, Wolin maintains that the American political system was produced by those "who were either skeptical about democracy or hostile to it."[62] There were no ordinary farmers or workers among the drafters of the Constitution. The propertied class and elite statesmen of the time drafted the Constitution and viewed it as a means to regulate the amount of democracy permitted to enter the American political system.[63] This attempt to restrict or limit democracy is a consistent pattern in the Western political tradition in which the people (*demos*) have been ruled mainly by various aristocracies, oligarchies, and plutocracies. Wolin argues that enshrining democracy in a constitutional form has served as one of the primary mechanisms of managing the passions of the people. He observes,

> It is no exaggeration to say that one of the, if not the, main projects of ancient constitutional theorists, such as Plato (*The Laws*), Aristotle, Polybius, and Cicero, as well as modern constitutionalists, such as the authors of *The Federalist* and Tocqueville, was to dampen, frustrate, sublimate, and defeat the demotic passions. The main devices were: the rule of law and especially of a sacrosanct "fundamental law" or constitution safeguarded from the "gust of popular passions"; the idea of checks and balances; separation of powers with its attempt to quarantine the "people" by confining its direct representation to one branch of the legislature; the "refining" process of indirect elections; and the suffrage restrictions. The aim was not simply to check democracy but to discourage it by making it difficult for those who, historically, had almost no leisure time for politics, to achieve political goals.[64]

Because Wolin defines the distinctive mark of democracy as the direct experience of power, those realities that bar access to this experience serve an antidemocratic function. Historically, the tradition of constitutionalism has represented one of the most potent means of constraining and restricting the participation of citizens in power-sharing. According to Wolin, the fundamental structures of American government served to erect barriers to democratic rule by limiting direct popular elections to one branch of government (the House of Representatives), the election of the Senate and the presidency to indirect means, and the appointment of federal judges by the president.[65] This separation of powers and the constitutional framework

62. Wolin, *Democracy Incorporated*, 228.
63. Wolin, *Democracy Incorporated*, 277.
64. Wolin, "Democracy: Electoral and Athenian," 476.
65. Wolin, *Democracy Incorporated*, 229.

that enshrined it has served as a bulwark against popular rule, the result of which is that the task of governing has been delivered over to an elite class with sufficient leisure time to devote to the political.[66]

Wolin maintains that where constitutionalism utilized legal and political mechanisms to constrain democracy, capitalism has deployed economic power to manipulate and manage democracy. Democracy and capitalism emerged in the modern world at the same time and worked together as occasional allies because of their shared opposition to feudalism, monarchy, and aristocracy. However, this tactical alliance gave way to tensions concerning how much inequality each system would tolerate. Capitalism emerged victorious from this confrontation and has now made democracy subservient to capital.[67] The paradox Wolin highlights is that where the competitive individualism of the capitalist social order destroys common purpose in society, the politics of American empire rebuilds this purpose through the "symbolic gratifications of patriotism, collective self-righteousness, and military prowess."[68]

Given this bleak diagnosis, it is little wonder that commentators have noted that a mood of pessimism pervades Wolin's work.[69] Wolin admits as much, and yet offers a defense of this pessimism in a text titled "What Revolutionary Action Means Today." He observes that in a country where optimism appears to be a "patriotic duty," pessimism is interpreted as an act of resignation. He contests this view and instead argues that pessimism is "the sign of suppressed revolutionary impulses. It is the mood inspired by the reasoned conviction that only a revolutionary change can ward off the consequences that are implicit in contemporary American society." The revolutionary change demanded by the current conditions cannot be envisaged, however, along Marxist lines as violent insurrection.[70] Instead, revolution should be imagined along the lines proposed by John Locke— as the enduring possibility that individuals can come together in order to "reinvent the forms and practices that will express a democratic conception of collective life."[71]

66. Wolin, *Democracy Incorporated*, 230.

67. Wolin, *Politics and Vision*, 597.

68. Wolin, *Democracy Incorporated*, 239.

69. Connolly, *Democracy and Vision*, 13ff., and Brown, "Democracy and Bad Dreams."

70. Wolin, "What Revolutionary Action Means Today," 253.

71. Wolin, "What Revolutionary Action Means Today," 254. Wolin observes, "If the right to revolt is about devising new institutions, citizenship is more than a matter of being able to claim rights. It is about a capacity to generate power, to cooperate in it, for that is how institutions and practices are sustained" (254).

In a later essay entitled "Fugitive Democracy," Wolin provides a more detailed description of these forms and practices that reinvent democracy in a cultural situation dominated by the power of capital and empire.[72] In this text, he characterizes democracy as an "ephemeral phenomenon" that embraces several different "forms and mutations that are responsive to grievances on the part of those who have no means of redress other than to risk collectivizing their small bits of power."[73] Democracy is neither a settled form nor a governmental structure but the capacity of ordinary people to share power and create new political possibilities in response to their experience of marginalization and disempowerment. Wolin suggests that this was the experience of democracy among the people (the working class, small farmers, women, slaves, and indigenous populations) during the beginning stages of American history. Democracy "stood for a politics of redress, for common action to alleviate the sharp inequalities of wealth and power that enabled the more affluent and educated to monopolize governance."[74] Broadly defined, demotic action occurs when those marginalized by the system organize to tend to "a commonality of shared concerns" that range from "low-income housing, worker ownership of factories, better schools, better health care, safe water, controls over toxic waste disposals, and a thousand other common concerns of ordinary lives."[75]

The form of demotic action described by Wolin in "Fugitive Democracy" has occurred only episodically in the political history of the West. It emerged in incomplete and fragmentary form in Athens in the fifth century BCE (there it excluded women and foreigners and was limited to adult males—or around 14 percent of the population) as well as moments of "irruptive politics" in the nineteenth and twentieth centuries in the United States: the abolitionist movement, women's suffrage, the emergence of trade unions to protect the rights of workers, the civil rights movement, and various other movements of the 1960s that protested against "the Vietnam War, racism, sexism, environmental degradation, and corporate power."[76] For Wolin, these democratic moments were "doomed to succeed only temporarily" because they were the political action of the powerless whose only

72. Wolin, "Fugitive Democracy," 100–113.

73. Wolin, *Politics and Vision*, 602.

74. Wolin, *Democracy Incorporated*, 227.

75. Wolin, "Fugitive Democracy," 112. He observes, "What is at stake in democratic politics is whether ordinary men and women can recognize that their concerns are best protected and cultivated under a regime whose actions are governed by principles of commonality, equality, and fairness, a regime in which taking part in politics becomes a way of staking out and sharing in a common life" (*Democracy Incorporated*, 260).

76. Wolin, *Democracy Incorporated*, 277–78.

strength is the fact that they have "numbers" that can be utilized to "offset the power of wealth, formal education, and managerial experience."[77] The democratic ideal that voting and political parties could express the interests of the people largely has been eliminated by elites who have become adept at manipulating elections and controlling representative government. Because elites use their political and financial power to influence the electoral process and shape public policy, the only recourse available to the demos is to engage in political action that is "inevitably episodic" and "born of necessity" because it is practiced by "those who must work, who cannot hire proxies to promote their interests, and for whom participation, as distinguished from voting, is necessarily a sacrifice."[78]

In addition to its episodic character, Wolin argues that democracy is necessarily local because "small scale is the only scale commensurate with the kind and amount of power that democracy is capable of mobilizing" given the dominant forms of economic and political organization.[79] The political ecology of localism represents one of the few remaining sources of democratic renewal both because it is capable of mobilizing citizens to respond to the concrete needs of the local community and because it draws sustenance from its engagement with "family, friends, church, neighborhood, workplace, community, town, city. These relationships are the sources from which political beings draw power—symbolic, material and psychological—and that enable them to act together."[80] Those affected by political decisions at the local level are more willing to sacrifice their time and their security to tend to issues of common concern.[81] Furthermore, in a period in which the power of the state and capitalism has reached unforeseen levels, Wolin proposes localism as a form of politics that builds resistance at multiple sites of contestation, even if it is unable to topple the state and capitalism through direct confrontation. Wolin observes, "The power of democratic politics lies in the multiplicity of modest sites dispersed among local governments and institutions under local control (schools, community health services, police and fire protection, recreation). Multiplicity is anti-totality politics."[82]

Commentators have criticized the episodic, localist, and anti-institutional orientation of Wolin's approach to democracy for being incapable of

77. Wolin, *Democracy Incorporated*, 255.

78. Wolin, *Politics and Vision*, 602.

79. Wolin, *Politics and Vision*, 604.

80. Wolin, "What Revolutionary Action Means Today," 251.

81. Wolin, *Politics and Vision*, 604.

82. Wolin, *Politics and Vision*, 603.

generating the organizational forms needed to achieve long-term, structural transformation. Even a sympathetic critic like Wendy Brown suggests that "Wolin presents us with a scene of hegemonic, dispersed state and capitalist domination, and proposes counter-practices that offer, at best, episodic and partial experiences with powers whose production and circulation citizens will never control."[83] Similarly, Jeffrey Stout argues that fugitive democracy is too episodic to be adequate as a form of resistance to the politics of the nation-state and global capitalism. For him, Wolin's approach is incapable of building organizations that can produce sustainable democratic trans-formation. He observes, "Wolin's work on the evisceration of democracy, though admirably accurate in its treatment of the dangers posed by empire and capital, abandons the project of democratic accountability too quickly in favor of the romance of the fugitive."[84] Stout fears, in particular, that Wo-lin's interpretation of radical democracy as a temporary form of resistance refuses the responsibility of governance because it opposes all institutional forms as antidemocratic. Within Wolin's framework, it is impossible for de-mocracy to be anything other than ephemeral because he views institutions as little more than tools to be manipulated by elites to retain power.

Additionally, Stout worries that Wolin's bleak diagnosis of the contem-porary challenges faced by democracy engenders a sense of hopelessness in the face of the overwhelming power of capitalism and empire. As a result, Stout argues that Wolin fails at the most basic task of radical politics, which is to provide hope that another political order is possible.[85] He observes, "Like its close cousin, fugitive Christianity, it threatens to become a mere 'ought' that has lost both its roots in the soil of social life and any hope of effecting change in the institutions it criticizes."[86] When everyday citizens surrender the hope that by changing their behavior they may "be able to use governmental structures to exercise a greater degree of control on the economy" than they now do, they resign themselves to "ever-increasing domination by corporate elites."[87] If institutions are viewed as inherently corrupt and incapable of fundamental reform, this ultimately delivers "un-constrained global power to capital" and cedes control of the "judiciary to people who believe that the Bill of Rights became obsolete on 9/11."[88]

83. Brown, "Democracy and Bad Dreams."

84. Stout, "Spirit of Democracy," 3.

85. Stout, "Spirit of Democracy," 7. On democratic hope, see Stout, *Democracy and Tradition*, 40ff.

86. Stout, *Blessed Are the Organized*, 254.

87. Stout, *Blessed Are the Organized*, 255.

88. Stout, "Spirit of Democracy," 17–18.

Stout concludes that because a "strictly" fugitive democracy abandons the hope that institutional structures of government can be held accountable, it serves to "reinforce the tendencies it officially opposes."[89]

As an alternative to Wolin's fugitive approach, Stout argues that it is necessary to attend to the relationship between political action at the local level and the broader commitment to creating durable organizations capable of sustaining the gains of fugitive democracy at a macropolitical level. He points to community-based organizations as a model of radical democracy that offers a more sustained model for social transformation than the "subterranean" resistance and "anarchist insurgencies" of fugitive democracy.[90] For example, Stout maintains that the grassroots organizing of the Industrial Areas Foundation (IAF) represents a more effective model for democratic renewal than the anarchist politics of Occupy Wall Street. Stout observes, "I talk to community organizers like Ernesto Cortes and Sister Judy Donovan of the Industrial Areas Foundation. For in their work, I see not only the sort of grassroots democratic practices that provide Wolin with some hope at the local level, but also a concerted attempt to link up local citizens' organizations in networks that might be capable of affecting political outcomes at the state and national levels. It matters a great deal whether these attempts at network-building succeed."[91] For Stout, the work of the IAF would scarcely exist without Christianity: "If one subtracted the churches from IAF and other similar organizing networks, then grassroots democracy in the United States would come to very little."[92]

As with the Hardt/Negri and Laclau/Mouffe debate, the postliberal conversation in the United States has occurred as a debate between a withdrawal or anti-institutional option (Wolin) and grassroots or institutional approach (Stout). Each of these approaches possesses distinctive strengths as well as liabilities. As we noted in the introduction to this book, at times Hardt and Negri and Mouffe express crude and reductionistic approaches to religion that restrict their commitment to pluralism. And while Wolin offers a critique of the state that paradoxically delivers enormous political power over to capital and empire, Stout is insufficiently attentive to the importance of fugitive experiences of resistance to democratic renewal. In view of these

89. Stout, "Spirit of Democracy," 18.

90. Stout, "Spirit of Democracy," 19.

91. Stout, "Spirit of Democracy," 18. Stout sees the religious support for radical democracy as particularly critical: "If the religious Left does not soon recover its energy and self-confidence, it is unlikely that American democracy will be capable of counteracting either the greed of its business elite or the determination of many whites to define the authentic nation in ethnic, racial, or ecclesiastical terms." Stout, *Democracy and Tradition*, 300.

92. Stout, *Blessed Are the Organized*, 5. On this point, see Hauerwas and Coles, *Christianity, Democracy, and the Radical Ordinary*, 227ff.

shortcomings, the position adopted in this work is similar to William Connolly's pluralist approach to radical democratic politics in its attempt to displace binaries that inhibit the development of multilayered resistance to the
politics of empire. Connolly not only affirms the importance of "withdrawal"
and "engagement" frameworks but also advocates for the integration of religious voices within radical democratic politics.

Generally, Connolly affirms the work of Hardt, Negri, and Wolin, but
he also expresses reservations about specific features of their projects. In
particular, along with Stout, Conolly expresses concern that the anti-statist
and anti-reformist tenor of their reflections ultimately delivers too much
power over to the right. He observes, "It is tempting for critics to forgo electoral politics because it is so dysfunctional. But to do so cedes too much
independent power to corporate action and the radical right with respect to
state power. The right loves to *make* politics dysfunctional to make people
lose confidence in it and to transfer their confidence to the private sector."[93]
Connolly suggests another path that, while affirming the importance of
fugitive experiments in insurgent and grassroots democracy, attempts
to move beyond it by linking these local experiments with national and
transnational movements. His diagnosis is that we live in the midst of an
interregnum between national and post-national politics and so "positive
democratic movements on behalf of egalitarianism, ecology and diversity
must be active at several sites, including local involvement, country-wide
social movements, direct pressure on corporate structures and church organizations, participation in national party politics, and cross-state citizen
networks to challenge the American state from inside and outside at the
same time."[94] It is when these diverse movements resonate at multiple sites
that widespread democratic transformation becomes possible.[95] This approach is compelling because it attempts to construct a vision of politics
that takes into account the complexity of the multiple sites (local, state,
transnational) and constituencies (secular and religious) needed to facilitate social and political transformation. Connolly specifically maintains that
because the left has been hampered by its tone-deafness to the important
role that spirituality and religion play in cultural life, a central imperative of
any politics on the left is to engage religious believers as a means of building

93. Connolly, *Fragility of Things*, 182. Emphasis original. See also Connolly, *Facing
the Planetary*, 23, in which he observes, "In an era replete with neofascist potential we
thus must both participate in electoral politics and break the political grid of intel-
ligibility it secretes."

94. Connolly, "Wolin, Superpower, and Christianity." See also Connolly, *Ethos of
Pluralization*, 23.

95. Connolly, "Evangelist-Capitalist Resonance Machine," 870; Coles, *Beyond Gated
Politics*, 150; Coles, "Of Tensions and Tricksters," 549.

a pluralist coalition.[96] The right has dominated this work in recent years and invokes "Christianity to support the politics of torture, the suspension of due process, a unitary presidency, preemptive wars, and the extension of inequality in income, job security, workers' rights, and retirement," and so "it is indispensable for dissenting Christians, Jews, Muslims, and nontheists to cite publicly the sources from which they find inspiration to oppose those policies."[97] Connolly contends that to build a broad-based assemblage on the left, Christians and members of other religious traditions must offer alternative interpretations of the political implications of these faith traditions. In subsequent chapters on black prophetic thought, feminist theology, Latin American liberation theology, and peaceable theology we will examine one such pluralist theo-political assemblage.

In this chapter we have examined debates within two trajectories of radical democratic theory: post-Marxist and postliberal. Beyond laying the groundwork for subsequent chapters, this chapter has permitted us to describe some of the fundamental issues debated in radical democratic theory. Notably, the theologians examined in this work have been more attracted to the withdrawal axis of radical democratic theory than the engagement axis. Thus, we find Wolin, Hardt, and Negri appearing as interlocutors more frequently than Laclau or Mouffe; the probable reason for this is that Wolin, Hardt, and Negri locate the site of radical democratic politics in civil society rather than the state, and because civil society is the space occupied by religion, it stands to reason that theologians would find some affinity with political theorists who emphasize its significance. The task in subsequent chapters will be to analyze how Christian thinkers have generated unique approaches to radical democracy in their attempt to retrieve radical forms of ekklesial witness: the black church (West), ekklesia of wo/men (Schüssler Fiorenza), the church of the poor (Sobrino), and the peaceable church (Hauerwas).

---

96. Connolly, "Interview with William Connolly," 331. See also Connolly, "Confronting the Anthropocene and Contesting Neoliberalism," 268.

97. Connolly, *Christianity and Capitalism*, 36.

CHAPTER 3

Black Prophetic Thought

IN THE 1960S BLACK theology emerged as a form of liberation theology (alongside Latin American and feminist theologies) that offered a critique of structural racism and the retrieval of the emancipatory politics of the Christian tradition to confront racism in American history. Cornel West was an early advocate of black theology and offered his own distinctive challenge to it in two essays, "Black Theology and Marxist Thought" and "Black Theology and Liberation as Critique of Capitalist Civilization," as well as his first book, *Prophesy Deliverance! An Afro-American Revolutionary Christianity*.[1] West engaged black theology not as a theologian but as a Christian, observing, "I have always shunned the role of theologian because I have little interest in systematizing the dogmas and doctrines, insights and intuitions of the Christian tradition." In reflecting on his own work West describes it as an attempt to retrieve "Christian resources, among others, to speak to the multi-layered crises of contemporary society and culture."[2]

In this chapter we approach West's writing as a form of black prophetic thought that utilizes philosophy, critical theory, and resources from the Christian tradition to offer a pragmatic approach to radical politics. West's approach to black prophetic thought focuses on the relationship between racism, American empire, and radical democracy. For West, racism is the foundational lens through which to confront the contradictions of American empire, even as he finds it necessary to link the effects of racism to other forms of oppression—capitalism, military imperialism, and other social evils (which he often lists as sexism, homophobia, anti-Semitism, and Islamophobia). Additionally, as a Christian pragmatist who recognizes the formative power of religion in the public sphere, West criticizes imperial

1. West, "Black Theology and Marxist Thought"; West, "Black Theology of Liberation as Critique of Capitalist Civilization"; and West, *Prophesy Deliverance!*
2. West, *Ethical Dimensions of Marxist Thought*, xxix.

or Constantinian forms of Christianity that legitimate empire by providing religious cover for a politics of oppression. West maintains that because Constantinian Christianity serves a central role in legitimating empire, the struggle over the meaning of Christianity represents a critical site of struggle for the contemporary left. He characterizes the left's tendency to reject religion and to generate political coalitions on purely secular grounds as "tantamount to political suicide" because "a purely secular fight cannot be won."[3] Constructively, West draws the link between Constantinian Christianity and the politics of American empire, on the one hand, and between prophetic Christianity and radical democracy, on the other hand. These coordinates serve as the central points of creative tension in West's analysis and serve as the framework for explicating his thought in this chapter.

In the first section of this chapter we analyze West's description of the politics of American empire as a complex interaction between racism, capitalism, imperialism, and social crimes (mass incarceration and police brutality) that receive a popular base of support among Constantinian Christians. In the second section, we explore his religious retrieval of prophetic Christianity, particularly as it is manifest in the radical politics of the black church, as a potent force for democratization in society. In the final section, we analyze his distinctive contribution to radical democratic theory and practice through his articulation of a prophetic-pragmatist approach to radical politics. Furthermore, we examine a Hauerwasian criticism of West's pragmatist approach to Christian politics. For Hauerwas, West's approach is in danger of relinquishing the distinctiveness of Christian witness for the sake of political relevance. And while West possesses resources to contest this interpretation of his work, it is true that even as he offers the most expansive engagement with radical democratic politics among the Christian thinkers examined in this work, he offers the least developed set of theological reflections to support a Christian engagement with radical democratic politics.

Empire and Racism

In his analysis of the current configuration of American empire, West follows the broad outlines of Martin Luther King Jr.'s "A Time to Break the Silence" (1967), in which King argued that racism, militarism, and classism represent the central features of American empire. West recalibrates King's approach by arguing that empire now consists of free market fundamentalism (neoliberalism), militarist imperialism, and the racialized

3. West, *American Evasion of Philosophy*, 234, and West, *Democracy Matters*, 146.

contradictions of the American criminal justice system (social crimes). We focus here on West's distinctive contribution to our previous discussion of neoliberalism and neoconservatism in the first chapter by analyzing the role that racism and Constantinian Christianity play in the formation and legitimation of American empire.

For West, the United States represents a fragile experiment in democracy as well as a project in expansionist imperialism. Although he points to deep democratic energies throughout American history—from resistance to British imperialism and the abolitionist movement to the suffragist and the civil rights movements in the twentieth century—West also observes that empire exists alongside these movements, stretching from the imperialist projects of settler colonialism and the transatlantic slave trade to the Jim Crow laws of disenfranchisement, *de jure* segregation, racially biased policing, redlining, policy brutality, and mass incarceration. West observes of this history that the "repressive face of the American state" has served as a dominant mechanism of racial oppression in American history and stretches from "the whip on the plantation to the lynching of the lynching tree, to the trigger-happy policing, on to the death penalty and the criminal justice system and the prison-industrial complex."[4] For him, race specifically constitutes the critical "intersecting point" of the constituent elements of empire and amplifies the oppressive features of capitalism, military imperialism, and social crimes.[5]

The first point of intersection that emerges in West's work concerns the relationship between racism and capitalism in which he extends the black radical tradition's analysis of racial capitalism. West's own critical engagement with capitalism is displayed most prominently in his early work (particularly *Prophesy Deliverance!* and several articles on Marxism and black theology in the 1980s) and develops alongside the critical body of literature on racial capitalism. The term *racial capitalism* was developed in South Africa in the 1970s and 1980s to describe the racialization of political and economic structures under apartheid. It was subsequently popularized by Cedric Robinson in *Marxism and the Black Radical Tradition* (1983), in which he argued that capitalism always operates through existing forms of racism.[6] Against Marx, Robinson argued that capitalism did not dramatically

4. West, "Empire, Pragmatism, and War," 55.

5. West, *Democracy Matters*, 14. As a result, he posits that the plight of African Americans should serve as the "fundamental litmus test" of the health of American democracy, and by this standard it must be acknowledged that "the history of American democracy in regard to black people from 1776 to 1965 was a colossal failure." West, *Race Matters*, vii. See also Unger and West, *Future of American Progressivism*, 17–18.

6. Robinson, *Marxism and the Black Radical Tradition*.

break with feudalism, but rather strategically utilized its racialized categories of exploitation for capitalist purposes. Europe was racialized before the advent of capitalism—the first subjugated classes were racialized subjects (Gypsies, Roma, Jews, etc.)[7]—and so capitalism operated by appropriating these existing racial categories in order to expropriate indigenous land (settler colonialism), extract wealth from the labor of those deemed to be nonpersons (slavery), and exploit the labor of global immigrants. While there is no stable relation between racism and capitalism because these realities are interlaced in distinctive ways in every sociohistorical situation, one constant of capitalism is that it deploys race in order to institute hierarchies and normalize the differential value attributed to groups of people.[8]

In his own work, West affirms Robinson's work on racial capitalism but offers his own contribution to this discussion by initiating a dialogue between black theology and Marxist theory.[9] In his early essays, as well as his first book, *Prophesy Deliverance!*, West analyzed the shortcomings of both Marxism and black theology and called for a productive dialogue between these traditions as a means of generating a multilayered response to social oppression. West criticizes Marxism for its elision of racial oppression and its exclusive focus on the analytics of class domination. He resists this reductionism by arguing that "although racist practices were appropriated and promoted in various ways by modern capitalist processes, racism predates capitalism" and performs "multiple power functions" not reducible to class antagonism.[10] Black theologians have recognized what Marxists have failed to acknowledge, namely, that "racist practices are not reducible to a mere clever and successful strategy to divide and conquer" the underclass by economic elites.[11]

West also takes issue with the Marxist approach to religion. He largely exonerates Marx and Engels by arguing that their approach is more nuanced than often acknowledged, but blames the Marxism of the Second International for promoting a reductionistic interpretation of religion. Pragmatically, West criticizes the reductionism of Marxists because they fail to recognize the continued role that religion plays in the lives of the oppressed. He instead calls for Marxists to engage in a process of

7. Kelley, "What Did Cedric Robinson Mean by Racial Capitalism?"

8. See Lowe, *Intimacies of Four Continents*, 149–50.

9. West, *Prophetic Fragments*, 53.

10. West, *Cornel West Reader*, 258, and West, *Prophetic Fragments*, 100.

11. Thus, racism exceeds a "class analytic" and should be viewed as "an integral element within the fabric of American culture and society. It is embedded in the country's first collective definition, enunciated in its subsequent laws, and imbued in its dominant way of life." West, *Prophesy Deliverance!*, 116.

"de-secularizing" by which they disavow their paternalistic attitude toward religion and engage the oppressed not only as political and economic agents but also as productive agents who express meaningful resistance through their cultural and religious practices.[12]

In addition to highlighting the deficiencies of the Marxist tradition, West examines the efforts of black theologians to confront structural racism in American history. Generally, West praises black theologians' work on this front, but he cautions that a serious omission is their failure to attend to the exploitative structures of capitalism.[13] It is not a question of whether "racist practices should be stressed less by black theologians" but rather whether "these practices be linked to the role they play in buttressing the current mode of production, concealing the unequal distribution of wealth, and portraying the lethargy of the political system."[14] In particular, West challenges black theologians for failing to make the connection between "racist interpretations of the gospel" and a political and economic order that legitimates class-based inequalities.[15] The focus of black liberation theology has been on "including Black people within the mainstream of liberal capitalist America," and, as a consequence, black liberation theology largely remains "uncritical of America's imperialist presence in Third World countries, its capitalist system of production, and its grossly unequal distribution of wealth."[16] And because "class position contributes more than racial status to the basic form of powerlessness in America," the failure to seriously confront the class dynamics of the capitalist system in the United States undermines black theologians' capacity to offer a liberating political vision.

West's intervention aims to push Marxism beyond its class reductionism and to move black theology into a new discursive space as a "critique of capitalist civilization."[17] Constructively, West maintains that a black theology of liberation as a critique of capitalist civilization must take "into account the complex ways in which racism (especially white racism) and sexism (especially male sexism) are integral to the class exploitative system of production as well as its repressive imperialist tentacles abroad; and to

12. West, "Religion and the Left," 20.

13. West, *Prophesy Deliverance!*, 106. West observes, "An undisputable claim of Black theology is America's unfair treatment of Black people. What is less apparent is the way in which Black theologians understand the internal dynamics of liberal capitalist America, how it functions, why it operates the way it does, who possesses substantive power, and where it is headed" (*Prophesy Deliverance!*, 113).

14. West, *Prophesy Deliverance!*, 113–14.

15. West, *Prophesy Deliverance!*, 113.

16. West, "Black Theology and Marxist Thought," 413.

17. West, *Prophesy Deliverance!*, 106.

keep in view the crucial existential issues of death, disease, despair, dread, and disappointment that each and every individual must face within the context of these present circumstances."[18] As we shall see in the final section of this chapter, West's distinctive contribution to Christian theological engagement with radical democracy is a prophetic-pragmatist vision for politics that responds to this shortcoming by offering a more concrete vision for a black politics of liberation.

West's analysis of the relationship between racism and capitalism is linked to his critique of imperialism because for him it is impossible to comprehend the mechanisms of racialized capitalism without situating it within the broader context of American imperial violence abroad. In his early works, West offered a variation on the classical Marxist approach to imperialism by arguing that "at present, capitalism is inseparable from imperialism in that the latter is an extension of capitalism across national boundaries."[19] The historical legacies of colonialism have persisted through neocolonial projects of economic coercion by which the global North controls the "land and means of production" of "less developed countries. This control has been protected by the military and political resources of developed countries."[20] In his recent work, West has focused less on the Marxist interpretation of imperialism and more on the military dimension of American imperialism by which the United States exerts control over foreign countries. He specifically points to this process in Latin America, where the United States intervened militarily "over three hundred times in the last hundred years" and, in the process, offered support and assistance to "antidemocratic regimes, sometimes overthrowing democratic regimes, as in Guatemala, Brazil, the Dominican Republic."[21] The United States policy in Latin America in the 1970s and 1980s has been repeated in the United States policy in the Middle East in the 2000s, a policy which, according to West, is characterized by "unilateral intervention, colonial invasion, and armed occupation."[22] West observes that in order to support these and other military operations the United States has built an expansive military presence around the world, with "650 military facilities in 132 countries, a ship in every major ocean, a presence on every major continent other than Antarctica, and 1,450,000 soldiers around the globe."[23] Finally, there exists

18. West, *Prophesy Deliverance!*, 106.

19. West, *Prophesy Deliverance!*, 122.

20. West, *Prophesy Deliverance!*, 122.

21. West, "Prisoner of Hope," 124.

22. West, *Democracy Matters*, 5.

23. West, "Empire, Pragmatism, and War," 49.

a domestic analogue to imperialism abroad in terms of the proliferation of punitive forms of structural racism at home. Nikhil Pal Singh and others have pointed to the discursive resonance in the American imagination between militarism and criminality. On the one hand, military action abroad is justified through the criminalization of foreign countries as rogue states or as a threat to American security. On the other hand, internal threats to the social order are similarly criminalized and used to justify militarization of the police and border security.[24] This dual process of criminalization legitimates the use of the American military and security apparatus to manage, suppress, and eliminate racialized threats to American security.

Domestically, West characterizes the United States as a scene of contradiction in which the legal system fails to penalize corporate (Wall Street violators) and military crimes (torturers, wiretappers), while bringing the full force of the law to bear against minoritized and marginalized populations.[25] The contradictions in the criminal justice system represent a constant feature of American history now most "graphically seen in the prison-industrial complex and targeted police surveillance in black and brown ghettos, rendered invisible in public discourse."[26] In 1980 the prison population in the United States was approximately three hundred thousand people. By the 1990s that figure grew to almost one million. By the 2000s it reached 2.4 million people. Presently, one in thirty-five adults in the United States are in prison or on parole or probation.[27] The United States accounts for approximately 5 percent of the global population but warehouses 25 percent of the global prison population. These statistics are jarring and raise a number of disquieting questions about the rapid development of the United States' vast carceral apparatus. In general, there have been two primary positions that attempt to account for the explosion of mass incarceration over the past forty years: structural racism and neoliberalism.

The persistence of structural racism in American history is often identified as the primary cause of the rise of mass incarceration in the United States. Michelle Alexander offers the most famous example of this interpretative approach in *The New Jim Crow: Mass Incarceration in an Age of Colorblindness* (2012). In *The New Jim Crow* Alexander describes how mass incarceration succeeded Jim Crow policies as a new means of social control

24. Singh, *Race and America's Long War*, 128–29. In *Democracy Matters*, West observes that there exists a relationship between American militarism abroad and the militarization of "police power" in relation to "criminal" populations in urban centers in the United States (6).

25. West, *Black Prophetic Fire*, 163.

26. West, introduction to King, *Radical King*, xi–xii.

27. Camp, *Incarcerating the Crisis*, 3, and Alexander, *New Jim Crow*, 60.

of black bodies after the end of the formal Jim Crow system. She contends that after the Civil Rights Act of 1964 there emerged a political backlash by disaffected whites who feared that their jobs, educational access, and social standing were threatened by the social transformations associated with the civil rights movement. The Republican Party saw this disaffection as an opportunity for electoral advantage and seized upon it. They developed and then successfully deployed the so-called Southern strategy, which utilized coded forms of racism to appeal to whites' racial resentments. After the civil rights movement it was no longer socially acceptable to employ explicit forms of racism in public, so politicians employed "dog whistles" to signal to voters that their policies would serve white interests and punish minoritized populations.[28] Richard Nixon, Ronald Reagan, George H. W. Bush, and Bill Clinton all built a winning electoral strategy around policy proposals to cut welfare, enact a war on drugs, and get tough on crime. As politicians achieved electoral success with dog-whistle strategies they attempted to deliver on their campaign promises by passing legislation facilitating the war on drugs and tough-on-crime policies that swept unprecedented numbers of African American men into the criminal justice system. Alexander surveys the results: "More African American adults are under correctional control today—in prison or jail, on probation or parole—than were enslaved in 1850, a decade before the Civil War began."[29]

Alexander argues that the exploitation of racial resentment by politicians drove the rise of mass incarceration.[30] Others have suggested alternative explanations that, without rejecting Alexander's thesis, supplement it by pointing to economic factors behind the expansion of the American carceral complex. Ruth Wilson Gilmore, Angela Davis, Cedric Johnson, and Loïc Wacquant suggest that the crisis of capitalism in the late 1970s and the neoliberal restructuring of society in the 1980s worked in concert with structural racism to create the prison-industrial complex. For these thinkers, the relation between racism and neoliberalism most adequately explains mass incarceration's genesis.[31] There are two notable features of this relation: (1) the management of surplus populations through criminal

28. López, *Dog Whistle Politics*.

29. Alexander, *New Jim Crow*, 180.

30. It is important to note that Democrats as well as Republicans contributed decisively to this process. Bill Clinton's administration was as instrumental as Reagan's in building the mass incarceration system in the United States. For the broader history that stretches back to the presidencies of John F. Kennedy and Lyndon Johnson, see Hinton, *From the War on Poverty to the War on Crime*, and Murakawa, *The First Civil Right*.

31. Wacquant, "Class, Race, and Hyperincarceration," 74.

justice rather than welfare, and (2) the management of neoliberal crises through the security state.

First, as a result of neoliberal reforms and the attendant processes of deindustrialization, globalization, and deregulation, sizable portions of the population have been rendered unemployable and useless by market standards. During the era of industrial capitalism, rises in unemployment were dealt with by expanding the welfare state. Similarly, declines in unemployment meant restriction of welfare benefits in order to push recipients back into the labor market. In their classic work *Regulating the Poor* (1971), Frances Fox Piven and Richard Cloward argue that this expansion-retraction cycle served to manage the poor and mitigate any social disorder that might result from unemployment.[32] The neoliberal restructuring of economy and the state undermined this approach from two sides by assaulting the Keynesian ideal of full employment and enacting severe cuts to welfare and antipoverty spending.[33] Under neoliberalism, the welfare state has been replaced with a punitive state. Wacquant explains, "Incarceration has de facto become America's largest government program for the poor."[34] It has been estimated that increased prison populations during the rise of mass incarceration shaved almost two percentage points off of US unemployment statistics. Angela Davis detects in mass incarceration something even more insidious: prisons serve to inoculate society from disturbing questions about structural racism and the inequalities generated by capitalism. Prisons "function ideologically as an abstract site into which undesirables are deposited, relieving us of thinking about real issues afflicting those communities from which prisoners are drawn in such disproportionate numbers . . . The prison has become a black hole into which the detritus of contemporary capitalism is deposited."[35] Both spatially and ideologically, prisons warehouse societal problems generated by the nexus between structural racism and neoliberal capitalism.

Second, mass incarceration relates to neoliberalism's tendency to create insecurity for white working-class and minoritized populations alike. A defining feature of neoliberalism is its susceptibility to constant crisis.[36] The felt sense of precarity produced by neoliberal reforms and their attendant crises, especially among working classes, could be dealt with by

32. Piven and Cloward, *Regulating the Poor*. See Wacquant *Punishing the Poor*, 290.

33. Gottschalk, *Caught*, 46. In *Golden Gulag*, Ruth Wilson Gilmore contends that the dramatic rise in incarceration in California was a response to four surpluses: finance capital, labor, land, and state capacity.

34. Wacquant, *Prisons of Poverty*, 69.

35. Davis, *Are Prisons Obsolete?*, 16.

36. Harvey, *Seventeen Contradictions,* and Harvey, *The Enigma of Capital.*

resisting neoliberalism and demanding a more extensive redistribution of wealth, greater economic protections, and the revitalization of unions. The neoliberal approach has been to translate economic insecurity into political insecurity and to reduce the state's function to criminal security provision. Wacquant details this approach: "By elevating criminal safety *(sécurité, Sicherheit, sicurezza,* etc.) to the frontline of government priorities, state officials have condensed the diffuse class anxiety and simmering ethnic resentment generated by the unraveling of the Fordist-Keynesian compact and channeled them toward the (dark-skinned) street criminal, designated as guilty of sowing social and moral disorder in the city, alongside the profligate welfare recipient."[37] In this sense, securitization represents a political strategy of deflection and redirection that immunizes neoliberal policy from critique. Furthermore, it serves as a potent political strategy that assembles white resentment against minoritized communities.

For West, mass incarceration is the result of the confluence of structural racism with neoliberal reforms, processes of securitization, and the militarization of the police. As such, mass incarceration represents an example of the destructive nexus between racism, capitalism, imperialism, and state violence. And even though his critique of American empire is primarily directed at political formations on the right, it is important to note that West also criticizes the politics of the center-left as embodied, most recently, in the Clinton and Obama administrations. The Clinton administration's support of NAFTA (1994), the Violent Crime Control and Law Enforcement Act (1994) and the Personal Responsibility and Work Opportunity Reconciliation Act (1996), and the repeal of Glass-Steagall (1999) led to policies that eliminated social supports for the working class, contributed to the decimation of communities of color through policies that intensified mass incarceration, and deregulated the banking industry.[38] According to West, the worst elements of Clintonism reemerged in the Obama administration in a cabinet filled with "Clintonites on the economic front so the Keynesian neoliberalism would still hold, and recycled the Clintonites on the imperial front so you get the liberal neoconservatism."[39] Despite Obama's emancipatory language and democratic rhetoric, his administration watched over what amounted to a "Wall Street government" that showed relative indifference to "the New Jim Crow (or prison-industrial complex)" and

37. Wacquant, *Punishing the Poor,* 299.

38. West, "Why Brother Bernie Is Better for Black People than Sister Hillary."

39. West, "Left Matters," 359.

expanded "imperial criminality in terms of the vast increase of the number of drones since the Bush years."[40]

Although the center-left shares a broad policy orientation with the right in terms of economic and foreign policy, the right distinguishes itself from the center-left in terms of the intensity of its commitments and its strategic appeal to white conservative Christians as a populist base of support.[41] West maintains that Constantinian Christianity represents the moral arm of the Republican Party and provides a base of support for American militarism, neoliberal capitalism, as well as racist and misogynist discourses and practices.[42] The basic charge West levels against Constantinian Christianity is that it functions as a form of idolatry that raises the flag above the cross.[43] As such, it stands at fundamental "odds with the prophetic legacy of Jesus Christ" and "has supported the worst moments in American history from manifest destiny to the justification of slavery and the denial of women's equality."[44] Just as Constantine used Christianity "partly out of political strategy and imperial exigency" to maintain imperial power, political and economic elites in the United States use Christianity to support racist, militarist, and anti-egalitarian policies.[45] West is careful here to distinguish between elites who manipulate Christians by enlisting them in the politics of empire and the Christians themselves, whom he describes as largely "sincere in their faith and pious in their actions" but "unaware of their imperialistic identity because they do not see the parallel between the Roman Empire that put Jesus to death and the American flag that they celebrate."[46] As we shall see in the next section, although West claims that Constantinian Christianity has been co-opted by capitalism and white supremacy and serves as a base of support for imperialism abroad, he describes the black church—and more broadly all prophetic forms of religion—as important sites of resistance to empire.

40. West, *Black Prophetic Fire*, 163 and 3. West observes that the Obama presidency resulted in "563 drone strikes, the assassination of US citizens with no trial, the 26,171 bombs dropped on five Muslim-majority countries in 2016 and the 550 Palestinian children killed with US supported planes in 51 days, etc." West, "Ta-Nehisi Coates Is the Neoliberal Face of the Black Freedom Struggle."

41. "America's two main political parties, each beholden to big money, offer merely alternative versions of oligarchic rule." West, introduction to King, *Radical King*, xiii.

42. West, *Democracy Matters*, 149–50. According to West, certain forms of Christianity serve as "a fundamental pillar for imperial America." West, "Empire, Pragmatism, and War," 61, and West, "Prisoner of Hope," 123.

43. West, *Hope on a Tightrope*, 80.

44. West, *Democracy Matters*, 148, 152.

45. West, *Democracy Matters*, 148.

46. West, *Democracy Matters*, 150 and 148.

THE BLACK CHURCH

In *Democracy Matters* West observes that "the battle for the soul of American democracy is, in large part, a battle for American Christianity."[47] The reason for this is straightforward—the strength of American empire is derived largely from the support it gathers from Constantinian Christians. It follows that in a very real sense the future direction of American democracy is dependent on the future direction of Christianity in America.[48] The success of the struggle for democratization in the face of American empire depends on the extent to which prophetic forms of Christianity generate opposition to Constantinian forms of Christianity. This diagnosis offers a unique challenge to the left because its position has been largely one of suspicion and hostility toward religion. West argues that the pervasive secularism on the left is an important reason it has failed to build effective coalitions of resistance to the right since the 1970s. He observes, "The inability of the left, especially in the USA, to deal adequately with the crucial issues of everyday life such as racism, sexism, ecology, sexual orientation, and personal despair may indeed have something to do with its refusal to grapple with the complex role and function of religion. Needless to say, since the majority of American people remain religious in some form or other, the American left (black or white) ignores religious and cultural issues at its own peril."[49] For West, religious thinkers on the left must offer an interpretation of religion that contests imperialist forms of religiosity on the right (Constantinian Christianity) and establishes alliances with other groups that support radical democracy.

West's approach to these matters differs from the theologians examined in subsequent chapters because he is not a theologian and approaches religion from the perspective of his pragmatic philosophical commitments. His pragmatist approach departs from traditional or doctrinal approaches to Christianity on two fronts. First, he views metaphysical truth claims that attempt to disclose the essence of things as untenable and argues that there is simply no way to know "whether one's Christian beliefs correspond to some given metaphysical, transcendent, or ahistorical divine referent." It is necessary to view all talk of "truth" as a "contextual affair, always related to human aims and human problems, human groups and human communities."[50] Second, West's critique of metaphysical truth

47. West, *Democracy Matters*, 146.

48. West, *Democracy Matters*, 146. See also West, "Empire, Pragmatism, and War," 60.

49. West, *Prophetic Fragments*, 68. See also West, *Democracy Matters*, 159.

50. West, *Keeping Faith*, 134.

is linked to his concern about the political implications of "dogmatic pro-
nouncements" that reinforce the tendencies among "homogenous constituencies" to persecute and exclude.[51]

As a result of his critique of the correspondence theory of truth as
well as his concern about the political and social implications of religious dogmatism, West has developed an approach to Christianity that
is pragmatist with respect to truth claims and prophetic with respect to
its political implications.[52] West views truth as serving a pragmatic function that entails a commitment to a particular set of practices and forms
of life. To proclaim that Jesus Christ is "Truth," as West does, means that
Christians "should look at the world through the eyes of its victims, and
the Christocentric perspective that requires that one see the world through
the lens of the Cross—and thereby see our relative victimizing and relative
victimization."[53] As with his Christology, West offers minimal ecclesiological reflections, and when he has written about the church his focus has
been on the capacity of the black church to generate forms of life that resist
racism and other forms of social violence.[54] From the slave insurrections in
the nineteenth century to the civil rights movement in the 1960s the black
church has served as the most important site of Christian prophetic witness in American history.[55] Because the black churches retained "relative
control over their churches," even in the midst of enslavement and other
forms of racial persecution, black Christians created a unique spirituality
that creatively embodied a life between tragedy and hope.

In his work, particularly *The American Evasion of Philosophy*, West
assesses different discourses in terms of whether they move in a tragic or
romantic (or hopeful) direction. West characterizes his own prophetic-
pragmatist approach as an attempt to work through this tension and finds
an important precedent for this in the black church's dual commitment to
"religious transcendence and political opposition, belief in God and liberation themes, faith in the ultimate trustworthiness of human existence and

---

51. West, *Keeping Faith*, 126.

52. West, *Cornel West Reader*, 285. West acknowledges that "prophetic Christian
conceptions of what it is to be human, how we should act, and what we should hope
for are neither rationally demonstrable nor empirically verifiable in a necessary and
universal manner." West, *Ethical Dimensions of Marxist Thought*, xxviii.

53. West, *Keeping Faith*, 133.

54. Jeffrey Stout offers a provocative attempt to make explicit some of West's theological and ecclesiological commitments in "A Prophetic Church in a Post-Constantinian Age."

55. West, *Prophetic Fragments*, 67.

the negation of racism in the prevailing social order."[56] The black church cultivated "strategies of survival and visions of liberation" by simultaneously pursuing "tactics of reform and dreams of emancipation."[57] This creative interplay between the utopian imagination of total emancipation and the concrete and pragmatic commitment to incremental reform represents a central feature of West's thought.

In *Prophesy Deliverance!* West maintains that two prophetic norms ground the black church experience: individual human dignity and democracy. The norm of individual dignity is granted by God and, as a natural right, supports the principle of egalitarianism or radical equality before God. West invokes the biblical tradition of the *imago Dei* to defend the proposition that all persons are equal before God, a claim that is expressed in the Christian tradition as the call to identify with "the downtrodden, the dispossessed, the disinherited, with the exploited and the oppressed."[58] Moreover, this religious vision of fundamental equality before God necessitates the creation of political institutions that allow people to have some measure of control over their lives.[59] West invokes democracy as the political form best suited to the work of protecting the capacity of people to rule themselves. He argues, "Radical democracy is the best we finite, fallen creatures can do. Democracy is the ethical implication of the Christian conception of what it is to be human."[60] It is of some importance that West describes a secular political form—democracy—as an internal norm of black Christianity. As we shall see in the next section, this view contrasts sharply with Christian theologians like Yoder and Hauerwas, who argue that the alignment of the Christian church with secular political forms leads to the Constantinian erosion of authentic Christian witness.

In West's view, the black church has served as the central witness to prophetic (and therefore radical democratic) politics in American history. West observes that radical politics

> must inspire progressive and prophetic social motion. One precondition of this kind of social movement is the emergence of potent prophetic religious practices in churches, synagogues, temples, and mosques. And given the historical weight of such practices in the American past, the probable catalyst for social motion will be the prophetic wing of the black church. Need

56. West, *Prophetic Fragments*, 67. See also West, *Prophesy Deliverance!*, 149n3.

57. West, *Prophetic Fragments*, 44.

58. West, "Prophetic Theology," 224.

59. West, *Prophesy Deliverance!*, 19–20.

60. West, "Prophetic Theology," 225.

we remind ourselves that the most significant and successful organic intellectual in twentieth-century America—maybe in American history—was a product of and leader in the prophetic wing of the black church?[61]

Even as West identifies the prophetic orientation of the black church as critical to the retrieval of a contemporary radical politics, he offers an interpretation of prophetic Christianity as ecumenical and a natural ally of the pluralist orientation of radical democratic politics.[62] This pluralist approach is evident in his inclusive approach in which he views not only prophetic Christians as exemplars of this tradition (Sojourner Truth, Elizabeth Cady Stanton, Walter Rauschenbusch, Dorothy Day, Martin Luther King Jr.) but also Jewish (Abraham Joshua Heschel), Muslim (Malcolm X), and nonreligious figures (one thinks here of his extensive engagement with the black prophetic tradition of W. E. B. DuBois and James Baldwin).[63] In this regard, while West describes the black church as the most important carrier of prophetic discourse and practice in American history, he detaches the prophetic from its roots in the Judeo-Christian tradition and applies it to any discourse or social practice that defends the rights of the marginalized in society. And while the Christian community has specific reasons for cultivating this approach to the world, West maintains that it can be embodied by any person or community insofar as it is defined as those discourses or practices that "let suffering speak, let victims be visible and let social misery be put on the agenda of those with power."[64]

61. West, *American Evasion of Philosophy*, 234. West maintains, "This prophetic Christianity adds a moral fervor to our democracy that is a very good thing. It also holds that we must embrace those outside of the Christian faith and act with empathy towards them. This prophetic Christianity is an ecumenical force for good." The black church is at the root of the prophetic tradition in the United States: "Much of prophetic Christianity in America stems from the prophetic black tradition." West, *Democracy Matters*, 158.

62. West observes of his approach that it "worships at no ideological altars. It condemns oppression anywhere and everywhere, be it the brutal butchery of third-world dictators . . . or the racism, patriarchy, homophobia, and economic injustice in the first-world capitalist nations." West, *American Evasion of Philosophy*, 235.

63. West, *Democracy Matters*, 152. See also West, *American Evasion of Philosophy*, 234–35.

64. West, "Prophetic Religion," 99.

Prophetic-Pragmatist Democracy

In this final section of the chapter we turn to West's pragmatist approach to radical democratic politics, which combines elements of Wolinian radical democracy, the American pragmatist commitment to social reform, and the prophetic orientation of black Christianity and the black radical tradition. West offers a pragmatic trajectory in radical democratic theory and Christian thought that provides the most concrete political vision among the Christian thinkers analyzed in this book. Even more importantly, West articulates an approach to radical democracy that foregrounds the issue of race by maintaining that it represents the critical point of intersection between other forms of domination: capitalist exploitation, militarist violence, and punitive mechanisms of exclusion (mass incarceration).

West observes that if there is a "master term" in his writings it is democracy.[65] As with other radical democratic theorists, West defines democracy as a political form that is more radical than the classical liberal commitment to "bourgeois freedom" (individual rights, property rights, etc.) and "formal equality."[66] Furthermore, West suggests that democracy should be viewed as "more a verb than a noun" in that it represents a form of politics that has more to do with collective movements of resistance than institutions or systems of governance. Democracy entails a praxis undertaken on behalf of those disempowered by dominant cultural, economic, and political systems.[67] It is rooted in the attempt to provide those who have been marginalized by the dominant social order with a voice in determining the policies that shape their lives. West observes,

> Democracy is just the voice of everyday people being lifted in such a way that they have a role in decision-making processes in the institutions that regulate their lives. We begin with the least of these, raising their voices to make sure that their voices are heard when it comes to the economy, nation-state, culture, mass media, and so on. That is a deep democracy, a radical democracy that has everything to do with the Christian view that

65. West, *Prophesy Deliverance!*, 8.

66. For West, the entanglement between liberalism and democracy has placed American democracy within "racist, sexist, and class constraints." He observes, "I recognize that every democracy we know has been predicated on some kind of empire, going back to the Greeks. Predicated on patriarchal households, predicated on subordination of working people, usually predicated on marginalizing gay brothers and lesbian sisters and so forth." Strube and West, "Pragmatism's Tragicomic Jazzman," 293.

67. West, "Empire, Pragmatism, and War," 50.

puts a premium on voices of the least of these and the dignity of
the least of these.[68]

Because radical democracy represents a political form that prioritizes the
voices of those who suffer the consequences of the decisions made about how
society is organized, the removal of structural barriers (classism, racism, sexism, homophobia, and ethnocentrism) to participation serves as a fundamental task of radical democracy.[69] Historically, the target of democratic revolt has
been the consolidation of political and economic power among elites.[70] This
is as true of the organized revolt of peasants against the powerful oligarchs of
Athenian society as the organized resistance of a multiracial coalition against
structural racism during the civil rights movement.[71]

West's approach to democracy shares similarities with Wolin's insofar as the goal of democratic action is to eradicate political hierarchies that
inhibit participation.[72] Furthermore, as with Wolin, West expresses a measure of pessimism about the prospects for radical democratic transformation within the current political climate, observing that radical democratic
projects "remain on the cross—fugitive efforts rendered nearly impotent
and trapped in plutocratic, pigmentocratic, patriarchal, and heterosexist
constraints."[73] This type of language, as well as his sense of the significant
limitations of social action under the constraints of neoliberalism and empire, move West's work close to the pessimism of Wolin's fugitive democracy.
West describes this pessimistic feature of his work as a "sense of the tragic"
which he views as entailing the recognition that it is impossible to rid "the
world of *all* evil."[74] West differs from Wolin, however, insofar as this tragic
orientation is set alongside a "romantic" sensibility that supports "the auda-
cious projection of desires and hopes in the form of regulative emancipatory

68. West, "Politics, Virtue, and Struggle."

69. West, *Cornel West Reader*, 151.

70. West, *Democracy Matters*, 203–4.

71. West, *Democracy Matters*, 205. West argues that radical democracy is "operative
only when those who must suffer the consequences have effective control of institutions
that yield the consequences, i.e., access to decision-making processes." West, *American
Evasion of Philosophy*, 213.

72. In 2011 West called Sheldon Wolin "the greatest theorist of radical democracy
alive" ("Left Matters," 369).

73. West, "Afterword," 357. He contends that the effort to generate more inclusive
and egalitarian political forms constitutes a fugitive affair that often ends in failure
because more often than not elite powers try "to either kill you, try to absorb you and
incorporate you, or lie about you or try and undermine your movement." West, *Black
Prophetic Fire*, 84.

74. West, *American Evasion of Philosophy*, 229. Emphasis original.

ideals."[75] The romantic axis of West's thought is present in his engagement with the Christian tradition as well as the American pragmatic tradition. The pragmatic tradition, in particular, represents an important supplement to his Wolinian proclivities in terms of its concrete commitment to social experimentation and political reform.

West's most extensive engagement with the American pragmatist tradition, *The American Evasion of Philosophy*, contains both important genealogical and constructive elements. West's genealogy of pragmatism includes the usual suspects—Ralph Waldo Emerson, John Dewey, William James, C. S. Peirce, and Richard Rorty—but incorporates the voices of Roberto Unger and W. E. B. DuBois as important correctives to the tradition. Constructively, West argues that in contrast to traditional philosophical inquiry, which attempts to validate the correspondence theory of truth, the pragmatist tradition rejects any ahistorical understanding of truth and instead ascribes it a practical function by viewing it as the use of critical reflection to resolve concrete problems that restrict human flourishing. In this sense, pragmatism has "evaded" philosophy as traditionally practiced by approaching philosophy as an experimental tradition that engages in a theoretical critique of oppressive structures and seeks to cultivate "options and alternatives for transforming praxis."[76]

Substantively, West defines pragmatism as having "to do with trying to conceive of knowledge, reality and truth in such a way that it promotes the flowering and flourishing of individuality under conditions of democracy."[77] In the previous section, we noted that for West human dignity and democracy represent the two internal norms of black prophetic Christianity. It is not surprising, therefore, that West views pragmatism as an important philosophical ally to this tradition in its support of democratic movements that defend the basic dignity of each individual in society. Importantly, though, West is not uncritical of the American pragmatist tradition and points to a number of inadequacies. First, he criticizes pragmatism as trapped within a "racist" American political culture, observing that "American philosophy has never taken the Afro-American experience seriously. Even during the golden age of Royce, James, Santayana, and Dewey it remained relatively unaffected by the then rampant lynchings and widespread mistreatment of Afro-Americans."[78] If one expands the pragmatist tradition to include W. E. B. DuBois, as West does in *The American Evasion*

75. West, *American Evasion of Philosophy*, 215.

76. West, "Prophetic Theology," 23–24.

77. West, "Prophetic Theology," 32.

78. West, *Prophesy Deliverance!*, 11.

of Philosophy, alternative readings of the tradition become possible with respect to the issue of race. But even with this supplement, the fact remains that the mainstream of the pragmatist tradition remains insufficiently attentive to the dynamics of racial oppression in American history. Second, West criticizes pragmatic thought as a tradition that remains constrained by bourgeois and middle-class commitments concerning economic justice. He argues that Dewey's approach is confined to "the professional and reformist elements of the middle class" and also contends that Rorty's philosophy could be utilized to legitimate "liberal bourgeois capitalist societies."[79] West specifically maintains that Rorty's devotion to the United States caused him to turn away from the task of criticizing "the civilization he cherishes."[80] Finally, West objects to the pragmatist approach to resolving social problems, which he views as far too sanguine about the capacity for education and dialogue to effect social change. As a result, he maintains that pragmatists fail to attend to the significance of "confrontational politics and agitational social struggle."[81]

As a corrective to these deficiencies, West recovers resources from the prophetic tradition as a supplement to the pragmatist tradition. West insists on the importance of the pragmatic focus on experimentalism and reformism but links these elements with the prophetic emphasis on critique, protest, and resistance in order to ground the pragmatic commitment to democracy within a framework that recognizes the plight of the oppressed as a central feature of emancipatory politics. West observes,

> So here I am saying prophetic—that's the work that prophetic is doing, that adjective—the work that that adjective is doing, is saying: This is going to be a vantage point that even James, Dewey, Peirce, and the others—given all their philosophical talent and genius—didn't really attend to. And from this vantage point you begin to see that democracy actually means something much deeper, much richer, because it's going to be calling into question imperialism, patriarchy, white supremacist constraints on democracy, homophobic constraints on democracy, and yet still root it in this pragmatist tradition that was always historical, contextual, concerned about making the future a better place, concerned about the dignity of everyday

79. West, *American Evasion of Philosophy*, 206. In this regard, West maintains that the pragmatism of Rorty needs to be braided to the "moral vision, social analysis and political engagement of the liberation perspectives of Gutiérrez, Daly, and Cone" to be an effective model for social engagement. West, *Keeping Faith*, 116.

80. West, *American Evasion of Philosophy*, 206.

81. West, *American Evasion of Philosophy*, 102.

people as that circle broadens, and includes all of humanity, especially the wretched of the earth![82]

At one level, the prophetic tradition serves to ground pragmatism in the experience of the oppressed and to place it in an adversarial relationship with the cultural, political, and economic structures of American society that dispossess and marginalize vulnerable populations. At another level, the colorblind and bourgeois orientation of the pragmatist tradition receives an important corrective through West's creative appropriation of the American black prophetic tradition.[83] West's constructive contribution to pragmatism is to bring the commitment to social experimentalism and the reformist orientation of the pragmatist tradition into conversation with the radical elements of the black prophetic tradition.

This synthesis of American pragmatism and black propheticism, set alongside Wolinian pessimism, provides a framework for working through the tensions that exist between utopianism and incremental reform. West describes this framework as prophetic pragmatism and argues that from a prophetic-pragmatist perspective the achievements of liberal democracy need to be radicalized and not rejected. Elements of liberalism should be reconceptualized—participatory citizenship and redistribution of wealth by civil as well as legal means—but this approach "constitutes a radical democratic interpretation of liberalism, not a total discarding of it."[84] Concretely, this means that West's approach to radical democracy is driven by "revolutionary intent," even if it leads only to "reformist consequences."[85] At a theoretical level, West's radical reformism is on display most clearly in his engagement with the Brazilian social theorist Roberto Unger. In *The American Evasion of Philosophy* West describes Unger's project as a post-Marxist and postliberal approach to democracy similar to West's own prophetic pragmatism that stakes out a unique position in the field of leftist politics.[86]

82. Strube and West, "Pragmatism's Tragicomic Jazzman," 293.

83. West observes, "The Black prophetic tradition accents the fightback of poor and working people, be it in the United States against big money, be it in the Middle East against Arab autocratic rule or Israeli occupation, be it against African authoritarian governments abetted by US forces or Chinese money, be it in Latin America against oligarchic regimes in collaboration with big banks and corporations, or be it in Europe against austerity measures that benefit big creditors and punish everyday people. In short, the Black prophetic tradition is local in context and international in character" (*Black Prophetic Fire*, 4–5).

84. West, *Keeping Faith*, 181.

85. West, *Cornel West Reader*, 167.

86. West, *American Evasion of Philosophy*, 214. In his engagement with Unger's work prior to this publication, West criticized the fact that Unger's project remains "inscribed within a Eurocentric and patriarchal discourse that not simply fails to

In *The Leftist Alternative* Unger rejects the approaches on the left that attempt to slow down the processes of neoliberal globalization without offering an alternative (the recalcitrant left) or that accept neoliberalism as "unavoidable" and attempt to humanize it (the humanizing left). He instead maintains that it is necessary to offer an alternative in the form of a "reconstructive Left." A critical feature of this political orientation is the imaginative effort to describe visions of a "reordered social world, with its poetic attempt to connect present personal experiences to hidden social possibilities."[87] A visionary element to politics serves to enlarge imaginative possibilities and provide people with an alternative picture of the social and political world that can produce "(slightly) different people, with (slightly) revised understandings of our interests and ideals." Unger views this visionary element as a necessary prerequisite for social transformation, observing that "we must be visionaries to become realists." But he also promotes the use of the practical imagination as a means of approximating concrete institutional alternatives.[88]

In this respect, Unger advocates for a focus on both institutional experimentalism and what he refers to as "political prophecy."[89] He depicts this as a revolutionary approach to reform that overcomes the traditional impasse between revolution and reform by avoiding the problematic utopianism of revolutionary politics as well as the trivialism of reformist politics. This is done by resisting approaches to social transformation that claim either that a "decisive crisis" will lead to "the total substitution of one way of organizing society by another" or that fragmentary and piecemeal reforms are sufficient. Unger calls instead for a "permanent revolution" and the "practice of repeated and cumulative institutional reconstruction."[90] In the context of American democracy, the privileged model for enacting social change has been institutional reform that takes place within the existing system. Unger's project represents a form of radical reformism: "Reform is radical when it addresses and changes the basic arrangements of society: its formative structure of institutions and enacted beliefs. It is reform because it deals with one discrete part of this structure at a time."[91] Reform, then, is

---

theoretically consider racial and gender forms of subjugation, but also remains silent on the antiracist and feminist dimensions of concrete progressive political struggles." West, *Cornel West Reader*, 152–53.

87. Unger, *Democracy Realized*, 12.
88. Unger, *Democracy Realized*, 74.
89. Unger, *Democracy Realized*, 12.
90. Unger, *Democracy Realized*, 74.
91. Unger, *Democracy Realized*, 18–19.

a critical dimension of the work of replacing "the whole system" because it creates the conditions for broader and deeper change.[92]

With Unger, West coauthored *The Future of American Progressivism*, in which they offered a practical description of "radical reformism" in relation to the American political system. West and Unger maintain that "the work of progressives is to speak, within and outside the Democratic Party, for a clear alternative. Not for some impossible, romantic dream of a different 'system' . . . [b]ut for a practical view of how, step by step, and piece by piece, to democratize the American economy and reenergize American democracy."[93] To this end, they offer a number of policy proposals that seek to democratize the American economic system, proposing an overhaul of the tax system by advocating for a deeply progressive consumption tax (consumption up to a certain level would be untaxed) and more substantial taxation of wealth accumulation and inheritance. Furthermore, they maintain that American democracy should support a generalized principle of "social inheritance" by which every person in the United States is provided with a basic resource inheritance that can be spent on education, a down payment on a house, or some other social good. Just as family inheritance provides educational and resource opportunities for the wealthy, American society should provide a similar resource for the poor and working class.

The Future of American Progressivism was written in 1998, and as a result many of its policy prescriptions are dated. Nevertheless, it provides a sense of what radical reformism looks like in a cultural context dominated by neoliberal policies. West's current political commitments and activism are characterized by a multifaceted attempt to support "fugitive" projects of democratic resistance (Occupy Wall Street, Black Lives Matter, and Standing Rock) and to push the institutional apparatus of American democracy (e.g., the Democratic Party) to the left. This attempt to move the Democratic Party to the left is evident in West's sustained critique of the Obama presidency and endorsement of Bernie Sanders's candidacy in both 2016 and 2020.[94] West has a long-standing association with the Democratic Socialists of America, but he supported Sanders in 2016 as a "neopopulist" response to Clinton's "neoliberalism" and Trump's "neofascism."[95]

92. Unger and West, *Future of American Progressivism*, 29.

93. Unger and West, *Future of American Progressivism*, 93.

94. For a very fine analysis of the West-Obama engagement, see Springs, "The Prophet and the President." For West's analysis of Sanders's platform as consistent with the vision of Martin Luther King Jr., see West (with Mehdi Hasan), "Cornel West on Bernie, Trump, and Racism."

95. West, "Black Lives Matter Is an Indictment of Neoliberal Power." On West's socialism, see Dorrien, *Social Ethics in the Making*.

In terms of the religious dimension of his approach, West maintains that prophetic pragmatism "neither requires a religious foundation nor entails a religious perspective."[96] This follows from his approach to religion in which he judges its authenticity by its capacity to inspire and support liberating praxis. For West, what matters most is not creedal affiliation, liturgical practice, or orthodoxy, but rather resistance to domination and oppression wherever it is found.[97] Thus, while the commitment to justice that emerges out of the prophetic tradition of black Christianity is central to West's prophetic pragmatism, he utilizes the category of the prophetic to describe diverse movements that resist the dominant social order on behalf of the oppressed. West's approach to religion focuses, therefore, on the transformation of society rather than the cultivation of virtues of members of an ecclesial body. This focus has led some theologians to question the adequacy of his project from a Christian theological perspective.[98]

One way to approach these criticisms is to examine John Howard Yoder and Stanley Hauerwas's framework for analyzing Christian engagement with the secular political order. As we will see in more detail in the sixth chapter, Hauerwas and Yoder identify Constantinianism as a pervasive error in the history of the church by which Christians identify civil or political authorities as agents of God's cause.[99] Yoder claims that this has led Christians to identify themselves "with the power structures of their respective societies instead of seeing their duty as that of calling these powers to modesty and resisting their recurrent rebellion."[100] Yoder's critique of Constantinian Christianity differs from West's because in West's view Constantinianism is characterized by the historical collusion between the Christian church and the dominant social order that supports oppressive political formations.[101] While Yoder (and Hauerwas) would certainly recognize this as one form of Constantinianism, they view the operation of Constantinianism as more expansive and as infecting political orientations on both the right and the left. In Yoder's assessment a variety of currents in twentieth-century theology exist that while putatively opposing empire, nevertheless represent

---

96. West, *American Evasion of Philosophy*, 233.

97. West observes, "It is possible to be a prophetic pragmatist and belong to different political movements, e.g., feminist, Chicano, black, socialist, left-liberal ones. It also is possible to subscribe to prophetic pragmatism and belong to different religious and/or secular traditions." West, *Cornel West Reader*, 170.

98. See, for instance, Anderson, "Wrestle of Christ and Culture," 141ff.

99. Yoder, *Priestly Kingdom*, 143.

100. Yoder, *Original Revolution*, 150.

101. West, *Democracy Matters*, 146–51.

forms of Constantinianism by adopting the view that the primary task of the church is to serve secular political aims.[102]

In his work, Hauerwas describes liberal democracy as the primary Constantinian temptation for the church in the United States. While his criticism of democracy in its liberal form is complex and will be examined in more detail later, what should be noted here is that for Hauerwas when the church supports the political project of liberal democracy it disavows its own distinctive politics in the service of secular political aims. Put otherwise, when Christians view it as their responsibility to ensure the functioning of the liberal democratic order they begin "to detach themselves from the insights, habits, stories, and structures that make the church the church."[103] In his genealogy of Constantinianism in the United States, Hauerwas identifies Walter Rauschenbusch as representative of the tendency by which the distinctiveness of a Christian vision for life is relinquished in favor of a form of Christian engagement that seeks to democratize the social order. According to Hauerwas, "Democracy for Rauschenbusch was not an external social system with which Christianity must come to terms, but a system integral to the very meaning of Christianity."[104] Rauschenbusch thought it self-evident that Christians were called to use politics to achieve a more just social order and, furthermore, thought it obvious that democracy was the most effective system for generating this justice.

The fundamental aim of Rauschenbusch's political theology is remarkably similar to that of West in that, like Rauschenbusch, West describes democracy as an internal norm of Christianity. He names Rauschenbusch as a pivotal figure alongside Sojourner Truth, Elizabeth Cady Stanton, Dorothy Day, Martin Luther King Jr., and Abraham Joshua Heschel in his description of prophetic witness in American history. Furthermore, because West defines what it means to be Christian in terms of the bedrock commitment to justice for the oppressed, the cultivation of shared commitments across creedal differences—among Christians, Jews, Muslims, Buddhists, Hindus, as well as nonbelievers—is more central to how he conceives of prophetic pragmatism than cultivating distinctive virtues within the church community. From Hauerwas's perspective, West moves close to repeating the problematic Rauschenbuschian move of making democratization the fundamental aim of the Christian church. In a footnote in State of the University Hauerwas

102. Yoder observes of this form of Constantinianism that "God's cause and Christians' loyalty [align] with a regime which is future rather than present: with a 'revolution' or 'liberation' which, being morally imperative, is sure to come" (Priestly Kingdom, 143). Emphasis original.

103. Hauerwas and Willimon, Resident Aliens, 116.

104. Hauerwas, Better Hope, 96.

praises West for his critique of the Constantinianism of "conservative Christians" but cautions that "Rauschenbusch was in his day as implicated in the Constantinian project as the religious right is today."[105] He further notes that while Yoder (and, one presumes, Hauerwas himself) was sympathetic to Rauschenbusch's critique of American capitalism, "Rauschenbusch's blessing of democracy as *the* form of Christian government would appear to Yoder as a Constantinianism of the left."[106]

For his own part, West positively characterizes Hauerwas's approach as a form of "prophetic ecclesiasticism" that aims "to preserve the integrity of the prophetic church by exposing the idolatry of Constantinian Christianity and bearing witness to the gospel of love and peace."[107] West agrees with Hauerwas's critique of American empire and his concern to retrieve the prophetic witness of the church but takes issue with Hauerwas's focus on the purity of Christian witness over against a corrupting secular political order. West observes of Hauerwas, "His prophetic sensibilities resonate with me and I agree with his critique of Constantinian Christianity and imperial America. Yet he unduly downplays the prophetic Christian commitment to justice and our role as citizens to make America more free and democratic."[108] In the midst of "American empire" West avers that Hauerwas finds "solace only in a prophetic ecclesiological refuge that prefigures the coming kingdom of God."[109]

As an alternative to Hauerwas's approach, West invokes the legacy of Martin Luther King Jr., suggesting that for him "to be a prophetic Christian is not to be against the world in the name of church purity; it is to be in the world but not of the world's nihilism, in the name of a loving Christ who proclaims the this-worldly justice of a kingdom to come."[110] West appropriates King's criticism of inequality, militarism, and racism in "A Time to Break Silence" as the basic framework for his own approach to Christian politics. Furthermore, he endorses the pluralist approach to social transformation pursued by King, pointing to King's democratic socialist commitments as support for his own association with the Democratic Socialists of America. By way of contrast, Hauerwas engages King's legacy only a few times in his writings, and when he does his approach to King differs

---

105. Hauerwas, *State of the University*, 60n6.

106. Hauerwas, *State of the University*, 152n25. Emphasis original.

107. West, *Democracy Matters*, 161–62.

108. West, *Democracy Matters*, 162.

109. West, *Democracy Matters*, 162.

110. West, *Democracy Matters*, 162.

markedly from West's.[111] In Hauerwas's work, King becomes an exemplar not of a prophetic witness to an intersectional approach to justice, but rather an exemplary witness to a Christian politics of peace.[112] In *The Peaceable Kingdom*, Hauerwas succinctly summarizes the differences between their approaches to Christian discipleship when he argues that the task of the Christian church "is not to make the world the kingdom, but to be faithful to the kingdom by showing to the world what it means to be a community of peace."[113] West argues that the task of prophetic Christians is to work for the "this-worldly justice of a kingdom to come," whereas Hauerwas suggests that it is to be faithful to the kingdom by witnessing to Christ's peace. This plays out, too, in terms of their concrete political commitments in that West endorses a variety of movements, policies, and even institutions as secular political forms consistent with his Christian commitment to justice, where Hauerwas offers an approach to radical democratic politics that eschews any strategic alliance with secular political institutions and holds up local efforts and "ordinary" actions of receptivity, dialogue, and care as representative of a Christian approach to radical democracy.[114]

How should we evaluate these divergences between West and Hauerwas with respect to the question of Christian political engagement with the democratic order? In particular, does West commit the Constantinian error of prioritizing democracy over the particularity of Christian political witness? West himself denies that this criticism applies to his own work by insisting that his commitment to democracy is secondary to his commitment to Christianity. In *Democracy Matters* he observes, "I speak as a Christian whose commitment to democracy is very deep but whose Christian convictions are even deeper. Democracy is not my faith. And American democracy is not my idol."[115] West maintains that his commitment to democracy is subordinate to his commitment to Christianity—even if he describes his politics in terms of a "democratic faith"—because he views democracy as a contingent instrument that works to protect the dignity of each individual: "Democracy itself is a means. And it is a means for the flowering of individuality. Why do I see it this way?

111. For a trenchant critique of Hauerwas's failure to take up King's legacy, see De La Torre, "Stanley Hauerwas on Church."

112. Hauerwas, *War and the American Difference*; Hauerwas, "Remembering Martin Luther King Jr. Remembering"; Hauerwas, "The Dilemma of Martin Luther King, Jr."

113. Hauerwas, *Peaceable Kingdom*, 104.

114. See Hauerwas and Coles, *Christianity, Democracy, and the Radical Ordinary*.

115. West, *Democracy Matters*, 171. Hauerwas notes this quote approvingly in his brief engagement with West in *State of the University*, 152n25.

Because I stand fundamentally on the profoundly Christian notion that we are equal in the eyes of God."[116]

Even in view of West's defense of "democratic faith" as a political commitment that refuses to fetishize or idolize democracy, it remains true that West fails to offer a full account of the theological warrants for his Christian political commitments and as a consequence is vulnerable to this type of Yoderian and Hauerwasian criticism. While Hauerwas offers a charitable interpretation of West's thought in *The State of the University*, it is not difficult to read Hauerwas's trenchant critique of Jamesian pragmatism and Niebuhrian liberalism in *With the Grain of the Universe* as applicable to West's thought. Hauerwas is scathing in his assessment of Niebuhr's theological liberalism, which he claims sacrificed a substantive theological account of Christian belief for political relevance. Hauerwas contends that Niebuhr's approach achieved the unfortunate result of failing both to convince nonbelievers of the relevance of Christianity and to provide adequate theological warrants "for Christians to sustain their lives."[117] Again, while Hauerwas has not applied these criticisms of theological liberalism to West's thought directly, it is difficult not to conclude that his sharp opposition to pragmatist (James) and liberal (Niebuhr) approaches to religion is applicable in some way to West's prophetic pragmatism.[118]

West has not developed a theological justification for his politics—recall that he rejects the label of "theologian"—but in "A Prophetic Church in a Post-Constantinian Age: The Implicit Theology of Cornel West," Stout argues that in West's writings there exists an impressive set of theological fragments that have yet to be fully thematized or systematized. Stout acknowledges a christological deficit in West's writings but points to an implicit pneumatology that traces the movement of the Spirit through the prophetic witness of the black church. Although Hauerwas has a more developed Christology, Stout argues that West offers "a more fully developed conception of the Spirit than many academic theologians."[119] And for Stout, this approach to theology, even with its underdeveloped Christology, is preferable to Hauerwas's approach because it offers a more substantive engagement with American political life. He specifically argues that "there is nothing Constantinian, however, as Hauerwas sometimes seems to imply,

116. West, *Prophetic Thought*, 63. West observes that "democratic faith consists of a Pascalian wager (hence underdetermined by the evidence) on the abilities and capacities of ordinary people to participate in the decision-making procedures and institutions that fundamentally regulate their lives." West, *Cornel West Reader*, 186.

117. Hauerwas, *With the Grain of the Universe*, 139.

118. Stout raises this point in "Prophetic Church in a Post-Constantinian Age," 43.

119. Stout, "Prophetic Church in a Post-Constantinian Age," 43.

about holding a people responsible for the condition of its government, nor about believing that one essential task of the church is to hold its own members responsible for neglect of their responsibilities as members of nations. On both of these points, West has provided a clearer articulation of basic Christian themes than Hauerwas has."[120] It is unclear whether a more explicit development of this pneumatology in West's thought would satisfy Hauerwas's theological concerns about West's approach to Christian political theology, but it would serve to provide a fuller account of the relationship between the beliefs and practices of the Christian community and West's political commitments than has been offered to date.

Although West does not offer extensive theological warrants for his approach to politics—at least in comparison to theologians examined in subsequent chapters—he does offer the most robust engagement with secular political forms of the Christian thinkers examined in this work. This is the case both discursively and in terms of his participation in fugitive (Occupy Wall Street, Black Lives Matter, Standing Rock) and institutional forms of radical democratic politics (Democratic Socialists of America). And where the Christian theologians examined in subsequent chapters prioritize the significance of civil society for radical politics, West is unique in his call for a radical reformist engagement with the state. Furthermore, in a period in which politics have become more overtly white nationalist, West's focus on race as the critical intersecting point between neoliberalism and the militarism of empire constitutes an important challenge to not only these white nationalist political formations, but also to the lack of focus on race by both secular radical democratic theorists and Christian theologians. Finally, in the midst of a cultural situation in which the left is often divided between so-called struggles for recognition and struggles for economic justice, West's argument that a class-based politics constitutes an indispensable feature of antiracist struggle opens an important horizon for Christian political engagement that theorizes socialism and antiracism as "inseparable yet not identical" features of Christian political engagement.[121]

---

120. Stout, "Prophetic Church in a Post-Constantinian Age," 44.

121. West, *Prophetic Fragments*, 107.

CHAPTER 4

Feminist Theology

BECAUSE FEMINISM IS A pluralistic and variegated discourse both in terms of its multiple waves and its diverse expressions, it is most accurate to speak of feminisms rather than feminism. This situation is further complicated when one examines the feminist discourses associated with Christian theology because feminist theology simultaneously appropriates and resets secular feminist theory. So that where the first wave of feminist theology (which, according to the standard periodization of feminist theory, responds to second-wave secular feminism) focused on the gender roles of mostly white women in the church in the North Atlantic world, the second wave emerged as a critique of white feminist theology by African-American (womanist), Latina (Latina and mujerista), and Asian (minjung) theologians (this is commonly referred to as the third wave in secular feminism). The feminist theologians in the theological second wave emphasized the intersectional character of oppression on the basis of the relation between gender, race, class, sexual orientation, and ethnicity.[1] Feminist theology has moved in different directions recently with the emergence of third (international or global) and fourth (interfaith) waves.[2] A significant area of development in recent feminist theology—some, like Rosemary Radford Ruether, have labeled it the fifth wave—has been the turn to transnational approaches that support practices of justice that exceed the nation-state and contest the transnational political formations of neoliberalism and global militarism.[3]

In this chapter, we examine Elisabeth Schüssler Fiorenza's work as a form of transnational theology pursued in conversation with liberationist and

1. On the significance of intersectionality for feminist theology, see Schüssler Fiorenza, "Introduction: Exploring the Intersections of Race, Gender, Status and Ethnicity in Early Christian Studies."

2. Ruether, "Feminist Theology: Where Is It Going?"

3. Schüssler Fiorenza, *Transforming Vision*, 13–14.

feminist discourses. Schüssler Fiorenza is critical of each of these movements on their own and argues for the need to bring them together as a "critical, political the*logy of decolonizing liberation" that seeks to abolish "systems of domination" and to create "radical democratic conditions and attitudes."[4] Schüssler Fiorenza advocates for an ekklesial politics that is intersectional in its critique of multiple forms of oppression as well as transnational in its concern to advocate for justice beyond the borders of the nation-state. She specifically calls for a radical form of globalization from below comprised of a "transreligious" coalition of Christians, Jews, Buddhists, Hindus, Muslims, as well as atheists, agnostics, and nonbelievers.[5]

In this chapter we first analyze the relationship between patriarchy and kyriarchy in Schüssler Fiorenza's work with a specific focus on her critique of empire, which she depicts as the interrelation between neoliberalism, nationalism, and the gendered politics of the religious right. Second, we examine her description of the ekklesia of wo/men as a social and imaginative space of struggle against kyriarchy. Schüssler Fiorenza acknowledges the Christian resonances of ekklesia but pushes for an inclusive and pluralistic application of ekklesia as a political form that includes all those who resist kyriarchal forms of domination. In this section we examine three forms of the ekklesia of wo/men in the early Jesus movement, nineteenth-century suffragists, and transnational coalitions of wo/men. Third, we examine Schüssler Fiorenza's distinctive approach to a form of feminist-transnational democracy and bring her work into conversation with Cornel West's approach to Christian engagement with radical democracy.[6]

KYRIARCHY AND EMPIRE

In Memory of Her (1983) inaugurated the publication of a series of innovative studies of early Christianity in which Schüssler Fiorenza criticized traditional historiography by pursuing a creative reconstruction of Christian origins from a feminist perspective.[7] Against the positivistic commitments of traditional historiography, which attempted to offer an "accurate" account of the past, Schüssler Fiorenza maintained that feminist historiography serves as a "perspectival discourse that seeks to articulate a living memory

4. Schüssler Fiorenza, "Critical Feminist The*logy of Liberation," 26.

5. Schüssler Fiorenza, *Congress of Wo/men*, 19.

6. Schüssler Fiorenza, "Feminist Studies in Religion and the The*logy In-Between," 119.

7. Schüssler Fiorenza, *In Memory of Her*.

of the present and the future."[8] Schüssler Fiorenza insists that all biblical interpretation and theological discourse serves a political agenda whether this is stated explicitly or not. The political aim in *In Memory of Her* was to retrieve the egalitarian model for discipleship characteristic of the early Jesus movement.[9] Schüssler Fiorenza maintains that while this egalitarianism was distinctive in relation to the patriarchal norms of the surrounding Greco-Roman culture, "the Christian vision and praxis of 'equality from below'" gradually merged with this Greco-Roman culture, which effected a shift by which the church became "more Roman than Christian" as well as more patriarchal and less egalitarian.[10]

While Schüssler Fiorenza focused on the patriarchal features of Christianity in *In Memory of Her*, in subsequent works she targeted all forms of domination and subordination. In *But She Said* (1992) Schüssler Fiorenza introduced the neologism *kyriarchy* (derived from the Greek word *kyrios*) to denote the "rule of the emperor/master/lord/father/husband over his subordinates."[11] This term was utilized in order to represent an intersectional approach to feminist struggle that resists all forms of oppression and domination: sexism, colonialism, classism, racism, heterosexism, nationalism, and militarism.[12] Thus, although the critical feminist hermeneutic utilized in *In Memory of Her* remains present throughout her writings, *But She Said* marks the point at which her critique becomes more explicitly intersectional. Schüssler Fiorenza observes,

> The neologism *kyriarchy-kyriocentrism* (from Greek *kyrios* meaning lord, master, father, husband) seeks to express this interstructuring of domination and to replace the commonly used term *patriarchy*, which is often understood in terms of binary gender dualism. I have introduced this neologism as an analytic category in order to be able to articulate a more comprehensive systemic analysis, to underscore the complex interstructuring of domination, and to locate sexism and misogyny in the political matrix or, better, patrix of a broader range of oppressions.[13]

8. Schüssler Fiorenza, *In Memory of Her*, xxii.

9. Schüssler Fiorenza, *In Memory of Her*, 34.

10. Schüssler Fiorenza, *Discipleship of Equals*, 224.

11. Schüssler Fiorenza, *Jesus: Miriam's Child, Sophia's Prophet*, 14.

12. Schüssler Fiorenza, *Transforming Vision*, 105–6, and Schüssler Fiorenza, *Bread Not Stone*, 3.

13. Schüssler Fiorenza, *Rhetoric and Ethic*, 5. See also Schüssler Fiorenza, *Power of the Word*, 14.

Oppression is not just multiple but multiplicative because racism, sexism, and classism work together and reinforce each other.[14] Furthermore, kyriarchy exploits not only women but also "subaltern women's and men's experience of domination by elite women and men."[15] The term *wo/men* serves, therefore, as a description of all of those women, men, and children who experience oppression and marginalization as a result of their gender, sexual orientation, class, race, nationality, or religious affiliation.[16]

Schüssler Fiorenza identifies kyriarchal structures in diverse political formations, from the Roman Empire to American democracy,[17] but in her most recent book, *Congress of Wo/men*, she argues that the dominant form of kyriarchy today is "neoliberal kyriarchy." It follows that "the common sociopolitical space of all feminist theories and the*logies is neoliberal *globalization*," and while different "geographical or identity-centered" approaches to feminist the*logy remain critical, Schüssler Fiorenza argues that resistance to neoliberalism should be the focal point for these various forms of struggle.[18]

In her engagement with neoliberalism, Schüssler Fiorenza broadly indicts the inegalitarian effects of neoliberal policies, observing that these policies have created "a future where a handful of the world's most well-to-do families may pocket more than 50 percent of the world's $90 trillion in assets and securities (stocks, bonds, etc.)."[19] But she remains focused on the role that gender plays in the legitimation of neoliberalism. In particular, she identifies two ways in which neoliberalism has used gender to disseminate neoliberal values and policies: (1) by exploring specific developments within second-wave feminism that aided the spread of neoliberalism, and (2) by analyzing the use of gender by the religious right to legitimate the neoliberal organization of society.

The relationship between feminism and neoliberalism is complicated by the fact that there exist at least three divergent feminist responses to neoliberalism: resistance to it, unintentional support for it, and the use of

14. Schüssler Fiorenza, *But She Said*, 115.

15. Schüssler Fiorenza, *Power of the Word*, 13.

16. Schüssler Fiorenza, *Power of the Word*, 13.

17. Schüssler Fiorenza, "Introduction: Exploring the Intersections," 9.

18. Schüssler Fiorenza, *Congress of Wo/men*, 19. Emphasis original. She observes, "I see *the* major task of theology and religion as creating and sustaining a different vision of hope in the face of the dehumanization and exploitation of neoliberalism. Creating a vision of a different world of justice, care, and well-being is the task of religion." See Schüssler Fiorenza, "Articulating a Different Future." Emphasis added. See also Schüssler Fiorenza, *Congress of Wo/men*, 28–29 and 103–5.

19. Schüssler Fiorenza, *Democratizing Biblical Studies*, 102.

feminist discourse to realize neoliberal ends. We shall focus on the latter two here because in the final section of the chapter we take up the issue of how Schüssler Fiorenza theorizes feminist resistance to empire.

Following the work of Nancy Fraser, Schüssler Fiorenza argues that second-wave feminism unintentionally aided the rise of neoliberalism.[20] In an essay from which Schüssler Fiorenza draws heavily, "Mapping the Feminist Imagination," Fraser describes two trajectories in second-wave feminist theory.[21] The first phase, "redistribution," was characterized by an attempt "to 'engender' the socialist imaginary" in response to inequality in society (an inequality that disproportionately affects wo/men). The second phase, "recognition," sought recognition for identities marginalized by the dominant social order and moved the locus of struggle from political economy to culture. According to Fraser, the transition from "redistribution" to "recognition" took place at precisely the time of the ascendency of neoliberalism and coincided with the neoliberal desire to "repress all memory of social egalitarianism."[22] Fraser contends that some feminists "absolutized the critique of cultural sexism" at the exact moment in which what was required was a renewed "critique of political economy." A critique that emerged as a legitimate corrective to reductionistic forms of economism "devolved into an equally one-side culturalism." And while the emergence of a feminist cultural politics of recognition opened the possibility for joining a politics of recognition to a politics of redistribution, second-wave feminists "effectively traded one truncated paradigm for another."[23] Fraser concludes that the task for contemporary feminist theory is to generate an integrated feminism that combines the struggle for recognition with an egalitarian commitment to economic justice. Additionally, it is necessary to ensure that wo/men have a political voice at national as well as transnational levels. Fraser describes this integrated form of feminism as "transnational" and argues that it combines the demand for "representation" with "recognition" as well as "redistribution." Schüssler Fiorenza affirms this conclusion and argues that Fraser's analysis of recent feminist theory and practice provides a framework for

20. Schüssler Fiorenza, *Democratizing Biblical Studies*, 102, and Schüssler Fiorenza, *Sharing Her Word*, 108.

21. Schüssler Fiorenza analyzes this text in *Power of the Word*, 22–25. See Fraser, "Mapping the Feminist Imagination." Fraser has also made similar arguments in "Feminism, Capitalism, and the Cunning of History" and "How Feminism Became Capitalism's Handmaiden."

22. Fraser, "Mapping the Feminist Imagination," 296. Fraser observes that the feminist politics of recognition "dovetailed with neoliberalism's interest in diverting political-economic struggles into culturalist channels."

23. Fraser, "How Feminism Became Capitalism's Handmaiden."

constructing a "transnational" approach to religion and theology. We will return to this point later in the chapter.

If the shift toward recognition in feminist discourse provided unintentional support for the rise of neoliberal capitalism, the emergence of an explicitly neoliberal form of feminism represents an even more problematic development. In *Feminism for the 99%: A Manifesto*, Cinzia Arruzza, Tithi Bhattacharya, and Nancy Fraser contend that where the turn to "identity" in second-wave feminism aided the rise of neoliberalism, a new form of feminism has emerged and it explicitly aims to make "feminism . . . a handmaiden of capitalism." They argue that this brand of "lean-in feminism" seeks to dismantle barriers to women's access to power without contesting the structures of disempowerment. The effect is that this brand of feminism offers a vision for society in which exploitative structures are managed by both men *and* women. Thus, lean-in feminism asks people to celebrate the fact "that it is a woman, not a man, who busts their union, orders a drone to kill their parent, or locks their child in a cage at the border."[24] In *The Rise of Neoliberal Feminism*, Catherine Rottenberg explores the contours of neoliberal feminism, noting that it is an ideology shared by elites on the left and the right (from Hillary Clinton and Ivanka Trump to Sheryl Sandberg and Anne-Marie Slaughter).[25] She argues that the feminisms of Clinton, Slaughter, Trump, and Sandberg do not and cannot take into account the struggle of the majority of women globally, let alone the majority of American women. Rottenberg identifies neoliberal feminism as a "self-help" program for elite women who seek to maintain a balance between career and family. In this regard, neoliberal feminism represents a shift away from a critical analysis of the structural dynamics of inequality, emancipation, and rights and moves toward an individualized project focused on "affect, behavior modification, and well-roundedness."[26]

Whether by coincidence or design, neoliberalism has encased dominant forms of feminist discourse and practice within the logic of market individualism. In addition to analyzing these shifts in feminist discourse during the neoliberal period, Schüssler Fiorenza argues that neoliberalism has used a cultural politics of neoconservatism as a means of undermining egalitarian political and social projects.[27] She contends that

24. Arruzza, Bhattacharya, and Fraser, *Feminism for the 99%*, 2.

25. Rottenberg, *The Rise of Neoliberal Feminism*.

26. Rottenberg, *Rise of Neoliberal Feminism*, 42.

27. She observes, "The response to the increasing economic insecurity and deadly violence has been a global political shift to the right, which promises to mitigate public anxiety and insecurity by appealing to unacknowledged fears and scapegoating the weakest among us." Schüssler Fiorenza, *Sharing Her Word*, 107–8.

the right in the United States has paired a "capitalist politics of regressive economic redistribution" with coded language about gender, race, and nationalism to achieve electoral and political victories.[28] The religious right, in particular, prepared the cultural ground for the spread of neoliberalism by utilizing a number of strategies intended to obstruct efforts to create a more egalitarian social order.

First, Schüssler Fiorenza observes that "neoconservative fundamentalist groups" use the Bible as a weapon to erode the essential features of democracy: "basic individual rights; pluralism; freedom of speech; equal rights of women; the right to housing, health care, and work; equal compensation for equal work; social market measures; a democratic ethos; sharing of power and political responsibility."[29] Biblical religion has "strengthen[ed] antidemocratic" elements in society by "reproducing ancient patriarchal structures of inequality and slavelike conditions in the family and the economy."[30] This description of the relation between neoliberalism and neoconservatism comports with Melinda Cooper's account in which a normative moral vision dominates the neoliberal approach to public policy (from housing and welfare policy to education and incarceration). Schüssler Fiorenza supplements Cooper's analysis by detailing how the religious right uses the Bible to sustain an inegalitarian social order. Specifically, she highlights the ways in which conservative Christianity has cultivated dispositions of "obedience and submission to antidemocratic powers."[31] This ethos of submission emerges in distinctive ways among different denominations, so that where conservative Catholics demand submission to an all-male hierarchy ("hierarchical Catholicism"), Protestant fundamentalism demands submission to the inerrant authority of Scripture ("biblicist Protestantism").[32] Furthermore, in both Protestant and Catholic theology, specific biblical texts (the household codes in Paul's letters or the First Epistle of Peter 2:13–17, 18–25, and 3:1–6) have been utilized to legitimate the hierarchical organization of not only religious life but also family, political, and economic life. Schüssler Fiorenza argues that the cultivation of this ethos of submission and hierarchy among Christians has real-world consequences because it "compel[s] religious wo/men who suffer from both

28. Schüssler Fiorenza, *Power of the Word*, 24.

29. Schüssler Fiorenza, *Jesus: Miriam's Child, Sophia's Prophet*, 9.

30. Schüssler Fiorenza, *Bread Not Stone*, 69.

31. Schüssler Fiorenza, *Congress of Wo/men*, 60. In "American Nightmare," Brown similarly argues that fundamentalist Christianity cultivates a submissive posture toward authority that has been exploited by neoconservatives and neoliberals alike. See Brown, "American Nightmare," 708.

32. Schüssler Fiorenza, *Power of the Word*, 45.

globalized market capitalism and sexual exploitation not to struggle against such death-dealing injustice but to submit to it."[33]

Second, and relatedly, Schüssler Fiorenza maintains that the right has used Evangelical Christianity to manage the insecurity created by neoliberal policies through its dissemination of a therapeutic political spirituality. Again, Schüssler Fiorenza follows Fraser here and the argument that the security offered to individuals by "religious fundamentalism" and "Christian Evangelicalism" serves as a means to manage the pervasive state of "social insecurity" generated by neoliberalism.[34] Evangelical Christianity sustains the neoliberal order by offering a cultural discipline that systematically avoids structural analysis of the causes of insecurity by instead training individuals to manage these insecurities at a spiritual level. She specifically argues that Christians have been trained to manage their insecurities by invoking a religious worldview that instructs them that even though failure and defeat are part of life, what remains constant is that "God still loves you."[35] God's forgiveness, not structural reform, is the privileged Evangelical response to neoliberal precarity. And it is Foucault's rather than Marx's framework that is utilized to analyze this phenomenon because Evangelical Christianity serves a therapeutic rather than opiatic function in the neoliberal world.

As with Cornel West, Schüssler Fiorenza describes empire as the complex, multilayered political formation that brings together neoliberalism, nationalism/militarism, and cultural politics of the religious right, observing that American empire is a project of "capitalist globalization . . . secured by the military-industrial complex and justified in Christian religious terms."[36] In a 2005 essay titled "Feminist Studies in Religion and the The*logy In-Between Nationalism and Globalization," Schüssler Fiorenza argued that "patriotic nationalism is the most powerful discourse of the day." During the height of the war on terror she identified nationalism as the "kyriarchal structure that determines all of our discourses." Her assessment of the situation has shifted because she now views neoliberalism as the most pervasive kyriarchal structure in the world. But the critique of nationalism offered in the mid-2000s continues to occupy a critical space in her recent work. She argues that militaristic nationalism derives much of its power from the strategic use of religion and gender to draw constituencies into its

33. Schüssler Fiorenza, *Congress of Wo/men*, 60.

34. See Fraser, "Mapping the Feminist Imagination," 302–3, and Schüssler Fiorenza, *Power of the Word*, 24–25.

35. Fraser, "Mapping the Feminist Imagination," 303.

36. Schüssler Fiorenza, *Empowering Memory and Movement*, 497.

worldview. Specifically, she argues that Christianity in America functions as a civil religion that conflates the authority of God with the authority of the American empire. This confusion has become so widespread that it has become virtually impossible to discern whether "obedience" and "submission" is demanded "in the name of G*d or in the name of patriotism."[37] Even more problematically, when religion is absorbed by nationalistic rhetoric and practices it legitimates destructive projects of racialized exclusion and "dangerous militarism."[38] Concretely, Schüssler Fiorenza contends that the religious nationalism cultivated by the Moral Majority in the 1970s and the Christian right in the 1980s played a critical role in mobilizing support for the United States' "interference in the governments of Haiti or other Latin American States" as well as the "occupation of Iraq."[39]

More broadly, Schüssler Fiorenza maintains that feminism has been used to defend American imperialism abroad, arguing that "gender symbols, control of wo/men, the well-being of the heterosexual patriarchal family, appeals to religious scriptures and laws, specific cultural codes of dress and behavior—all these become central to the maintenance of traditional values and the construction of national identity."[40] For instance, she notes that George W. Bush's electoral victory in 2004 relied on the deployment of a "gender-coded politics" of "family values" to hide regressive economic policies and to cultivate support for American imperialism abroad.[41] This argument has been made by other theorists as well, so that where Nancy Fraser expresses concern that feminism has become the "handmaiden" of neoliberal capitalism, Saba Mahmood argues that "feminism runs the risk of becoming more of a handmaiden of empire in our age than a trenchant critic of the Euro-American will to power."[42] Politicians on both the left (Hillary Clinton) and the right (Condoleezza Rice) have used women's rights discourses to rally support for American military interventions abroad in what amounts to a form of "imperial feminism" (Angela Davis). As we shall see in the third section, Schüssler Fiorenza views the politics of transnational feminism as a movement that is critical to the creation of alternatives to neoliberal globalization as well as the violence of racialized exclusions and militaristic nationalisms.

37. Schüssler Fiorenza, "Reading Scripture in the Context of Empire," 158.

38. Schüssler Fiorenza, *Empowering Memory and Movement*, 100.

39. Schüssler Fiorenza, *Power of the Word*, 115. See also Schüssler Fiorenza, "Reading Scripture in the Context of Empire," 157.

40. Schüssler Fiorenza, "Feminist Studies in Religion and the The*logy In-Between," 112.

41. Schüssler Fiorenza, *Transforming Vision*, 14.

42. Mahmood, "Feminism, Democracy, and Empire," 82.

Overall, Schüssler Fiorenza's analysis of empire parallels West's, but where he focuses on race as the critical point of intersection between neoliberalism, nationalistic militarism, and the cultural politics of the Christian right, she argues that gender is the reality that stitches these elements of empire together. As a pluralist, Schüssler Fiorenza recognizes that resistance to empire must emerge at multiple sites, and yet, as a theologian and biblical scholar, she remains focused on the role that religion plays in the legitimation of empire. The fundamental concern of her work, which she recognizes as inescapably political, is to challenge religious communities to enter the field of struggle against kyriarchy and to support political experiments in radical democracy. To this end, she suggests that religious communities face the following alternative: "We can strengthen the power of neoliberal kyriarchal globalization or we can support the growing interdependence of people around the globe in and through alternative globalization 'from below.' We can spiritually sustain the exploitation of capitalist globalization, or we can engage the possibilities of radical democratization for greater freedom, justice, and solidarity."[43] We turn to this radical democratic alternative "from below" in the next two sections.

Ekklesia of Wo/men

Schüssler Fiorenza performs a dialectic between deconstruction and reconstruction in her work. In the previous section we traced the deconstructive movement in which Schüssler Fiorenza identified, denaturalized, and contested kyriarchal structures in society. The second element of Schüssler Fiorenza's project is reconstructive and seeks to offer egalitarian alternatives to kyriarchal structures of oppression. At a theological level, she maintains that it is necessary both to identify sources of imperial ideology in biblical texts and to "trace languages and imaginations of radical democratic equality" within the Christian tradition that can serve as an alternative to kyriarchy.[44]

For Schüssler Fiorenza the constructive theological task is political. So that just as defenders of the status quo interpret the Bible and Christian theology from a perspective that legitimates imperial formations, the task of feminist discourse is to engage in a reconstruction of the Christian tradition in order to elevate those projects "that have engendered radical

43. Schüssler Fiorenza, *Congress of Wo/men*, 63.

44. Schüssler Fiorenza, *Power of the Word*, 158. See also Schüssler Fiorenza, *Power of the Word*, 9; Schüssler Fiorenza, *Jesus and the Politics of Interpretation*, 74; and Schüssler Fiorenza, *Rhetoric and Ethic*, 10.

egalitarian Christian visions and movement through the centuries."[45] Schüssler Fiorenza's method is complex in that it does not attempt to ground feminist theology in Jesus's option for the poor.[46] She explicitly rejects the "sado-masochistic attachment to the man Jesus"[47] and instead argues that "scripture, tradition, theology and Jesus research should be analyzed and tested as to their ideological-political functions in legitimating or subverting multiplicative kyriarchal structures of domination."[48] The experience of a particular community—those who participate in liberative struggles for justice against kyriarchal structures—serves as the provisional norm for theology and religious practice from a feminist perspective. This move has drawn criticism from proponents of classical or traditional approaches to norms.[49] Where some theologians seek to ground the normativity of their interpretation in the magisterium and others in Jesus's life and ministry (Sobrino and Hauerwas), Schüssler Fiorenza criticizes these approaches for reinforcing patriarchal norms and argues instead that ekklesia of wo/men is the site of "divine revelation and grace" and "not the Bible or the tradition of a patriarchal church."[50]

In her work, ekklesia of wo/men serves as a utopian social space that opens the possibility for wo/men to imagine and to struggle to realize egalitarian alternatives to kyriarchal structures in society. These spaces are referred to as the "standpoint of women" in secular feminist literature. Schüssler Fiorenza utilizes ekklesia of wo/men as a theo-political term to serve this function in her work and to contest a number of problematic binaries.[51]

First, this social space challenges the view that only two options are available to feminists in relation to the Christian tradition: either submission to patriarchy or exodus from the church. Schüssler Fiorenza confronts this dilemma; in her work, she asserts, she has "sought to displace the feminist alternative: either affirm church and religion as your spiritual home or leave them behind as totally oppressive in an exodus to a liberated community on the margins (Rosemary Radford Ruether) or in a leap into the 'other world' (Mary Daly). I have sought to deconstruct this 'either-or' alternative into a constructive 'neither-nor but different' position by articulating the *ekklesia*

45. Schüssler Fiorenza, *Sharing Her Word*, 120.

46. Schüssler Fiorenza, *Jesus: Miriam's Child, Sophia's Prophet*, 48.

47. Schüssler Fiorenza, *Empowering Memory and Movement*, 333–34.

48. Schüssler Fiorenza, *In Memory of Her*, 32.

49. See, for instance, Hampson, *Theology and Feminism*, for criticism of Schüssler Fiorenza's work as humanism dressed up in theological garb.

50. Schüssler Fiorenza, "Will to Choose or to Reject," 128.

51. Schüssler Fiorenza, *Transforming Vision*, 17.

of wo/men as a radical democratic alternative site where feminists can denounce and deconstruct kyriarchal religious texts, traditions, and practices and at the same time reclaim their religious heritage on feminist terms."[52] Schüssler Fiorenza points to the fact that the English word *church* is derived from the Greek word *kyriarche*, which, as noted in the previous section, connotes a sense of belonging to the lord, master, or father. Ekklesia of wo/men exists both within and outside of the kyriarchal church because it is a social space where wo/men gather "as the people of God, to claim our own religious powers, to participate fully in the decision-making process of the church, and to nurture each other as women Christians."[53]

Second, while ekklesia of wo/men retains Christian roots, Schüssler Fiorenza maintains that ekklesia of wo/men displaces commonly drawn distinctions between the religious and the political because "ekklesia is not just a Christian religious notion; rather it expresses a sociopolitical radical democratic vision. The expression does not refer primarily to 'church' but seeks to convey the notion of radical democracy. This egalitarian vision has never been fully realized in history since in Western traditions wo/men have not been accorded full-citizenship and self-determination."[54] Ekklesia of wo/men offers a radical vision for politics that seeks to accord "all non-citizens of modernity" equal status in society.[55] Again, there exist similarities with West's work here because the struggle for justice constitutes the mark of authenticity rather than belief in specific doctrines or the engagement with particular liturgical practices. But where West generalizes the prophetic by using it as a term to signify the work of those who labor for a more just social order, Schüssler Fiorenza utilizes ekklesia of wo/men as a term to describe the communities of wo/men that struggle against kyriarchy.

For Schüssler Fiorenza, ekklesia of wo/men represents a space of social, political, and religious struggle that is "at once historical and an imagined reality, already partially realized but still to be struggled for."[56] In an analysis that parallels Sheldon Wolin's genealogy of fugitive democracy, Schüssler Fiorenza describes three emancipatory movements of resistance to kyriarchal oppression as historical examples of the ekklesia of wo/men: (1) the

52. Schüssler Fiorenza, *Empowering Memory and Movement*, 299. The task is to "interrogate biblical texts, Christian traditions, and institutional practices for religious visions that foster equality, justice, and the logic of the *ekklesia* rather than that of patriarchal domination." Schüssler Fiorenza, "Bible, the Global Context, and the Discipleship of Equals," 96.

53. Schüssler Fiorenza, *In Memory of Her*, 344.

54. Schüssler Fiorenza, *Sharing Her Word*, 112.

55. Schüssler Fiorenza, *Transforming Vision*, 51.

56. Schüssler Fiorenza, *Bread Not Stone*, 130.

early Jesus movement's commitment to *basileia*, (2) the women's suffrage movement in the United States, and (3) ekklesia of wo/men as an interfaith, grassroots movement of liberation.[57]

First, Schüssler Fiorenza engages in a critical-reconstructive retrieval of early Christian origins to rediscover the egalitarian politics of the first followers of Jesus of Nazareth. As noted above, *In Memory of Her* offers an analysis of the politics of the community that gathered around Jesus. Schüssler Fiorenza argues that a feminist approach moves away from focusing on Jesus as "exceptional man and charismatic leader" and toward "the emancipatory Divine Wisdom movement of which he was a part."[58] The women and men who gathered around Jesus were committed to the *basileia* of G*d. While *basileia* is often translated as "kingdom," she observes that a more accurate rendering of it would be "empire" (or "commonweal"). "Empire" serves to avoid the kyriarchal resonances of "kingdom" and accents the oppositional nature of the early Jesus movement in relation to the Roman Empire.[59] Thus, the *basileia* of G*d, which promised an egalitarian future, served as a direct alternative to the *basileia* of Rome as a potent kyriarchal structure of domination. Schüssler Fiorenza argues that *basileia* of G*d invokes "a range of ancestral democratic-religious traditions that proclaimed God's kingship and power of salvation. It was also an anti-imperial political symbol that appealed to the oppositional imagination of the Jewish people victimized by the Roman imperial system. The gospel of the *basileia* envisioned an alternative world free of hunger, poverty, and domination."[60] Because the early Jesus movement's commitment to a discipleship of equals stood in sharp contrast to the hierarchical and patriarchal structure of Roman empire, Schüssler Fiorenza concludes that the "self-description of the early Christian communities was a radical democratic one."[61]

Second, Schüssler Fiorenza describes feminist movements of democratic struggle in American history as examples of the ekklesia of wo/men, from "wo/men's struggle for the abolition of slavery, for religious freedom, for voting rights" to wo/men's movements "against sexual violence, and

57. Schüssler Fiorenza, *Power of the Word*, 73.

58. Schüssler Fiorenza, *In Memory of Her*, 21.

59. Schüssler Fiorenza, *Jesus and the Politics of Interpretation*, 169.

60. Schüssler Fiorenza, *Sharing Her Word*, 116, and Schüssler Fiorenza, *Jesus and the Politics of Interpretation*, 171.

61. Schüssler Fiorenza, *Power of the Word*, 77. Schüssler Fiorenza is careful to distinguish between the reality of the early Jesus movement and its ideals, noting that the followers of Jesus did not "all conform to a radical democratic ethos, for the texts that transmit this ethos are frequently prescriptive texts indicating that not all the disciples observed such a radical ethos of equality" (*Sharing Her Word*, 114).

against global capitalism."[62] She notes that while critics often have situated her project in relation to contemporary trends in hermeneutics (Ricoeur), critical theory (the Frankfurt School), or the pragmatist tradition, she views her work as extending the project of the nineteenth-century suffragists. She observes that "while my own radical democratic understanding of the ekklesia of women is theorized quite differently and speaks to a different rhetorical situation and historical context, it nevertheless continues this nineteenth century suffragist tradition on the religious importance of democracy."[63] She specifically invokes the work of suffragists like Elizabeth Cady Stanton, Susan B. Anthony, Anna Julia Cooper, and Anna Howard Shaw, who described "democracy as a religious-biblical symbol in its struggle for justice."[64] The suffragists' concern to establish a positive relationship between religion and democracy represents an important precedent for Schüssler Fiorenza's own work. Secular feminists often reject the Bible and the Christian tradition as irredeemably sexist and argue that it is better to abandon religion as a backward remnant from the patriarchal past than view it as a site of feminist struggle. Schüssler Fiorenza points to the alternative perspective adopted by Cady Stanton and other suffragists:

> Cady Stanton argued that no serious reform of society in the interest of women's emancipation will be successful if one does not seek to advance the reform of biblical religion at the same time. If suffragists believe that they can neglect the revision of the Bible and the reform of religion because there are more pressing political issues at stake, Cady Stanton insists, then they do not recognize the impact of religion and the Bible upon society and especially on the lives of women.[65]

The suffragists argued that because religion was a critical site of feminist political struggle, it would be a strategic miscalculation to dismiss the role that religion plays in either legitimating patriarchy or contributing to democratic resistance to it. Feminists, whether they possess religious commitments or not, should be concerned with how the Bible is interpreted, if for no other reason than that it continues to play a formative role in society. Because "many wo/men not only consult the bible as an inspiring authority but also value and transmit it as a source of strength and hope," it is self-defeating for feminists to reject religion and to view secular political resistance as the exclusive site of struggle. The aim of feminist discourse and praxis is to

62. Schüssler Fiorenza, *Wisdom Ways*, 80.
63. Schüssler Fiorenza, *Bread Not Stone*, 178.
64. Schüssler Fiorenza, *Bread Not Stone*, 176.
65. Schüssler Fiorenza, *Transforming Vision*, 145.

transform the entire society and to work toward the liberation of all human beings from structures of kyriarchal domination. Religion should be viewed, therefore, as a critical site of struggle, because "one cannot reform one segment of patriarchal society without reforming the whole."[66]

Third, Schüssler Fiorenza describes the ekklesia of wo/men in contemporary terms as a "transreligious" movement comprised of all persons who struggle against kyriarchy. As noted above, the term *ekklesia of wo/men* undermines any dualistic construction that separates religious from nonreligious movements. And while acknowledging that ekklesia of wo/men is developed within the context of her own Catholic Christianity, Schüssler Fiorenza recognizes the need to develop spaces of feminist struggle in different "symbolic universes" and religious traditions. And so, in addition to ekklesia of wo/men, Schüssler Fiorenza points to the existence of a "synagogue of wo/men" and an "umma of wo/men."[67] Furthermore, in response to critics who claim that even ekklesia, synagogue, and umma of wo/men is not sufficiently pluralist, Schüssler Fiorenza has utilized the "kosmopolis of wo/men" or "congress of wo/men" to signify the inclusivity of feminist struggle against kyriarchy. These terms attempt to push the political struggle against kyriarchy beyond Christian identification and toward an understanding of it as a democratic assembly that works toward the realization of a world in which "religious, racial, and class, but also heterosexual markers no longer signify and legitimate status differences and relations of kyriarchal domination and subordination."[68] As we shall see in the next section, Schüssler Fiorenza contends that ekklesia, congress, or kosmpolis of wo/men takes form as a "transreligious," "transconfessional," and "transnational" form of resistance to kyriarchy.[69]

The community of the early Jesus movement, nineteenth-century suffragists, and transreligious grassroots movements around the world today embody both an "already" and "not yet" structure insofar as they serve as episodic expressions of radical egalitarianism in history yet to be fully realized.[70] In diverse ways, these movements resisted the dominant kyriarchal structures of their time and developed a communal politics that sought fuller equality and freedom. In the next section, we more fully

66. Schüssler Fiorenza, *Wisdom Ways*, 64.

67. Schüssler Fiorenza, *Power of the Word*, 77.

68. Schüssler Fiorenza, *Power of the Word*, 79.

69. Schüssler Fiorenza, *Congress of Wo/men*, 25.

70. Schüssler Fiorenza, "Critical Feminist The*logy of Liberation," 28. On this point, see Castelli, "*Ekklesia* of Women and/as Utopian Space," 45

explore Schüssler Fiorenza's feminist-transnational approach to the politics of radical democracy.

FEMINIST-TRANSNATIONAL DEMOCRACY

Schüssler Fiorenza invokes a number of different radical democratic theorists in her description of the politics of the ekklesia of wo/men: Chantal Mouffe, Sheldon Wolin, Antonio Negri and Michael Hardt, Simone Chambers, Ewa Plonowska Ziarek, Adriana Hernández, Nancy Fraser, and Chela Sandoval. Because she has generated a distinctive account of radical democracy in conversation with secular feminist theory as well as critical scholarship on the biblical and theological traditions of Christianity, it is difficult to situate her approach within any single paradigm of radical democratic theory.

As with the other thinkers examined in this book, Schüssler Fiorenza contends that democracy represents a contradictory political form predicated on a series of historical exclusions that undermine its stated aspiration to freedom, equality, and self-rule. She notes that the ancient Greek model offered access to power only to "imperial, elite, propertied, educated male heads of households."[71] The majority of people (wo/men, slaves, the poor, etc.) were excluded from the democratic project of self-rule.[72] This pattern of exclusion is consistent in the history of democracy, with subsequent iterations "structured as complex pyramidal political systems of superiority and inferiority, of dominance and subordination." According to Schüssler Fiorenza, the result is that every democratic structure is "stratified by gender, race, class, religion, heterosexism, and age."[73]

Schüssler Fiorenza describes three dominant forms of democratic theory and practice in the contemporary world: liberal democracy, Marxist/socialist democracy, and participatory democracy. She argues that where liberal democracy is constrained by its commitment to hierarchical forms of political representation, the focus of the Marxist/socialist model on class-based exploitation is not sufficiently pluralist. As a result, she advocates for a participatory form of democracy that ensures self-rule by securing "equal opportunities for all to take part in decision making in matters affecting not only the political realm but also the workplace, the community, and interpersonal relations."[74] The politics of ekklesia of wo/men affirms the Roman and medieval democratic axiom "That which

71. Schüssler Fiorenza, *Power of the Word*, 71–72.
72. Schüssler Fiorenza, *Transforming Vision*, 47.
73. Schüssler Fiorenza, *Changing Horizons*, 8.
74. Schüssler Fiorenza, *Democratizing Biblical Studies*, 8.

affects all should be determined by every one."[75] Radical democracy supports institutional arrangements that provide citizens with the capacity for self-determination, relationships of mutuality with others, and activities that support the "common good."[76] This form of democracy is qualified as "radical" in that it "sets the terms for critique of imperial power and institutions and creates the basis for their change."[77] Furthermore, it attempts to make real the claim to full citizenship for those excluded or viewed as less than human by generating a politics that seeks to realize the etymological meaning of democracy as "rule of and by the people."[78]

Schüssler Fiorenza shares with other radical democratic theorists the view that democracy is not primarily a system of governance but instead an ethos that seeks to generate an inclusive and egalitarian social order.[79] As a consequence, she places her approach at a critical distance from reformist political projects that aim to transform society via the mechanisms of centralized power of governmental structures. She observes that "as a radical democrat dreamer, I do not envision that change is going to take place from the top down but only from the bottom up" through community-based organizations, base groups, and people's organizations.[80] These grassroots movements seek to improve the lives of wo/men by generating nonhierarchical and nonpatriarchal practices in local communities and by being committed to "improving living conditions in a particular location and to promoting values associated with local radical democratic politics."[81] Schüssler Fiorenza specifically affirms localism as a critical site of the politics of the ekklesia of wo/men because it serves to situate feminist struggle within the context of the lived experience of concrete communities of wo/men around the world. But her localism differs from Wolin's because Schüssler Fiorenza advocates for the development of transnational networks from below capable of countering transnational forms of kyriarchy. Thus, in terms of the typology that we described in the second chapter, Schüssler Fiorenza's approach is situated squarely within the "withdrawal" space of Wolin, Hardt, and Negri because she focuses on civil society as

75. Schüssler Fiorenza, *Power of the Word*, 77.

76. Schüssler Fiorenza, *Democratizing Biblical Studies*, 8.

77. Schüssler Fiorenza, *Power of the Word*, 158.

78. Schüssler Fiorenza, *Democratizing Biblical Studies*, 7, and Schüssler Fiorenza, *Transforming Vision*, 238.

79. She observes, "I understand democracy not primarily as a representative form of government, but rather as a social vision and egalitarian ethos." Schüssler Fiorenza, *Transforming Vision*, 42.

80. Schüssler Fiorenza, *Democratizing Biblical Studies*, 7.

81. Schüssler Fiorenza, *Democratizing Biblical Studies*, 8.

the primary site of democratic conscientization and struggle. Her work is distinguished from these approaches by offering a transnational feminist approach to radical democracy.

Transnational feminism is a movement that is inclusive of a diverse set of theoretical and practical orientations. At its core, transnational feminism explores the ways in which globalization has generated new possibilities for solidarity beyond the boundaries of the nation-state. The term transnational feminism was first used by Inderpal Grewal and Caren Kaplan in their text *Scattered Hegemonies: Postmodernity and Transnational Feminist Practices* (1994). Grewal and Kaplan described transnational feminism as a critical response to global feminism's tendency to propose a "Western model of women's liberation" as normative for all women.[82] Global feminists made the argument that because patriarchy is universal, it is possible to construct "a theory of hegemonic oppression under a unified category of gender." For them, it followed that the common experience of patriarchal oppression across geographical, cultural, and racial difference creates the conditions for a "global sisterhood" of women. While supportive of the effort to move beyond the restricted confines of North Atlantic experience, Grewal and Kaplan criticize the tendency of global feminists to offer a monolithic account of gender oppression. The claim that patriarchy represents the primary form of oppression of women around the world fails to account for the complicated intersection of patriarchy with racism, neoliberalism, nationalism, and religious fundamentalism. Accordingly, in a move representative of the pluralist commitments of radical democratic theory, Grewal and Kaplan call for the creation of coalitions and transnational solidarities among "diverse feminisms without requiring either equivalence or a master theory."[83] In *Feminist Genealogies, Colonial Legacies, Democratic Futures* (1997), M. Jacqui Alexander and Chandra Mohanty also argue that transnational feminism is distinguished from global feminism in its support of forms of feminist struggle that exceed the borders and boundaries of the nation-state. They observe, "To talk about feminist praxis in global contexts would involve shifting the unit of analysis from local, regional, and national culture to relations and processes across cultures. Grounding analyses in particular local, feminist praxis is necessary, but we also need to

82. Grewal and Kaplan, *Scattered Hegemonies*, 17. In this text, the term was used to signify a shift in feminist discourse that recognized "how people in different locations and circumstances are linked by the spread of and resistance to modern capitalist social formations even as their experiences of these phenomena are not at all the same or equal" (5).

83. Grewal and Kaplan, *Scattered Hegemonies*, 19.

understand the local in relation to larger, cross-national processes."[84] Mohanty and Alexander focus on the oppression caused by global capitalism as the basis for a "common context of political struggles" and "common interests" that serve to generate transnational solidarity movements among subaltern women. Alexander and Mohanty describe this transnational politics as a form of "feminist democracy" rooted in "an anticolonialist, anticapitalist vision of feminist practice."[85]

Nancy Fraser offers yet another approach to transnational feminism that situates the arguments of Grewal, Kaplan, Alexander, and Mohanty in the context of the contemporary struggle for recognition and redistribution. Fraser maintains that feminists should respond to the tension between cultural (recognition) and economic (redistribution) approaches, as well as challenges associated with representation and political agency, by adopting a transnational perspective. Fraser describes her approach as a transnational feminist politics of "representation" that seeks to create a political culture in which those affected by a decision are empowered to express their viewpoint through debate, protest, and political procedure. In a move similar to Schüssler Fiorenza's retrieval of the Roman and medieval maxim of inclusive political participation, Fraser describes this as the "all-affected principle" in which "all those affected by a given social structure or institution have moral standing as subjects of justice in relation to it."[86] This is particularly important in an era of globalization when transnational elites make political and economic decisions without any form of democratic accountability from below. Fraser observes that transnational feminists argue that it is not possible to challenge gender injustice if their work remains situated within the "frame" of the modern nation-state: "Because that frame limits the scope of justice to intrastate institutions that organize relations among fellow citizens, it systematically obscures transborder forms and sources of gender injustice."[87] According to Fraser, truly radical forms of democracy necessitate that representation extend beyond the nation-state as a transnational form of political empowerment.

Schüssler Fiorenza adopts the broad outlines of Fraser's approach and notes that "recognition," "redistribution," and "representation" do not constitute "three sequential steps" but a "dynamic model defined by simultaneity." Accordingly, feminists should work at the cultural, economic, political, and transnational level simultaneously in order to build a global democratic

84. Alexander and Mohanty, *Feminist Genealogies*, xix.
85. Alexander and Mohanty, *Feminist Genealogies*, xxvii.
86. Fraser, *Scales of Justice*, 24.
87. Fraser, *Scales of Justice*, 112.

order of inclusion and justice. Schüssler Fiorenza notes, however, that in religious studies and the*logy insufficient attention has been paid to this turn in feminist theory and practice. Schüssler Fiorenza observes, "Six years ago, for example, I was in India. In Kerala, I had the opportunity of meeting with a woman union leader who was fully immersed in organizing fishworkers from around the world, trying to make people conscious of the fact that what happens in one place affects people in other places, that what happens in India, for example, has an impact on people in Spain, in North America, everywhere, because of the global market. It was really quite impressive." But she cautions that "among us in religious studies, however, I see no theoretical movement that would take global interdependence seriously. This we very much need." At the present political conjuncture, Schüssler Fiorenza argues that a feminist the*logy must become a "transnational the*logy" that resists "prescribing a nationalistically colored feminist politics of identity" and instead "organize[s] transnationally."[88] Schüssler Fiorenza pursues this argument at multiple registers in her work.

First, she contends that a feminist transnational theology takes aim at all forms of nationalism because, by artificially dividing communities, it creates oppositional relationships between "natives" and "others." Schüssler Fiorenza has argued that feminists should view themselves as "resident alien[s]" or as immigrants and foreigners who resist identifying with forms of community that perpetuate discourses and practices of exclusion.[89] Furthermore, she expresses concern about the consequences of feminists identifying with geographical or regional identities:

> Insofar as they tend to define and construct identity in terms of continents—Asian, African, South American, African American, or North-American feminist the*logy—these discourses tend to reinscribe nationalistic tendencies. Hence, we need to engage in critical reflection on the nationalist undercurrents of such self-naming and the different understandings of nationalism. The danger exists that a feminist identity politics centered on continents ends at best in a liberal pluralism that leaves each group ensconced in its own discourse and at worst in feminist antagonisms that diminish the little power for change that we have. If, however, we could remain conscious of the pitfalls of territorial nationalism, many of our theoretical and the*logical disagreements could be understood as political contradictions shaped by the discourses of nationalism.[90]

88. Schüssler Fiorenza, *Empowering Memory and Movement*, 64.

89. Schüssler Fiorenza, *Empowering Memory and Movement*.

90. Schüssler Fiorenza, "Feminist Studies in Religion and the The*logy In-Between," 119.

Schüssler Fiorenza expresses concern that an identity politics of recognition among feminists either leads to antagonisms between groups or yields an anemic pluralism that fails to link diverse forms of struggle. She argues instead that feminists should recognize their own particularity in ethnic, racial, national, and religious terms, while at the same time building transnational strategies for resisting "kyriarchal globalization."[91]

Second, we noted above that Schüssler Fiorenza argues that because we live in the midst of "capitalist globalization under nationalist American hegemony," the form of theology required to counteract this kyriarchal formation is a transnational feminist the*logy "from below."[92] Globalization-from-above is defined by its "hypermasculinity expressed in militarism, corporate exploitation, sexual conquest, religious fanaticism . . ." Furthermore, globalization-from-above is characterized by a set of antidemocratic commitments resistant to any attempt by the people to exercise control over its mechanisms.[93] Importantly, Schüssler Fiorenza also recognizes that globalization has created new possibilities for transnational solidarities and grassroots political movements. She observes that "such globalization also presents possibilities for a more radical democratization worldwide. It also makes possible the interconnectedness of all being and the possibility of communication and organization across national borders on the basis of human rights and justice for all."[94] Schüssler Fiorenza's construal of transnational feminist politics draws close to Hardt and Negri in their claim that neoliberal globalization (or Empire) constitutes a new form of global domination that represents an opportunity for radical politics because it opens the space for new forms of global resistance. Schüssler Fiorenza characterizes this mode of resistance to neoliberalism as a form of "globalization from below" and, once again, describes it as the attempt to empower wo/men beyond the "North-South antagonisms" and build coalitions across cultures on the basis of common ends rather than "identity based" commitments.[95]

Finally, because nationalism, militarism, and neoliberalism rely on conservative, patriarchal, and fundamentalist forms of religion for legitimation, Schüssler Fiorenza maintains that contemporary feminist

91. Schüssler Fiorenza, "Feminist Studies in Religion and the The*logy In-Between," 119.

92. Schüssler Fiorenza, *Congress of Wo/men*, 22.

93. Schüssler Fiorenza observes, "The danger of this shift from nation-state to international corporation is that democratic government no longer can be exercised and the system of global capitalism is not held democratically accountable" (*Transforming Vision*, 178).

94. Schüssler Fiorenza, "Power of the Word," 57.

95. Schüssler Fiorenza, *Congress of Wo/men*, 24–25.

theology must offer alternative interpretations that seek to correct a "one-sided vision of G*d."[96] We noted above that she is critical of theologians for failing to respond to the transnational turn in feminist theory and practice. But we should also recall her critique of secular feminists for failing to recognize religion as an important site of political struggle. This tendency among secular feminists represents a strategic error because religion continues to play a formative role in society and serves either to legitimate kyriarchy or to engender democratic political formations. In this regard, in addition to insisting upon the importance of grassroots transnational organizing, Schüssler Fiorenza argues that discursive struggle over the contemporary significance of religion represents a central component of contemporary feminist politics.

We have paired West with Schüssler Fiorenza in these two chapters because they identify democracy as an internal norm of the Christian tradition, share a common focus on pluralist coalition building, and describe radical democracy as the most appropriate instrument to realize an intersectional vision of justice. In view of these commonalities, it is not surprising that West and Schüssler Fiorenza have been criticized for similar reasons. Because Schüssler Fiorenza avoids invoking scriptural, doctrinal, or liturgical markers as normativity and appeals instead to the experience of wo/men, critics have characterized her work as a reduction of Christianity to politics.[97] These critics argue that Schüssler Fiorenza's approach to feminist theology is driven by ideological commitments rather than either fidelity to the doctrinal tradition of the church or the objectivity of scholarly neutrality.[98] Schüssler Fiorenza's response has been to insist that there is no neutral or objective approach to theology, and those who profess to offer such an approach seek to mask their own ideological agenda. Every interpretation of Scripture is a political act. Thus, scholars or theologians committed to doctrinal-dogmatic or historical-critical approaches obscure the ideological and political commitments that their interpretive choices authorize.

Schüssler Fiorenza distinguishes her approach from these alternatives in that she makes explicit the ideological and political framework that animates her theological reflections. She names this framework a "rhetorical-emancipatory" model and describes its political aim as building a future "in which none are hungry, strangers, or outcasts but each cherishes the earth

96. Schüssler Fiorenza, *Transforming Vision*, 15.

97. This charge most famously was articulated by Luce Irigarary when she observed of *In Memory of Her* that "sociology quickly bores me when I'm expecting the divine." Irigaray, "Equal to Whom?," 80.

98. *Rhetoric and Ethic, Jesus and the Politics of Interpretation*, and *Democratizing Biblical Studies* are the works that respond to these critics.

and struggles in solidarity with those who are oppressed by racism, nationalism, poverty, neo-colonialism, and hetero-sexism."[99]

Notably, Schüssler Fiorenza shifts the audience for theology from the church to society. Accordingly, she contends that the fundamental imperative is to position these discourses in "the public sphere of the polis" in order "to further the well-being of all inhabitants of the *cosmo-polis* today."[100] This attempt to situate the ekklesia of wo/men in the *polis* parallels West's use of the "prophetic" as a description of all those who labor for justice in society. From an ecclesiological perspective, the potential problem with this move is that it makes the church invisible as a distinctively Christian institution. Because ekklesia is identified as any group or community that struggles for justice in society, critics claim that Schüssler Fiorenza's approach fails to offer the shared beliefs, rituals, or practices that bind a community together. The result is that ekkelsia of wo/men exists as an abstract "ought" or an idealized community, rather than a concrete community assembled on the basis of shared beliefs and practices.

Although it is difficult to identify ekklesia of wo/men with any extant community, Schüssler Fiorenza does generate theological warrants for her approach. In a sense, the legitimacy of her approach hinges on the relationship between God and the world and what role the church plays in facilitating the experience of God. Is the primary purpose of the church to cultivate distinctive practices and virtues among the Christian community? Or, as Schüssler Fiorenza and West suggest, is the task to mobilize its members to participate in a struggle for an intersectional form of justice in a pluralistic society? Schüssler Fiorenza pushes the pluralist commitments of this position in a radical direction insofar as she imagines the ekklesia as a site of political struggle for Christian and non-Christian alike. This vision for ekklesia is supported by her claim that the divine does not reside in an authoritative text or the practices of the church, but rather among wo/men who struggle for justice in the world.[101] Schüssler Fiorenza argues that Pentecost represents a Christian precedent for this approach in that it describes how diverse peoples from different regions of the world encounter the Spirit in the context of their own cultural traditions and languages. Schüssler Fiorenza observes that the image of Pentecost "invites Christian wo/men in the power of the Spirit to struggle together with wo/men from other religions and persuasions for the realization of the kosmopolis of wo/men, as G*d's alternative world of justice and well-being."[102]

99. Schüssler Fiorenza, *Power of the Word*, 77–78.

100. Schüssler Fiorenza, *Rhetoric and Ethic*, 11.

101. Schüssler Fiorenza, *Bread Not Stone*, 140.

102. Schüssler Fiorenza, *Congress of Wo/men*, 116.

Even as West and Schüssler Fiorenza share similar discursive and political sensibilities, they differ in a number of important respects. First, where West invokes the prophetic legacy of the Bible as a warrant for his approach to Christian political engagement, Schüssler Fiorenza is critical of any attempt to retrieve a biblical paradigm as normative. Schüssler Fiorenza criticizes Rosemary Radford Ruether's attempt to retrieve the prophetic discourse of the Bible as a norm for feminist theology by arguing that Ruether employs an overly abstract and idealized approach to prophetic traditions that fails to confront their androcentric and patriarchal elements.[103] While West notes this criticism in his review of *In Memory of Her*, he has continued to use the prophetic tradition of the Bible.[104] Second, they diverge with regard to the question of whether radical politics should pursue reformist or revolutionary strategies. West adopts a pragmatic and reformist approach to politics, even as his approach aspires to revolutionary effects. In his writings as well as his public advocacy he aligns himself with concrete political movements and calls for policy reforms that seek to open more radical possibilities within the realm of American politics. By way of contrast, Schüssler Fiorenza avoids entirely any concrete analysis of the political situation in the United States, except to criticize its politics as imperialistic, and focuses instead on local grassroots movements and transnational networks of organizing. In this regard, Schüssler Fiorenza's approach is consistent with the withdrawal axis of radical democratic theory in its focus on civil society as the site of political struggle and in its articulation of a utopian horizon for radical democracy (Hardt and Negri).

Of course, the differences between West and Schüssler Fiorenza are minimal in relation to the common concerns they share—to support a liberationist approach to Christianity and to affirm radical democracy as an internal norm of the Christian tradition. In the next two chapters we shift to approaches that focus on the christological and ecclesiological warrants for an *ad hoc* engagement with radical politics. As we examine thinkers more concerned with Christian identity than West and Schüssler Fiorenza, we would do well to recall that the mandate of radical democratic politics is to affirm a diversity of approaches as a means of building coalitions capable of resisting empire. Thus, while West and Schüssler Fiorenza offer an approach that is obviously more oriented in this pluralist direction, the constructive task is to draw approaches that overlap on significant points into a broader theo-political assemblage.

103. Schüssler Fiorenza, *In Memory of Her*, 16–17.
104. West, "On Elisabeth Schüssler Fiorenza's *In Memory of Her*."

CHAPTER 5

Latin American Liberation Theology

IN AN INTERVIEW, ENRIQUE Dussel has observed that Latin American liberation theology "was a novelty in world history, because it was the first religious movement that was democratic, Left, and against capitalism."[1] Latin
American liberation theology was most certainly a movement on the left
with anticapitalist commitments, but the relationship between liberation
theology and democracy is complex and varied. At times, Latin American
liberation theologians have adopted a critical stance toward democracy, while
at other times they have expressed openness to its more radical manifestations. Those theologians who have adopted a critical stance toward democracy (Ignacio Ellacuría and Jon Sobrino) have done so because historically
democracy has been invoked by the United States to justify its military and
economic interventions in Latin America. So that where Christianization
served as the ideological justification for military and political intervention
in Latin America within the colonial period, democratization has served
that same function in the neocolonial period.

Since the 1970s, the United States has utilized two strategies in Latin
America to realize its strategic aims: the Salvador option and the Chile option.[2] The first, the Salvador option, refers to the process of farming out
imperial violence by using native militaries to exercise American interests
in Latin America. The United States utilized this option in El Salvador in
response to a civil war that pitted economic and military elites against the
poor and peasant farmers (*campesinos*). The United States trained, funded,
and armed a counterinsurgency in El Salvador that went on to commit
atrocities against unarmed civilians (most famously at the massacre in El

1. Dussel, "The Philosophy of Liberation: An Interview with Enrique Dussel (Part
II)."

2. Rosen, "Introduction," 3. The term "Salvador option" was coined by Michael
Hirsch and John Barry in a *Newsweek* article dated January 8, 2005.

Mozote) and planned and executed the assassination of Ignacio Ellacuría, five other Jesuits, their housekeeper and her daughter on the evening of November 16, 1989. Nineteen of the twenty-six members of the Salvadoran military who planned or participated in the assassination of the Jesuits were trained by the United States government at the School of the Americas in Fort Benning, Georgia. Greg Grandin notes that the Reagan administration spent more than a million dollars a day to fund the brutal counterinsurgency in El Salvador and that "all told, US allies in Central America during Reagan's two terms killed over 300,000 people, tortured hundreds of thousands and drove millions into exile."[3]

The second option, the Chile option, is an economic strategy. In Chile, the United States supported the military coup in 1973, provided support to the military junta of General Pinochet, and played a pivotal role in the subsequent neoliberalization of the Chilean economy under Pinochet. Milton Friedman and other proponents of neoliberalism trained economists at the Pontificia Universidad Católica de Chile in neoliberal economics and advocated for the reorganization of Chile as a neoliberal state via the mechanisms of "shock therapy." By repressive (imprisoning an estimated 80,000 to 100,000 Chileans) and violent means (torturing and murdering 3,200 political dissidents) the Pinochet regime worked to neoliberalize the state through privatization, deregulation, and extensive cuts to social services. Thus, in contrast to the standard narrative that links the spread of capitalism with democracy, the historical record points to the fact that one of the first global experiments in neoliberal capitalism involved a military coup and brutal political repression that aimed to silence those who advocated for a democratic socialist political order.[4]

Ellacuría and Sobrino offer a trenchant critique of American empire in view of this multifaceted history of American interventionism in Latin America in the 1970s and 1980s. In this chapter, we examine Ellacuría and Sobrino's approach to empire both as a critique of the civilization of capital and state-sanctioned violence and as an attempt to offer an alternative by revitalizing the church of the poor (as a Christian alternative) and the civilization of poverty (as a civilizational alternative).

In the first section of this chapter, we examine the writings of Ellacuría and Sobrino on the relationship between American empire, the civilization of capital, and the suffering of a crucified people. In the second section, we analyze their description of the church of the poor and the civilization of poverty as an alternative to the civilization of capital. In the final

3. Grandin, *Empire's Workshop*, 71.
4. Rosen, "Introduction," 3.

section on liberative-populist democracy, we bring Ellacuría and Sobrino's theological reflections into conversation with the liberation philosophy of Enrique Dussel. Although the politics of Ellacuría and Sobrino are not explicitly democratic, their reflections on civilizational alternatives to empire converge with contemporary radical democratic theory. In some ways, they draw close to the reflections of Hardt and Negri on poverty and a politics of the commons, but overlap most substantively with Dussel's liberative democratic politics in terms of their shared commitment to an anti-imperialist, populist, and liberative politics.[5]

EMPIRE AND THE CRUCIFIED PEOPLE

In "The Latin American Quincentenary: Discovery or Cover-Up?" Ellacuría describes the history of imperial violence in Latin America since the time of the Spanish and Portuguese empire, which was justified by the call to Christianize a "savage" people.[6] Where the Christian mission to save souls provided theological cover for the imperial violence of the Spanish and Portuguese crowns, imperialism is justified now in terms of the political project of democratization. According to Ellacuría, the affluent world comes to Latin America with an "ideological clothing whose only purpose is to spread a 'lovely' curtain over its real intentions. The powerful nations of today say they are coming to the third world to make us 'democratic.'"[7] The professed generosity of the United States' commitment to democratization only obscures its imperialist intentions.[8] The American commitment to democracy is little more than an illusion because "the democracy it defends is false, deceptive, and means absolutely nothing as a universal value."[9]

The historical record makes clear that the United States has supported brutal dictatorships in Guatemala, El Salvador, the Dominican Republic, and Chile when these regimes have served its economic and

5. Because it is impossible to understand Sobrino's theology independent of the work of Ignacio Ellacuría this chapter will move back and forth between Sobrino and Ellacuría. Ellacuría provides the philosophical horizon for Sobrino's theology even if Sobrino develops Ellacuría's thought in a more expansively christological and ecclesiological direction.

6. Ellacuría, "The Latin American Quincentenary," 27–38.

7. Ellacuría, "Latin American Quincentenary," 29.

8. Ellacuría, "Latin American Quincentenary," 30.

9. Ellacuría, "Latin American Quincentenary," 30. Ellacuría observes, "The ideologized propaganda about capitalist democracy, as the only and absolute form of political organization, becomes an instrument of cover-up and, at times, an instrument of oppression" ("Utopia and Propheticism," 21).

political interests. As a historical example, Ellacuría points to the United States' opposition to the democratically elected Sandinista government in Nicaragua in the 1980s. He maintains that the United States would have been indifferent to either the presence or lack of democracy in Nicaragua if it were an ally that supported the interests of corporations in the United States. The demand that the United States support regime change in Nicaragua became an urgent national imperative only when the Sandinistas appeared to represent a threat to the United States' economic interests in the region. Ellacuría observes that the United States' attempt to "democratize" Latin America does not "let the people determine their own political and economic model" but serves "to cover up the imposition of the capitalist system." He concludes, "Democracy is supported only insofar as those interests are presumed to be furthered."[10]

Ellacuría wrote "The Latin American Quincentenary: Discovery or Cover-Up?" in 1989. In 2003 Sobrino published "God and Empire," which extends the basic orientation of Ellacuría's argument in a context dominated by American interventionism in the Middle East.[11] For Sobrino, the United States' response to 9/11 makes it clear "the prostration of the planet as a whole can no longer be described in simple terms of injustice and capitalism. Iraq has made clear that there is an empire, and today's empire is the United States."[12] American empire is comprised of a military-industrial complex with no respect for life, a global economic system that imposes iniquitous trade policies and debt structures on the global poor, and a political system that manipulates facts and disseminates false information to serve its own self-interest.[13] In addition to these more overt features of empire, Sobrino argues that it enacts a subtle form of control over time and space. In relation to time, the "empire decides where and when time is something real" and determines which dates and events should be recognized as significant for the world.[14] The result of this capacity to determine the significance of time is that 9/11/1973 pales in significance to 9/11/2001 and barely registers as a noteworthy event in history. However, 9/11/1973 is an essential date in Latin American history. It is the date of the United States–backed overthrow of the democratically elected president of Chile, Salvador Allende, by General

10. Ellacuría, "Utopia and Propheticism," 21.

11. In *No Salvation Outside the Poor*, Sobrino observes that were he alive today Ellacuría "would denounce the savagery of preventive war and its theoretical justification, as well as the atrocity of using the term 'collateral damage' for what are in fact monstrous murders" (47–48).

12. Sobrino, *Where Is God?*, viii.

13. Sobrino, *Where Is God?*, viii.

14. Sobrino, *Where Is God?*, xi.

Pinochet, which led to Pinochet's torturous military regime and the imposition of neoliberal "shock therapy" on the people of Chile.[15] The generalized amnesia about 9/11/1973 and almost obsessive focus on 9/11/2001 make it clear that while "there have been many 9/11s" in history they "don't exist because they were never entered on the imperial calendar."[16] Furthermore, the United States exerts spatial control over the world through its manipulation of the processes of neoliberal globalization and its celebration of the world as smooth and round—a "blessed space"—"where there is room for everyone."[17] It defends globalization by invoking biblical concepts that justify neoliberal processes as delivering "good news" and even "salvation (*euaggelion*)" to the world.[18] Sobrino argues that this evangelical view of globalization refuses to acknowledge "the holes, the chasms" and "the sharp corners" that exist around the world.[19] He concludes that neoliberal globalization supports a politics of exclusion not inclusion, indifference not solidarity, dehumanization not humanization, and is rooted in imperial violence (*Pax Americana*) rather than the peace of the "biblical shalom."[20]

Central to Ellacuría and Sobrino's analyses of imperialism is the claim that military power is deployed to defend the interests of the civilization of capital. From this perspective, the civilization of capital is the foundational structure of violence that generates repressive and imperialist forms of violence. Thus, while Ellacuría and Sobrino rarely refer to neoliberalism explicitly, their description of the civilization of capital resonates with the Marxist and Foucauldian approaches to neoliberalism described in the first chapter.[21] The civilization of capital proposes a specific vision for society and the human person in which "the accumulation of capital" is viewed as "the engine of history, and the possession-enjoyment of wealth as the principle of humanization."[22] Furthermore, the civilization is rooted in structural violence insofar as it keeps "the immense majority of humanity in absolutely inhuman biological, cultural, social, and political

15. See, for example, Klein, *The Shock Doctrine*.

16. Sobrino, *Where Is God?*, x.

17. Sobrino, *Where Is God?*, 33.

18. Sobrino, *No Salvation*, 10, and Sobrino, *Where Is God?*, 33.

19. Sobrino, *Where Is God?*, xi.

20. Sobrino, *Where Is God?*, xi. The fundamental fear is that things might change or "that 'a different world is possible' in which everyone can eat, even if it means the affluent countries have to eat less. To put today's good life at risk, to reduce it significantly, is too much to ask. The fear is that this might happen" (*Where Is God?*, xii).

21. Although Sobrino does invoke neoliberalism from time to time, characterizing it as an "unjust, cruel and criminal economic system" (*Where Is God?*, 42).

22. Ellacuría, "Utopia and Propheticism," 40.

conditions."[23] Ellacuría and Sobrino focus on three problematic features of the civilization of capital.

First, they argue that the civilization of capital leads to intensified inequalities between the affluent and the poor. Historically, colonialism generated many of the inequalities that exist between the North Atlantic world and the global South, but new forms of colonialism persist today through the mechanisms of neoliberal structural adjustment policies that permit the North Atlantic world to dominate the global South by way of soft power and economic coercion. Ellacuría specifically criticizes the debt repayment structure of neoliberal policy as a hegemonic exercise of power through which affluent countries "export the evils of capitalism to the exploited periphery."[24] Often the loans offered by the International Monetary Fund and the World Bank were given to corrupt governments who used them to build the wealth of the "upper social classes" and not to serve the needs of the people. These structural adjustment policies have led to the consolidation of wealth and power of economic elites and foreign investors and the dispossession and impoverishment of "the poor majority."[25]

A second negative consequence of the civilization of capital is its destruction of the natural world. Ellacuría adopts a novel approach to environmental degradation by invoking Immanuel Kant's approach to morality to critique the civilization of capital. For Ellacuría, the basic principle of Kantian morality is that if an act cannot be universalized, it is not moral. If the lifestyle of a few cannot be generalized for the entire human family, then this lifestyle cannot be viewed as "moral or even human, all the more so if the enjoyment of a few is at the cost of depriving the rest." Ellacuría observes, "Since the United States' solution cannot be universalized to the whole world, it is not a human solution; it does not serve humanity. If everyone had a U.S. standard of consumption—of meat, electricity, petroleum, etc.—we would exhaust the existing resources in twenty years. So from a concrete, measurable, ecological perspective on world reality, that is not and cannot be the solution. It is at best a solution for them, which can make them feel happy and proud. Meanwhile we

23. Ellacuría, "Latin American Quincentenary," 36–37. Sobrino observes that the civilization of capital "generates extreme scarcities, dehumanizes persons, and destroys the human family: it produces impoverished and excluded people and divides the world into conquerors and conquered. Our world continues to be 'gravely ill.'" Sobrino, *No Salvation*, 37.

24. Ellacuría, "Utopia and Propheticism," 20.

25. Ellacuría argues, "In the case of foreign debt it can be seen concretely how the originating loans were often made one-sidedly and with the complicity of governments and the upper social classes, yet without any benefit whatever for the mass of the people" ("Utopia and Propheticism," 19).

and the whole third world are left with a great problem."[26] Because the civilization of capital is unsustainable from an ecological perspective and cannot be universalized, it should be judged as undesirable from a Christian perspective.[27] In addition to this Kantian argument, Ellacuría also points to the fact that the fundamental dynamics of the civilization of capital re-create the structure of colonialism by constructing the global South as an "exploited periphery" that is used to "dispose of waste of all sorts that the more developed countries produce."[28] Sobrino suggests that the dynamic created is such that the affluent world depends on the countries of the global South—it extracts their materials, exploits their people, and treats them as "a dumping ground for poisonous waste."[29]

Third, Ellacuría and Sobrino argue that the civilization of capital is dehumanizing even for those who succeed by its standards. Ellacuría argues that the civilization of capital possesses "an almost irresistible pull toward a profound dehumanization" in which individuals become preoccupied with their "own security and happiness by means of private accumulation, of consumption, and of entertainment; submission to the laws of the consumer market by advertising in every kind of activity, including the cultural; and a manifest lack of solidarity of the individual, the family, and the state with other individuals, families, or states."[30] Sobrino observes that persons in the affluent world might very well ask, "What's wrong with wanting a good life?" The answer is clear: it leads to "dehumanization" because "structurally speaking, 'the good life' is only possible at the cost of a 'bad life' and death for the poor."[31] Furthermore, they contend that to succeed within the civilization of capital virtually necessitates devotion to idols. Idols are those historical realities that "promise salvation and demand worship and orthodoxy. Their existence, and the worship they demand, are decisively verified by the victims they inevitably produce."[32] And while religious idols have existed from the time of the Old Testament and were at the center of the violence of the Crusades and colonialism in Latin America, secular idols exist as well, and they "demand the daily sacrifice of the masses and the violent sacrifice of any who resist them. These deities require victims in order

26. Ellacuría, "Latin American Quincentenary," 34.

27. Ellacuría, "Latin American Quincentenary," 35.

28. Ellacuría, "Utopia and Propheticism," 20.

29. Sobrino, *Principle of Mercy*, 73.

30. Ellacuría, "Utopia and Propheticism," 20.

31. Sobrino, *Where Is God?*, xiii.

32. Sobrino, *Where Is God?*, xxx.

to survive, and so they produce such victims."[33] For Ellacuría and Sobrino, the dominant idols that produce death (and as such should be named "the idols of death"[34]) are "capitalism and national security."[35] But it is capitalism (or the idolatry of money) that is foundational: "The idol by definition, originator of all the others, is the economic configuration of society, which is unjust, structural, lasting, with many other organs at its service: military, political, cultural, juridical, intellectual and often religious, partake analogously of the being of the idol."[36]

Ellacuría and Sobrino argue that because death is the material effect of idolatry the victims of the civilization of capital should be named a crucified people. Like Jesus of Nazareth, the crucified people are innocent victims who have been put to death by the empires of this world, killed in the name of national security or subjected to the "slow death of hunger" as a result of the structurally iniquitous world sustained by the civilization of capital.[37] At one level, this characterization of the crucified people reveals the structural dynamics of oppression in our world. At another level, it represents an attempt to describe the very structure of reality.[38] Ellacuría observes,

> Among the signs that are always appearing, some striking and others barely perceptible, there is an outstanding one in every age, in whose light all the others must be discerned and interpreted. That sign is always the historically crucified people, which remains constant although the historical forms of crucifixion are different. That people is the historical continuation of the servant of Yahweh, whose humanity is still being disfigured by the sin of the world, whom the powers of this world are still stripping of everything, taking away everything including his life, especially his life.[39]

The form of crucifixion shifts from age to age, but what remains constant is the sacrifice of the poor and the vulnerable to the idols of wealth and power.[40]

33. Sobrino, *True Church*, 166.

34. Sobrino, *Where Is God?*, 37.

35. Sobrino, *Where Is God?*, 132. Sobrino characterizes American empire itself as an idol. Sobrino, *No Salvation*, 87.

36. Sobrino, *Jesus the Liberator*, 186.

37. Sobrino, *Jesus the Liberator*, 186.

38. Sobrino observes that "the crucified people are one of the main features of our time, not merely something factual that we may consider, but something central that must be considered, without which we do not have a full grasp on reality" (*No Salvation*, 4).

39. Quoted in Sobrino, *No Salvation*, 3.

40. Sobrino observes, "Things change, paradigms change. But we may wonder if

Sobrino notes that while economists, sociologists, and politicians talk of poverty, injustice, and even oppression, Ellacuría was strategic in his decision to use the term "the crucified people" because it conveys the fact that these peoples are put to death by the sin of the world—their death is not natural but historical and "takes the form of crucifixion, assassination, the active historical deprivation of life, whether slowly or quickly."[41]

Ellacuría and Sobrino describe the crucified people both as a negative sign of the times as well as a positive reality that brings salvation to the world (both transcendent and historical salvation).[42] Sobrino argues that from a theological perspective, there is no salvation outside the poor (*extra pauperes nulla salus*). This does not mean that with the poor salvation is guaranteed, but rather that without the poor there is no salvation because, as the entire biblical tradition witnesses, the bearers of salvation are "poor and small: a childless old woman, the small people of Israel, a marginal Jew . . ."[43] From the perspective of historical salvation, this claim is true for several reasons. First, Ellacuría and Sobrino argue that the crucified peoples reveal the true health of the affluent world.[44] Ellacuría suggests that coproanalysis, or the examination of the feces produced by the affluent world, represents the most appropriate means for assessing the health of the civilization of capital. This analysis demonstrates that the affluent world is profoundly sick because the "waste" it produces is death for the poor. Paradoxically, however, Sobrino argues that death brings a light that "shines from the crucified people and it lights up the darkness of our world. It brings this world's evil to light."[45] This light reveals the extreme inequalities generated by the civilization of capital and, furthermore, discloses that the affluent world's solutions to the world's problems—globalization, liberalization, and even democratization—are not working. The existence of a crucified people makes it painfully clear that there is an urgent need for an alternative social order that prioritizes the needs of the poor over the priorities of the civilization of capital.[46] Second, the crucified people have the unique capacity to move others to conversion and therefore possess the capacity

---

there is not something trans-paradigmatic, if there are not principles of evil and sinfulness that run throughout history" (*No Salvation*, 7).

41. Sobrino, *No Salvation*, 4.

42. Sobrino, *No Salvation*, 56.

43. Sobrino, *No Salvation*, 49, 14, and 53–54. See also Sobrino, *True Church*, 95.

44. Sobrino, *No Salvation*, 5.

45. Sobrino, *Jesus the Liberator*, 262.

46. Sobrino, *Jesus the Liberator*, 261–62.

to humanize the affluent world.[47] Moreover, they offer hope by challenging "our understanding of social, environmental, and religious salvation in a world that does not belong to poor people but creates them; and they help to unmask the dogma that a poor people can only receive but not give."[48] Finally, Ellacuría and Sobrino maintain that the crucified people not only reveal that alternatives to the sacrifices of the civilization of capital exist but also serve as the agents who will bring about this alternative. Sobrino argues that both philosophers and theologians have failed to recognize the radicality of this teaching, with only Marx reflecting in any depth on the historical role that the oppressed play in the transformation of society. Sobrino views Marx's approach as inadequate insofar as Marx views the proletariat—a specific social class—as the historical agent of social transformation and fails to include "the most disinherited." In this regard, the approach offered by Ellacuría and Sobrino is "more radical" than Marx's approach because it describes the excluded poor (and not the working class) as the agents of history.[49] Sobrino concludes that the poor (*ptochos*), or those who lack "the necessities of life,"[50] represent the "unparalleled—and utopian—principle by which to turn history upside down and reshape it."[51]

Ellacuría and Sobrino maintain that empire (the civilization of capital and repressive political violence) is the dominant structure of sin and violence in our world. It is this sin that generates a crucified people sacrificed to the idols of wealth and power. Importantly, at the same time, the crucified people possess a salvific role in history because they reveal the need for an alternative to the civilization of capital, offer the affluent world the possibility of conversion, and play a pivotal role in bringing about the alternative civilization.

The Church of the Poor

Ellacuría and Sobrino argue that historically the church has been aligned with the empires of the world and, like West, trace the loss of the prophetic nerve of the church to the conversion of Constantine. For Ellacuría, this represents the point in history when the church transitioned from a persecuted

---

47. Sobrino, *No Salvation*, 61.

48. Sobrino, *No Salvation*, 6.

49. Sobrino, *No Salvation*, 6. For his critique of Marx, see also Sobrino, *Jesus the Liberator*, 127.

50. Sobrino, *True Church*, 292.

51. Sobrino, *Where Is God?*, 102.

church of the poor to a church that served the interests of the elite and the powerful in society. He observes,

> The post-Constantinian Western historicization takes the faith through the path of power, wealth, and worldliness. The faith has been shaped more by the needs and interests of those countries of worldly wealth and societies of worldly domination. A church that is preferentially for the poor and weak becomes a church preferentially for the wealthy and powerful, for the maintenance of an order that benefits it, and not for transformation.[52]

This post-Constantinian church has served as a "conservative element" in society and has supported the "established order."[53] In relation to the civilization of capital, Ellacuría observes that during the Cold War, while the church condemned Marxism with particular vigor, it adopted a posture that was far too tolerant of the injustices of capitalism. In 1989 he observed that the dominant fear of the Catholic Church was Soviet imperialism and not American imperialism.[54] Because of this fear the church colluded with a political formation that ultimately rivaled Soviet Communism in its dehumanizing and sacrificial politics. Ellacuría argues that the church should contest both communist and capitalist civilizations and call for an alternative civilization rooted in the protection of basic rights of all human beings. Furthermore, he argues that the church can play a critical role in building this civilization by taking the option for the poor seriously.

For Ellacuría and Sobrino, the church receives its mission from Jesus Christ and his subversive option for the poor should guide its practice. In his two-volume Christology, *Jesus the Liberator* and *Christ the Liberator*, Sobrino offers a detailed account of God's option for the poor based on the "good news" that Jesus offered the poor in the gospels. "To these poor," he writes, "Jesus showed undoubted partiality, so that what is now called the option for the poor can be said to start with him."[55] It follows that an ecclesiology that takes seriously Jesus's life and ministry and his own partiality with regard to the poor should press the church to become a church of the poor. In this regard, Ellacuría and Sobrino argue that it is necessary to move beyond Vatican II's democratic image of the "people of God" because of its failure to recognize inequality within the church. The "people of God" secures only formal and not substantive equality. As a result, Ellacuría and Sobrino contend that

52. Ellacuría, *Ignacio Ellacuría*, 133.

53. Ellacuría, *Ignacio Ellacuría*, 133–34.

54. Ellacuría observes, "The fear is still of the evils of Soviet imperialism rather than the evils of US imperialism" ("Utopia and Propheticism," 23).

55. Sobrino, *Jesus the Liberator*, 81ff.

the poor must be placed at the center of the church if their needs are to be met. Sobrino observes, "In a world made up mainly of poor people, not even equality (if they had it!) would ensure that they would be taken seriously. They must be placed at the center in order not to be 'expelled' from social and ecclesial citizenship."[56] This critique of ecclesial democracy is echoed in Ellacuría and Sobrino's criticism of political democracy. In both cases, they call for a more radical focus on the suffering of the crucified people as the foundational reality that should organize the church (the church of the poor) and the social order (the civilization of poverty).

In order to realize this vision for the church and society, Ellacuría and Sobrino call for a commitment to propheticism and utopia. Propheticism is a discourse that contrasts the kingdom of God with a concrete historical situation and criticizes the current configuration of society based on its tension with the kingdom of God. Utopia—specifically historical utopia—symbolizes the need to make the kingdom of God, however partial, present in history.[57] According to Sobrino, the utopia of the gospels involves building a world in which "a just and dignified existence become[s] a reality of poor people, so that the very real cruelty of their sufferings does not have the last word."[58] Sobrino insists, therefore, that Christians seek not merely utopia—*ou-topia*, a nonexistent place—but *eu-topia* or "the place of the good" (invoking Jesus's "good news") that affirms life amid structures of death.[59]

From an ecclesiological perspective, Ellacuría maintains that "the utopian exercise of prophecy can lead [the] church (up to now configured in great part by the dynamisms of Western capitalism as a church of the rich and of the powerful that, at best, directs toward the poorest the crumbs falling from the table of abundance) to become converted—in a genuine 'conversion'—into a church of the poor."[60] Ellacuría and Sobrino maintain that moving the church beyond Constantinianism and toward the poor is an essential feature of the struggle away from a civilization of capital and toward a civilization of poverty. They maintain that because the civilization of capital produces death those who are committed to the gospel of life must work to generate an alternative to it.[61] Thus, against neoliberals who say there is no alternative (TINA) and progressives who offer the relatively weak

56. Sobrino, *No Salvation*, 12.

57. Sobrino, *Jesus the Liberator*, 129.

58. Sobrino, *No Salvation*, 81.

59. Sobrino, *No Salvation*, 81.

60. Ellacuría, "Utopia and Propheticism," 54.

61. Ellacuría observes that "the fundamental principle on which to base the new order remains 'that all might have life and have it more abundantly' (Jn 10:10)" ("Utopia and Propheticism," 29).

statement "another world is possible," Ellacuría and Sobrino insist from a Christian perspective that "another world is necessary."[62] In a situation dominated by the violence of capital, this alternative "cannot be other than a 'civilization of poverty'" in which all share "austerely in the earth's resources so that they can stretch to everybody."[63] The civilization of capital has failed: it has been unable to satisfy the basic needs of the world's poor, it has created vast inequalities, it has generated immoral debt obligations, it has produced almost constant economic crises, and it has "promoted an immoral culture of consumption and of easy profit."[64] By way of contrast, the civilization of poverty "rejects the accumulation of capital as the energizer of history and the possession-enjoyment of wealth as principle of humanization, and it makes the universal satisfying of basic needs the principle of development, and the growth of shared solidarity the foundation of humanization."[65] Ellacuría describes the most basic commitments of the civilization of poverty as "proper nourishment, minimal housing, basic health care, primary education, sufficient employment."[66]

While Ellacuría and Sobrino only offer a broad sketch of the values that should animate the civilization of poverty, they draw from the tradition of Catholic social teaching in articulating their vision by retrieving the church's teaching on the universal destination of goods. The universal destination of goods concerns the proper relationship between private property and the just use of the goods of creation. This principle is rooted in the Bible and finds expression throughout the history of Christian theology (Ambrose, Chrysostom) but has been revitalized in the twentieth and twenty-first centuries by Vatican II, Paul VI, John Paul II, and Francis. What has become a central claim of modern Catholic social teaching—the proposition that the universal destination of goods should serve as the first principle of the social order—was first formulated by John Paul II in *Laborem Exercens* and has been repeated more recently by Francis in *Laudato Si'*. In *Laborem Exercens*, John Paul II observes that the church's tradition has never viewed the right to private property "as absolute and untouchable. On the contrary, it has always understood this right within the broader context of the right common to all to use the goods of the whole of creation: *the right to private property is subordinated to the right to*

---

62. Sobrino, "On the Way to Healing."
63. Sobrino, *Jesus the Liberator*, 262.
64. Ellacuría, "Utopia and Propheticism," 43.
65. See Ellacuría, "Utopia and Propheticism," 40.
66. See Ellacuría, "Utopia and Propheticism," 41.

common use, to the fact that goods are meant for everyone."[67] The goods of creation were intended by God to provide life for every human person, and the task is to ensure that each is given the capacity to live a dignified life. Ellacuría and Sobrino invoke this teaching as a means of criticizing the values of the civilization of capital, and in order to insist that the values and priorities of the civilization of poverty are rooted in Catholic social teaching. In an assertion that echoes John Paul II's writings, Sobrino maintains that "as long as that principle [of private property] is maintained as absolute and untouchable, every economy will be structurally configured by a dynamic of oppression, human beings will be classified according to their ability to produce wealth . . . and most certainly it will widen the distance between the haves and the have-nots."[68] In this sense, Ellacuría and Sobrino call only for a more consistent application of the basic principles of Catholic social teaching in the economic realm. The civilization of poverty represents an attempt to concretize the Catholic commitment to the universal destination of goods in a civilization that has reversed the priorities of this principle by privileging the rights of capital over the rights of the poor.

Here it is important to note that Ellacuría intentionally chose the term "civilization" in an attempt to signify the fact that the type of social transformation that is needed cannot be limited to one sphere alone, whether it be the economic, political, cultural, or religious. The civilization of capital, for instance, is not simply or only an economic system but also a political and cultural system. The response to it must be similarly holistic and offer a substantive alternative to the current civilization. As such, Ellacuría and Sobrino recognize that the civilization of poverty is a utopian project in the sense that it "has no place in our world." They maintain that "a true solution like this require[s] not only reforms" but a more fundamental reorientation of the direction of civilization because "it is not enough to change policies and coalitions . . . there must be radical changes."[69] The civilization of poverty is a revolutionary ideal. This ideal evaluates reformist approaches to social transformation as inadequate because the task is a utopian task: to bring the crucified down from their crosses.

---

67. John Paul II, *Laborem Exercens*, #14. In *Laudato Si'* Francis follows John Paul II when he writes, "The principle of the subordination of private property to the universal destination of goods, and thus the right of everyone to their use, is a golden rule of social conduct and 'the first principle of the whole ethical and social order'" (#93).

68. Sobrino, *No Salvation*, 39.

69. Sobrino, "Ignacio Ellacuría, the Human Being and the Christian," 26–27, and Sobrino, *Where Is God?*, vii.

LIBERATIVE-POPULIST DEMOCRACY

This final section of this chapter differs from those that have preceded it because Ellacuría and Sobrino never directly engage the work of radical democratic theorists. Furthermore, when they have analyzed democracy as a political form, they characterize it as an instrument of Western imperialism. It is still possible, however, to bring the work of Ellacuría and Sobrino into conversation with radical democratic theory based on both their criticisms of American-style liberal democracy as well as their anti-capitalist and anti-imperialist commitments. In this section, we analyze Ellacuría and Sobrino's thought alongside the political theory of Enrique Dussel. Dussel is an interesting interlocutor in this context, not only because his work as a Latin American liberation philosopher closely parallels Ellacuría and Sobrino's work in Latin American liberation theology but also because his recent work on populist and radical democratic politics converges with the fundamental orientation of the political commitments of Ellacuría and Sobrino.

There are several areas of commonality between Ellacuría, Sobrino, and Dussel in terms of their critique of liberal democracy as well as their shared constructive focus on materiality, liberation, and populism.

First, Ellacuría, Sobrino, and Dussel converge in their assessment of liberal democracy as an imperialist political formation. As discussed above, Ellacuría assessed the United States' commitment to democracy in Nicaragua (and more broadly Central America) in the 1980s as contradictory and hypocritical in that it sought to protect and preserve the civilization of capital and not the rights of the people. Similarly, Dussel argues that the real character of the United States' commitment to democracy was disclosed when Donald Rumsfeld, at the time a U.S. State Department official, invoked the historic example of Hitler's majoritarian election as a means of delegitimizing Hugo Chávez's democratic election by the majority of Venezuelans. The United States holds that it alone possesses the privileged position from which to "evaluate all democratic processes" and evaluated Chavez's election as illegitimate.[70] The only rule of American foreign policy when assessing the legitimacy of foreign elections is the following: if the election leads to an outcome in which the person elected is submissive to the dictates of the United States, then "he or she is declared to be *truly* democratic, whereas if the elected responds to the people by exercising obediential power (and as a result not obeying the Empire) then he or she is declared *undemocratic*."[71]

70. Dussel observes, "Empire appropriates the right to evaluate all democratic processes" (*Twenty Theses on Politics*, 143n58).

71. Dussel, *Twenty Theses on Politics*, 143.

Second, because they argue that materiality represents the most basic level of human experience, Ellacuría, Sobrino, and Dussel posit that securing biological survival of the people is the most fundamental task of any political order. Ellacuría notes that the right to existence and the protection of mere biological life "may be taken as self-evident in the wealthiest countries, where that right is guaranteed . . . but that is not true in most countries, either because of extreme poverty or because of repression and violence."[72] Accordingly, Ellacuría defines liberation as "liberation from the lack of basic necessities . . . what should be called liberation from material oppression."[73] This stands in marked contrast to the civilization of capital's focus on the generation of wealth over the protection of bare life. Dussel also maintains that the fundamental goal of politics is to generate a social order in which the very survival of the victims is not in question. He describes this focus on survival as the "material-political principle," which places the emphasis of any politics on "human life, the concrete lives of each person, or a sort of 'bare life' that is more concrete than Agamben's *nuda vita*."[74] Because the dominant economic-political hegemony has produced a social order that has put into crisis "the possibility of mere bare life," the task of "assuring the permanence of the life of the population of every nation of humanity on planet Earth is the first and fundamental function of politics, and this criterion of survival must be imposed as the essential criterion of all else."[75] Dussel invokes something akin to the Kantian maxim discussed above as a diagnostic tool to assess the morality of a society, observing that "because the political order is unable to distribute the benefits of the current order to everyone, it manifests its ineffectiveness in its victims by the simple fact of their existence as victims."[76] It follows that the urgent political task is to "criticize, or reject as unsustainable, all political systems, actions, and institutions whose negative effects are suffered by oppressed or excluded victims!"[77]

Third, this material principle supports an approach to politics in which liberation from material deprivation is prioritized as a precondition for the individual liberties prized within liberal democracies. Ellacuría, Sobrino, and Dussel privilege a politics of liberation over North Atlantic political models rooted in the commitment to individual liberty, a commitment

72. Sobrino, *No Salvation*, 13

73. Ellacuría, *Ignacio Ellacuría*, 52. Sobrino similarly argues that God's will for humanity is "total liberation," which includes "very specifically, liberation from material poverty" (*Jesus in Latin America*, 107).

74. Dussel, *Twenty Theses on Politics*, 60.

75. Dussel, *Twenty Theses on Politics*, 47.

76. Dussel, *Twenty Theses on Politics*, 69.

77. Dussel, *Twenty Theses on Politics*, 85.

invariably reduced to the right to private property. Ellacuría and Sobrino argue for the prioritization of liberation over liberty for two reasons. First, they maintain that political liberalism has served historically as an ideology and political form that covers up atrocities committed in the name of capitalism.[78] Liberalism celebrates the freedom of the individual and the market but does so in a manner that generates "freedom for a few" and "the real negation of that same for the rest." Second, as a consequence of this first point, Ellacuría and Sobrino maintain that from a Christian perspective, liberation precedes liberty for the simple reason that an individual must be alive in order to exercise her freedom.[79] Ellacuría observes that "there is no freedom without liberation. There is no Christian freedom without Christian liberation, and this latter makes essential reference to the poor and poverty."[80] Liberation—specifically, the liberation from material deprivation—serves as the foundation for an authentic exercise of individual liberty. In contrast to proponents of liberal approaches to democracy for whom economic liberalization represents a panacea capable of solving the world's problems, Ellacuría contends that the civilization of poverty is rooted in an approach to freedom that comes from "liberation and not merely liberalization—whether economic or political liberalization."[81] Dussel also maintains that while the French Revolution spoke of "Equality, Fraternity, Liberty!" we should now "subsume that liberty and speak instead of *liberation*."[82] It is necessary to move "beyond liberalism" and cultivate a "new transmodern civilization" in which the excluded are given political access to decision-making processes.[83] A "liberatory democracy" entails the commitment to the substantive participation of the excluded as the fundamental mark of democratic legitimacy. Because the excluded have been most affected by past political decisions their voices should be given a privileged place in any discussion concerning future reforms.[84]

---

78. Ellacuría observes, "Liberalism . . . in Latin America, is the juridical and formal cover-up for those who have already been liberated from certain oppressions and dominations and who in turn see to it that others do not achieve the same through subsequent and more complex processes of liberation" ("Utopia and Propheticism," 30).

79. Sobrino, *Jesus in Latin America*, 107.

80. Ellacuría, *Ignacio Ellacuría*, 51.

81. Ellacuría, "Utopia and Propheticism," 49.

82. Dussel, *Twenty Theses on Politics*, 137. Emphasis original.

83. Dussel, *Twenty Theses on Politics*, xvi.

84. Dussel, *Twenty Theses on Politics*, 88. For Dussel, "the victims of the political system" must be given a prominent voice for the basic reason that "they are the most affected by the institutional decisions that were made in the past" (*Twenty Theses on Politics*, 88–89).

Fourth, Sobrino, Ellacuría, and Dussel share what can be described in broad terms as a populist approach to politics. We examined populism in the second chapter in our description of the democratic theories of Laclau and Mouffe. The formal structure of populist discourse involves the construction of an "underdog" (or, as the etymology suggests, "a people") in relation to an established power.[85] Ellacuría, Sobrino, and Dussel share this basic populist orientation, even as they differ in the way in which they construct the "underdog" vis-à-vis the established order.

Ellacuría and Sobrino argue that a Christian politics should always stand "against the established powers."[86] And, as we have already seen, they claim that the excluded poor serve as the transformative sociopolitical agent in history.[87] Sobrino argues in a fashion more radical than Marx that the world's excluded poor possess the capacity to "turn history upside down and reshape it."[88] This focus on the poor leads Ellacuría and Sobrino to privilege grassroots movements over political organizations because the poor possess more power in grassroots movements than is possible in large-scale political organizations. Sobrino observes of Ellacuría that "he recognized the need for and the legitimacy of the political front that sought power, but he gave priority to the organization of the base (grassroots), which did not seek to come to power."[89] At the same time, Ellacuría thought it strategically wise for these grassroots movements to align with progressive governments on an *ad hoc* basis in order to create the conditions for "new political forms of truly popular democracy."[90]

Where Ellacuría and Sobrino view the poor as the agent of social transformation, Dussel advocates for a pluralist approach to resistance that includes those who labor against militarism, racism, sexism, environmental destruction, and neocolonialism. Here Dussel departs from "the multitude" (Hardt and Negri) but invokes "the people" (Laclau), which he refers to variously as *plebs*, the excluded, or the historical bloc of the

85. See Laclau, "Populism: What's in a Name?," 39ff., and Laclau, *On Populist Reason*, 87. According to Laclau, "The conditions of possibility of the political and the conditions of possibility of populism are the same: they both presuppose social division; in both we find an ambiguous *demos* which is, on the one hand, a section within the community (an underdog) and, on the other hand, an agent presenting itself, in an antagonistic way, as *the whole* community." Laclau, "Populism: What's in a Name?," 48.

86. Sobrino, *No Salvation*, 18.

87. Sobrino, *No Salvation*, 12.

88. Sobrino, *Where Is God?*, 102.

89. Sobrino, *No Salvation*, 17.

90. Ellacuría, "Los modos sociales de participación social," quoted in Gould, "Ignacio Ellacuría and the Salvadorean Revolution," 313.

oppressed. The relevant shared experience of the people is that they consist of "those whose needs remain unsatisfied."[91] They "encompass the unity of all the movements, classes, sectors, etc." and specifically stand "in opposition to the elites, to the oligarchs, to the ruling classes of a political order."[92] Dussel's strategy here is quite similar to Laclau and Mouffe's in its attempt to establish chains of equivalence between different social groups. Dussel maintains that this pluralist assemblage (his term is "analogical hegemon") emerges because

> feminism discovers that women of color are treated worst, that female workers receive lower salaries, that female citizens do not occupy positions of representation, that women in peripheral countries suffer even more discrimination, etc. Similarly, the indigenous person discovers the exploitation of the community under capitalism, within the dominant Western culture, in subtle but nevertheless prevalent racism, etc. That is, through mutual information, dialogue, translation of proposals, and shared militant praxis, these movements slowly and progressively constitute an analogical hegemon . . . [93]

The birth of politics is traced back to the fact that there are a variety of demands made on the current social order by different groups that remain unfulfilled—from "feminist movements, anti-racist movements, movements organized by the elderly, by indigenous peoples, by the marginal and unemployed, by the industrial working class, by poor or 'landless' farmers, and movements of a geopolitical nature against the colonialist metropole, against Eurocentrism, against militarism, and those for pacifism and for the environment, etc."[94] The task is to assemble these diverse experiences of exclusion into a unified front against the established order. Dussel suggests that each historical epoch has prioritized specific demands to mobilize the people so that "in the process of emancipation from Spain in 1810, 'Liberty!' was given an indisputable primacy as a demand that unified all groups into the patriotic bloc of Latin America."[95] As noted above, in the current political situation, liberty has been co-opted by the neoliberal right in Latin America, and so it can no longer serve as the demand of the people and instead should be replaced with "*liberation*."[96] Concretely, the Pink Tide of

91. Dussel, *Twenty Theses on Politics*, 75.
92. Dussel, *Twenty Theses on Politics*, 73 and 75.
93. Dussel, *Twenty Theses on Politics*, 72–73.
94. Dussel, *Twenty Theses on Politics*, 72.
95. Dussel, *Twenty Theses on Politics*, 72–73.
96. Dussel, *Twenty Theses on Politics*, 137. Emphasis original.

Latin American populism (Néstor Kirchner, Tabaré Vásquez, Luiz Inácio Lula da Silva, Evo Morales, and Hugo Chávez) is representative of the type of liberative-populist politics for which Dussel advocates.[97]

There exist important differences between Ellacuría, Sobrino, and Dussel. They diverge in how they describe the agent of social transformation, with Ellacuría and Sobrino focusing on the excluded poor (a broader category than Marx's proletariat) and Dussel adopting a pluralist model that assembles diverse groups with unfulfilled demands in society. They also disagree on the extent to which a populist politics should be institutionalized, with Dussel offering more support than either Ellacuría or Sobrino for extant populisms in Latin America. It is this disagreement over populism and political parties that is symptomatic of a broader disagreement over the status of democracy in their politics, and the related question of whether to pursue reform or revolution as a political strategy.

Ellacuría and Sobrino advocate for something that draws close to the revolutionary approach of Hardt and Negri in that they focus on overturning the rule of capital—Empire (Hardt and Negri) or the civilization of capital (Ellacuría and Sobrino)—and describe an alternative civilizational order that prioritizes the defense of life over the right to private property—a politics of the commons (Hardt and Negri) or the civilization of poverty (Ellacuría and Sobrino). They place the emphasis on the articulation of a utopian vision of civilizational transformation rather than a concrete political strategy of reform. Where Hardt and Negri describe the alternative to Empire as radical democracy and do so for both strategic and substantive reasons, Ellacuría and Sobrino express concern about democracy as a political form that can support a politics of liberation. Sobrino goes so far as to argue that "democracy" does not constitute a sufficiently radical symbol to animate the type of action demanded by the suffering of a crucified world.[98] Sobrino's concern is that democracy offers only procedural and not substantive equality insofar as it is a political system that "make[s] poor people citizens with the same rights as others, but it does not place them, either in theory or in practice, at the center of society."[99] If democracy fails to integrate economic equality as a central good that must be protected by law, then it serves only as a symbol that legitimates injustice.[100] From a historical

97. See, for instance, Gonzalez, *The Ebb of the Pink Tide*.

98. Sobrino, *No Salvation*, x.

99. Sobrino, *No Salvation*, 136n53. Sobrino observes that "from a social viewpoint, it follows that any society that claims to be truly 'democratic' or egalitarian must be conceived and organized on the basis of the rights of the disadvantaged" (*No Salvation*, 12).

100. Sobrino, *No Salvation*, 135n33.

perspective, democracy has failed on this point, and so Sobrino concludes that "democracy has grave limitations: it expresses the political version of the civilization of wealth, and it can be manipulated." This manipulation does not seem to be an accidental feature but rather belongs to "the historical essence of democracy as it has been practiced in the West."[101] As a result, Ellacuría and Sobrino describe the civilization of poverty as the true alternative to empire and not democracy.

Dussel recognizes that democracy is a contradictory political form, but he nevertheless argues that the task is to improve upon its existing forms (welfare state, postcolonial, populist, etc.) rather than rejecting it wholesale.[102] In *Twenty Theses on Politics*, Dussel explicitly takes up the issue of reform or revolution. He first defines reform as "an accidental improvement" that does nothing to change the structure of institutions and does not respond to the popular demands of the excluded. Within this framework, reform is viewed as an action that merely "pretends to change." Dussel introduces the category of "transformation" to signify the process by which the political system responds to the demands of the oppressed or excluded. There exist two forms of transformation: partial and radical. Partial transformation occurs when institutions deliver more power to the people. Radical transformation is characterized by dramatic and revolutionary change that overturns the dominant social order—the bourgeois English Revolution (seventeenth century), the Maoist Revolution (1950s), and the Cuban Revolution (1959).[103] Although Dussel rejects the term *reformism* and opts for "partial" and "radical" transformation, his approach draws close to reformist approaches to radical democracy. He argues that liberative politics demand that "we must do the maximum *possible*—thereby appearing reformist to the anarchist and suicidal to the conservative—and having as the criterion of possibility in institutional creation (transformation) the liberation of the victims of the current system, the *people!*"[104] A political program for feasible transformations should be expressed in the short term or within a government cycle (four to six years), medium term (twenty-five

---

101. Sobrino, *No Salvation*, 39.

102. Dussel, *Twenty Theses on Politics*, 51. Dussel observes, "Because the people are the principle actors, critical, liberatory, or popular democracy calls into question the previous degree of achieved democratization, since democracy is a system to be perennially reinvented" (*Twenty Theses on Politics*, 89).

103. See Dussel, *Twenty Theses on Politics*, 111–12.

104. Dussel, *Twenty Theses on Politics*, 90. Emphasis original. He observes that once the "life of the victim" has organized itself and has arrived at a democratic consensus "the issue is to bring into practice, into historical reality, the effective institutionalization of the political project that has been germinating" (*Twenty Theses on Politics*, 90).

years), and "long-term projects for popular participation (especially with regard to ecological and transcapitalist economic questions)."[105] This is similar to Unger and West's "radical reformist" approach, which aspires to revolutionary change but which supports reform as a means of opening the space for a more substantive transformation of society. Thus, in contrast to Ellacuría and Sobrino, Dussel views democracy as the most suitable political form to support the project of pursuing both partial and radical transformations of the social order.

Ellacuría, Sobrino, and Dussel share a foundational commitment to a class-based populism that seeks to liberate the world's poor from the structural violence of material deprivation. In different ways, they invoke a liberative-populist approach to radical politics that not only offers a substantive critique of the civilization of capital but also necessitates a critique of the imperialist violence of American militarism in Latin America, the Middle East, and other colonized communities around the world. The primary difference between Ellacuría, Sobrino, and Dussel is that where Ellacuría and Sobrino offer a utopian vision for an alternative society (the civilization of poverty), Dussel's utopian vision of an alternative calls for the radical reform of existing democracies. If Dussel offers a more realistic approach in his commitment to a project of pluralist coalition building, it remains the case that there are features of Ellacuría's and Sobrino's work that overlap with Dussel's approach. In particular, Ellacuría's affirmation of the possibility of a "truly popular democracy" and Sobrino's claim that a "radical" form of democracy that prioritizes the needs and political participation of the poor represent commitments that could be viewed as consonant with Dussel's vision of radical politics.[106]

The christological and ecclesial approach to radical politics offered by Ellacuría and Sobrino differs in significant ways from West and Schüssler Fiorenza. This is the case even as justice remains the common horizon for their projects. West and Schüssler Fiorenza focus on the development of inclusive models for political engagement that seek to build coalitions based on their pursuit of justice for the oppressed. And while Ellacuría and Sobrino could be criticized for failing to offer a sufficiently pluralist approach

---

105. Dussel, *Twenty Theses on Politics*, 97.

106. While Ellacuría and Sobrino focus on material poverty, in his later writings Sobrino opens the possibility of developing a more inclusive approach to social suffering (and presumably coalition building). Sobrino observes, "I have only gradually begun to hear and understand the cries of women, indigenous people, and Afro-Americans. And I believe those cries have not only added—horizontally, we might say—new varieties or species of poverty; they have also enriched its depth: they have broadened and deepened the mystery of the poor" (*No Salvation*, 23). See also Sobrino, *Where Is God?*, 63ff.

to radical politics, the upside of their approach is that they provide a more robust description of the distinctively Christian commitments that support a Christian engagement with radical politics. As we shall see in the next chapter, this tendency is even more pronounced in Hauerwas's theology.

CHAPTER 6

Peaceable Theology

IN RESPONSE TO A question about Jeffrey Stout's criticisms in *Democracy and Tradition*, Stanley Hauerwas observed in a 2004 interview that it is imperative for Christians "to remember that our first task is to be the church of Jesus Christ, that's our politics. And that doesn't necessarily name Democracy."[1] Later, in 2006, Hauerwas observes, "I think I can claim to be a radical democrat."[2] These two statements express a central tension—although not an outright contradiction—in Hauerwas's theology concerning the political implications of his theology. This chapter attempts to make sense of this tension by analyzing the relationship between Hauerwas's long-standing criticisms of liberal democracy as well as his more recent constructive engagement with radical democracy.

In relation to the three other forms of Christian political engagement analyzed in this book, Hauerwas's approach is distinctive because it prioritizes nonviolence in a manner that departs from the prioritization of justice in the works of West, Schüssler Fiorenza, Ellacuría, and Sobrino. In the third chapter, we described the differences that exist between West and Hauerwas in terms of the approaches they adopt in response to Constantinianism. There we noted that a central area of disagreement between West and Hauerwas concerns the status of justice in their respective projects as well as the extent to which Christians should engage the liberal political order in pursuit of justice. Critics of Hauerwas have viewed engagements like this as evidence that his is a politics of Christian withdrawal. But, as will be evident from our discussion in this chapter, this represents a caricature of his position. In actuality, Hauerwas offers a rather sophisticated postliberal approach to democratic politics that both resonates with and recasts the postliberal approaches of Sheldon Wolin

1. Hauerwas, "An Interview with Stanley Hauerwas."
2. Hauerwas, *State of the University*, 163.

and Romand Coles and even, on a certain reading, the transnational politics of Michael Hardt and Antonio Negri.

In order to better understand the political implications of Hauerwas's theology it will be necessary to engage the work of John Howard Yoder in this chapter. Hauerwas places Yoder's work at the center of his theological development and narrates his conversion to christological pacifism in terms of the impact of Yoder's theology on his thought.[3] On the face of it, it appears that the relationship between Yoder and Hauerwas is similar to the relationship between Ellacuría and Sobrino, but there exist significant differences between Yoder and Hauerwas. Furthermore, Hauerwas alone has engaged in conversation with radical democratic theorists. So that where Romand Coles and Hauerwas view Yoder's work as a resource for radical democratic politics, Yoder himself never engaged the topic in his writings. By way of contrast, Hauerwas has offered one of the most sustained recent engagements with radical democratic theory, and that has generated a distinctive approach to the relationship between Christianity and democracy that differs in significant ways from the approaches offered by West, Schüssler Fiorenza, and Ellacuría/Sobrino. For these reasons, while Hauerwas's work will be the focus of this chapter, Yoder's thought will serve a supplemental role to clarify and challenge some of the assumptions of Hauerwas's own theological reflections.[4]

In the first section in this chapter we examine Yoder and Hauerwas's critique of Constantinianism with a particular emphasis on Hauerwas's argument that liberal democracy serves as the primary carrier of Constantinianism in the United States. Second, we analyze Hauerwas's analysis of the witness of the peaceable church as an ekklesial alternative to Constantinianism. Third, we describe Hauerwas's articulation of a postliberal and peaceable form of Christian political engagement that converges in important ways with Sheldon Wolin's postliberal approach to radical democratic politics.

---

3. See, for instance, Hauerwas, *Dispatches from the Front*, 118, and Hauerwas, *Peaceable Kingdom*, xxiv.

4. In addition to the reasons described above, the revelations about sexual violence by Yoder should give any theologian pause when engaging his thought on the topic of nonviolence. Yoder committed sexual violence—by some reports, forcible rape—against the women for whom he was responsible as a minister in the church, and there is simply no way to reconcile these private acts of violence with Yoder's public commitment to peace. Thus, as we examine Yoder's theology as a decisive influence on Hauerwas, we do so aware of the questions that this approach invites.

EMPIRE AND CONSTANTINIANISM

In his analysis of Constantinianism, Yoder describes two falls in human history—the fall in the garden of Eden and the fall of the church when it became subservient to the interests of the Roman Empire under Constantine.[5] The fall under Constantine transformed the church from a persecuted minority into the official religion of the Roman Empire.[6] This fall inaugurated a shift by which Christians moved from a community that embodied an alternative to empire to a community that legitimated it.[7] At its core, Yoder contends that the Constantinian error denies the political significance of Jesus by viewing the political ruler as the primary agent of divine action in history. This shift led Christians to support practices and policies that contradict the core commitments of the gospels. In particular, Christians identified "with a political project that does not favor the underdog, does not share bread, does not reconcile Jew and Gentile, does not share power, does not reach beyond the limits of empire, and does not love the enemy."[8] Furthermore, this tendency to identify God's work in history with political regimes set up an oppositional framework in which one side—a people, nation, or government—became identified with God's cause and felt impelled to force the other side into submission.[9] Thus, where pre-Constantinian Christians were pacifists who rejected violence because they viewed it as incompatible with their moral and religious commitments, post-Constantinian Christians "considered imperial violence to be not only morally tolerable but a positive good and a Christian duty."[10] Yoder evaluates this transition in the early church as an unmitigated disaster and suggests that the proper response to this situation is for Christians to disavow Constantinianism and to confess that "we were wrong. The picture you have been given of Jesus by the Empire, by the Crusades, by struggles over holy sites, and by wars in the name of the 'Christian West' is not only something to forget but something to forgive. We are not merely outgrowing it, as if it had been acceptable at the time: we disavow it and repent of it."[11]

5. Van Houtan and Northcott, "Nature and the Nation-State," 152.

6. Yoder, *Royal Priesthood*, 245.

7. Yoder, *Royal Priesthood*, 144.

8. Yoder, *War of the Lamb*, 174.

9. Yoder, *Royal Priesthood*, 155. For Yoder, this stands in tension with the most basic imperative of the New Testament, which "rejects most kinds of nationalism, militarism and vengeance for the Christian and calls Christians to return good for evil" (*Royal Priesthood*, 161).

10. Yoder, *Royal Priesthood*, 135.

11. Yoder, *Royal Priesthood*, 250–51.

Hauerwas adopts Yoder's framework and argues that what often is celebrated as the Christian church's greatest "historical triumph" is, in actuality, its "most calamitous defeat." The conversion of the Roman Empire to the Christian faith undermined Christian witness and eroded the capacity of Christians to serve as an alternative to the world.[12] Before Constantine, it was countercultural to be a Christian, but after Constantine it became commonplace as Christians adopted the habits, customs, and forms of life of the broader culture.[13] Furthermore, after Constantine, Christians sought to rule diverse societies and developed a language and morality acceptable to non-Christians, in the process dispensing with the distinctive practices of the Christian community, none more important than the commitment to love one's enemy. Because God's cause is identified with the empire (or the nation-state), ensuring that the empire continues to flourish emerges as the fundamental imperative of Christian discipleship. It follows that the validity of Christian action is judged on the basis of its effectiveness in managing the politics of the state and not its fidelity to the gospel. Furthermore, because violence is used to achieve the objectives of the state, pacifism—particularly the christological pacifism defended by Yoder and Hauerwas—becomes unintelligible.

For Hauerwas, political liberalism is the primary form of Constantinianism in the United States. Christians on both the left and the right grant the political order something akin to "a religious status." This is done in different ways; liberal Christians maintain that religion is necessary to build a more just social order, while conservative Christians argue that, as a community of virtue, the church is necessary to "sustain a free society."[14] In both cases, Constantinianism silences any form of Christian opposition to the secular political order by enlisting Christians in the project of sustaining liberal democracy.[15] This is a critical point in that for Hauerwas

12. Hauerwas observes, "The conversion of the Roman Empire, in which it was thought that the faith overthrew the powers of 'this age,' found that the faith itself had become subordinate to those very powers." Hauerwas, "Church Matters," 31.

13. Hauerwas and Wells, "How the Church Managed," 42.

14. Hauerwas, *Better Hope*, 33.

15. Hauerwas observes, "The conservative and the liberal church, the so-called private and public church, are basically accommodationist (that is, Constantinian) in their social ethic. Both assume wrongly that the American church's primary social task is to underwrite American democracy." Hauerwas and Willimon, *Resident Aliens*, 32. Hauerwas argues, for instance, that Jerry Falwell and Martin Luther King Jr. viewed it as necessary to engage the secular political order in order to achieve their vision of justice (whether it be to prevent abortions or to build a more inclusive social order). Hauerwas, "On Being a Church Capable of Addressing a World at War," in *Hauerwas Reader*, 463.

Christians contribute meaningfully to democratic politics when they resist adopting the norms of the broader culture and preserve the distinctiveness of their own witness.

Hauerwas's critique of liberalism targets the ways in which the market and the nation-state have become idols. Hauerwas's critique of capitalism is secondary to his critique of the violence of the nation-state. But he does note that his critical engagement with liberalism has always been a critique "of the dominance of capitalist modes of life."[16] Hauerwas specifically characterizes the liberal-capitalist social order as a "self-fulfilling prophecy" because it "is designed to work on the presumption that people are self-interested" and "tends to produce that kind of people."[17] Additionally, Hauerwas warns about the dire political consequences that emerge when a society is dominated by capital by explicitly invoking C. B. Macpherson's argument that the "liberal-democratic society is a capitalist market society, and the latter by its very nature compels a continual net transfer of part of the power of some men to others, thus diminishing rather than maximizing the equal freedom to use and develop one's natural capacities which is claimed."[18] As a system of unequal power, capitalism exercises control over political structures in a manner that can be described as oligarchic (or even plutocratic).[19] Because the American liberal political order is not democratic, Christians should disabuse themselves of the view that by supporting the American political system they are supporting democracy. We will take up this line of argumentation in the final section of the chapter when we examine Hauerwas's recent engagement with radical democratic politics. But what is evident already is that Hauerwas's primary concern is to decouple liberalism from democracy and explore ways in which Christians might contribute to a postliberal democratic politics.

Hauerwas's criticism of capitalism, as liberal democracy's economic form, is linked to his criticism of the nation-state as an institution sustained

16. Hauerwas, *Performing the Faith*, 228.

17. Hauerwas, *Better Hope*, 44.

18. Macpherson, *Democratic Theory*, quoted in Hauerwas, *Performing the Faith*, 228.

19. Recently, Hauerwas has linked the concentration of power among plutocratic elites to the rise of populism, observing, "Politically liberalism increases the concentration of power in the central state, as well as at the same time underwriting the assumption of the inevitability of a globalized market. The latter has the unfortunate effect of destroying a sense of place. In such a social order, the production of wealth increasingly is in the hands of a new, rootless oligarchy 'that practises a manipulative populism while holding in contempt the genuine priorities of most people'—as good a description of Trump as one could want." Hauerwas and Dean, *Minding the Web*, 101. The internal quote is from Milbank and Pabst, *The Politics of Virtue*, 1.

by political violence. His concern is that the nation-state is an idol that necessitates forms of loyalty that cause individuals to prioritize the demands
of citizenship over the demands of Christian discipleship. This issue comes
to a head in relation to the problem of violence. Hauerwas suggests that the
causes that individuals are willing to die for are "indicative of their most
basic conviction," and, by this standard, it is clear that the most fundamental
commitment for most American Christians is to the nation-state.[20] Christians no longer view their faith as something they are willing to die for but
instinctually view the nation-state as something for which they are not only
willing to die but to kill. Hauerwas concludes that American democracy
constitutes a "subtle temptation" because Christians "have never killed as
willingly as when they have been asked to do so for 'freedom.'"[21] They have
done so because American civil religion has been successful at building a
community that forms individuals in a way that the Christian churches have
failed to do. In our analysis of the relationship between neoliberalism and
neoconservatism in the first chapter, we observed that a commonly held
position among radical democratic theorists (Sheldon Wolin, Stuart Hall,
Wendy Brown, and David Harvey) is that nationalism rebuilds a social body
torn apart by the competitive individualism of neoliberalism. Hauerwas
adopts a parallel line of argumentation with respect to political violence;
he argues that war builds social cohesion in a liberal political order that has
destroyed virtually all other shared common goods.[22] In particular, war is
framed as a moral enterprise that creates a shared purpose among citizens
who have little in common beyond the fact that they oppose enemies who
threaten the American way of life. Hauerwas observes, "War remains for
Americans our most determinative moral reality. How do you get people
who are taught they are free to follow their own interest to sacrifice themselves and their children in war? Democracies by their very nature seem to
require that wars be fought in the name of ideals, which makes war self-
justifying." Of course, the "realists in the State Department and Pentagon"
have no illusions about the self-interested character of the United States'
commitment to perpetual warfare, but because the American public will
not fight wars as "cynics," noble ideals like freedom, liberation, and democratization are offered to justify militarism abroad.[23] It stands to reason that
it is "difficult to recall a time when America was not at war," because there
always exist new reasons for war: it is necessary to fight to "end all wars," it is

20. Hauerwas, *War and the American Difference*, 19.
21. Hauerwas, *Dispatches from the Front*, 134.
22. Hauerwas and Willimon, *Resident Aliens*, 35.
23. Hauerwas, *War and the American Difference*, 34.

necessary to fight to "make the world safe for democracy," or it is necessary to fight "to combat terrorism."[24]

Because Hauerwas argues that the idolatry of the nation-state poses the gravest threat to Christianity in America, he asserts that a fundamental task for Christians is to remember that "the democratic state is still a state that would ask us to qualify our loyalty to God in the name of some lesser loyalty."[25] Furthermore, because "war is a counter church" for Americans, and the rituals of American civil religion a "counter-liturgy," reasserting loyalty to God over nation necessarily involves a liturgical dimension.[26] In liturgy, Christians commemorate Christ's sacrifice at the eucharistic table, a sacrifice that ends all sacrifice insofar as it frees Christians from the compulsion to secure their existence by destroying the lives of others "on the world's altars."[27] The church is called to be a people who demonstrate that loyalty to God entails performing this "end of sacrifice" by witnessing to a politics of peace in their communities.[28] When the church offers this witness it succeeds in doing more than directing American foreign policy toward slightly less destructive ends (as realist and just war approaches often aim to do). It demonstrates that "there is an alternative to the sacrifices of war."[29] Because the visibility of the church has been marginalized under Constantinianism, restoring this visibility, as a peaceable alternative to the violence of the nation-state, is a central feature of the ekklesial politics that Hauerwas endorses. It is to this peaceable witness that we turn in the next section.

THE PEACEABLE CHURCH

Yoder and Hauerwas argue that pacifism is not a strategy to rid the world of violence and view any attempt to defend pacifism on the grounds of efficacy as improper for two reasons. First, it is utopian and betrays a "naïve faith in

24. Hauerwas, *War and the American Difference*, ix, xiv.

25. Hauerwas, *Dispatches from the Front*, 134.

26. Hauerwas, *War and the American Difference*, 34.

27. Hauerwas, *War and the American Difference*, 56.

28. As Hauerwas observes, "Christian commitment to nonviolence is a way of life for the long haul. Exactly because we understand how morally compelling war can be we know what a challenge we face. That is why we offer the world not simply moral advice designed to make war less destructive, but a witness to God's invitation to join a community that is so imaginative, so rich in its history that it gives us the means to resist the temptation to give our loyalties to those that would use them for war." Hauerwas, "Should War Be Eliminated? A Thought Experiment," in *Hauerwas Reader*, 424.

29. Hauerwas, *War and the American Difference*, 69.

the good will of men."[30] Second, a pragmatic form of pacifism is itself a form of Constantinian Christianity in its attempts to ensure that the world turns out right through the use of human power. Yoder points to the problematic Constantinian assumptions that animate the use violence to achieve political ends as an attempt "to be providence ourselves." This need to make history turn out right stems from the belief that *there is no other actor for good on the scene.*[31] When Christians take this role upon themselves they "short-circuit" the "providential potential" of God and inflict violence on others as a means of preventing history from "getting out of hand."[32]

Yoder offers an alternative approach to history in which cross and resurrection provide the paradigm for Christian engagement with the world. Yoder contends that the resurrection demonstrates that obedience and not a pragmatic calculus is central to Christian discipleship. God's providence, as revealed through the resurrection, demonstrates that Christians are never "boxed in" by a lesser-of-two-evils calculus because many events in history were unforeseeable at the time but somehow happened anyhow. Christians are called to read history as open to these unpredictable events because "the Resurrection was an impossible, unforeseeable new option, and it happened." While the resurrection represents the central example in Yoder's writings of the impossible realized in history, he also invokes more recent examples like the Montgomery bus boycott, observing that it should never have happened in terms of the normal social processes of the South in the United States in the 1950s. But when Christians acknowledge that the unforeseeable has occurred in history it leads to the recognition that "there is a power in history that reaches beyond the boxes in which we find ourselves. So one more reason that the cross is meaningful is that even though it fails, it does not fail if there is resurrection."[33] And even though any attempt to realize providence in history is at odds with resurrection faith, Yoder does not renounce efficacy altogether in favor of some vision of purity or "delayed gratification in heaven." He contends that Christians should support projects of "liberation" within the social order, but only by way of politics that "go with the grain of the cosmos."[34]

30. Hauerwas, "Stanley Hauerwas on John Howard Yoder," 251.

31. Yoder, *War of the Lamb*, 39. Emphasis original.

32. Yoder, *War of the Lamb*, 39.

33. Yoder, *Christian Attitudes*, 319–20. Yoder observes, "Most important events in the forward movement of history could not have happened. You could not have predicted them by extrapolating from the year before. Yet they did happen" (*Christian Attitudes*, 320).

34. Yoder, *Politics of Jesus*, 246.

Hauerwas shares Yoder's approach to peaceable witness by viewing the commitment to nonviolence as the only option available to Christians who confess that Jesus Christ is Lord. Hauerwas observes, "My pacifism, which is based upon christological presuppositions, does not look on our disavowal of war as a strategy to make the world less violent. Indeed, my own view is that Christians are called to nonviolence not because our nonviolence promises to make the world free of war, but because in a world of war we, as faithful followers of Jesus, cannot imagine being other than nonviolent."[35] Hauerwas's theology aims to demonstrate that nonviolence is a demand of all Christians and not merely a stance adopted by a few who wish to follow the more radical counsels. Because Hauerwas adopts a theological approach to pacifism he rejects efficacy as the criterion for assessing the adequacy of a particular action.[36] He contends rather that Christians should learn to "live out of control" by rejecting the temptation to manage history. Because Christians know that victory has been achieved in Jesus Christ, "the church is free to bear witness, peaceably and patiently, to that ending."[37] Patience, then, serves as a central virtue of Christian nonviolence because it enables Christians to place their hope in what God will realize in God's own time rather than what humans can achieve through coercive means. As we noted in the third chapter, Hauerwas describes the implications of this view for Christian political engagement when he observes that "the church must learn time and time again that its task is not to *make* the world the kingdom, but to be faithful to the kingdom by showing to the world what it means to be a community of peace."[38]

The political witness described by Hauerwas serves as an alternative to forms of Constantinianism that align with the powers of the world in the attempt to ensure that history turns out "right." Hauerwas maintains

35. Hauerwas and Neuhaus, "Pacifism, Just War, & the Gulf." Hauerwas contends, "To say one is pacifist gives the impression that pacifism is a position that is intelligible apart from the theological convictions that form it. But that is exactly what I wish to deny. Christians are non-violent not because certain implications may follow from their beliefs, but because the very shape of their beliefs form them to be non-violent." Hauerwas, "Pacifism: Some Philosophical Considerations," 100.

36. Hauerwas observes, "I am in fact challenging the very idea that Christian social ethics is primarily an attempt to make the world more peaceable or just. Put starkly, the first social ethical task of the church is to be the church—the servant community. Such a claim may sound self-serving until we remember that what makes the church the church is its faithful manifestation of the peaceable kingdom in the world. As such the church does not have a social ethic; the church is a social ethic." Hauerwas, *Peaceable Kingdom*, 99.

37. Hauerwas, *Performing the Faith*, 97.

38. Hauerwas, *Peaceable Kingdom*, 104.

that to resist Constantinianism is to adopt a position that is neither anti-Constantinian nor apolitical, but rather to create a political space in society that embodies an alternative to Constantinianism. Thus, for Hauerwas, the alternative to Constantinianism is "locality" and "place," because "only at the local level is the church able to engage in the discernment necessary to be prophetic."[39] Put otherwise, the alternative to Constantinianism is "to develop local forms of life that can sustain the necessary visibility of the church as an alternative to the world."[40] Hauerwas maintains that this visibility finds its most authentic expression in the church's capacity to witness to peace and thereby serve as an alternative to the violence of the world's politics.

It is important to emphasize here that the church's commitment to nonviolence does not entail a complete withdrawal from all political engagement. Hauerwas observes that his description of the church's politics does not necessitate an "indiscriminate rejection of the secular order."[41] Instead, he argues that "what is required for Christians is not withdrawal but a sense of selective service and the ability to set priorities. This means that at times and under certain circumstances Christians will find it impossible to participate in government, in aspects of the economy, or in the educational system."[42] Hauerwas frequently highlights the state's use of violence as the primary "circumstance" that should cause Christians to withdraw from the activities of the state. For example, in *The Peaceable Kingdom* he observes,

> Calling for the church to be the church is not a formula for a withdrawal ethic; nor is it a self-righteous attempt to flee from the world's problems; rather it is a call for the church to be a community which tries to develop the resources to stand within the world witnessing to the peaceable kingdom and thus rightly understanding the world. The gospel is a political gospel. Christians are engaged in politics, but it is a politics of the kingdom that reveals the insufficiency of all politics based on coercion and falsehood and finds the true source of power in servanthood rather than dominion.[43]

---

39. Hauerwas, *War and the American Difference*, 156–57.

40. Hauerwas, *State of the University*, 4.

41. Hauerwas, *Christian Existence Today*, 14–15.

42. Hauerwas, "Why the 'Sectarian Temptation' Is a Misrepresentation," in *Hauerwas Reader*, 106. Hauerwas observes, "While I am not opposed to trying to harness the resources of state power to alleviate the needs of people, I think it is unfortunate when we think only in those terms." Hauerwas, "Will the Real Sectarian Please Stand Up?," 90.

43. Hauerwas, *Peaceable Kingdom*, 102.

The call for Christians to embody a peaceable witness does not mean, as Hauerwas's critics often suggest, that Christians should pursue a separatist form of politics. Instead, it means that "the most creative strategy" for social and political transformation that Christians "have to offer is the church. Here we show the world a manner of life the world can never achieve through social coercion or governmental action."[44]

PEACEABLE POSTLIBERAL DEMOCRACY

In the third chapter, we described Hauerwas's criticisms of the Constantinian character of liberal democracy and examined how this criticism could apply to West's endorsement of democracy as an internal norm of Christianity. Furthermore, we noted that while West supports Hauerwas's prophetic critique of American empire, he has expressed reservations about the manner in which Hauerwas's approach could be construed as endorsing a politics of withdrawal from democratic politics. Jeffrey Stout offers a similar set of criticisms of Hauerwas in *Democracy and Tradition*.

First, he wonders whether, given the politics currently circulating in the United States, liberal democracy should be viewed as the primary object of critique. Specifically, Stout wonders whether this focus is wise strategically in an era in which the right stokes resentment among Christians by telling them every day that they represent "a beleaguered minority in an evil order."[45] There is no doubt that Stout shares some of Hauerwas's criticisms of liberal democracy, particularly his critique of the violence of American empire, but he thinks that it would be more useful to target racism, inequality, and political violence specifically rather than engage in a wholesale critique of liberal democracy. Second, he argues that Hauerwas's theological project has provided ideological cover for Christians who seek to preserve their place of privilege in society. Stout contends that "many of Hauerwas's readers probably liked being told that they should care more about being the church than about doing justice to the underclass. At some level, they knew perfectly well how much it would cost them to do justice. So they hardly minded hearing that justice is a bad idea for Christians."[46] Stout suggests that Hauerwas's claim in *After Christendom?* that justice is a "bad idea" is

44. Hauerwas and Willimon, *Resident Aliens*, 83.

45. Stout, *Democracy and Tradition*, 296.

46. Stout continues that one could imagine that for these Christians "following Jesus involves little more than hating the liberal secularists who supposedly run the country, pitying people from a distance, and donating a portion of one's income to the church" (*Democracy and Tradition*, 158).

problematic because, while it is a criticism of (the early) Rawls, it could be appropriated by groups that do not share Hauerwas's specific criticisms of Rawls and that seek to generate an oppositional relationship between Christianity and social justice. For instance, in light of our discussion of the "resonance machine" on the right in the first chapter, one could imagine how a Hauerwasian critique of justice could be deployed by neoliberals who, following F. A. Hayek, proclaim that social justice is a "mirage" that inhibits progress. Hauerwas's critique of justice is literally worlds apart from Hayek's, but the politics on the right (and the left, for that matter) rarely operate at the level of nuanced distinctions and instead gain traction by cultivating affective resonances among diverse constituencies. In this regard, one can sympathize with Stout's claim that Hauerwas should have been much more careful in his criticisms of Rawls in order to ensure statements like "justice is a bad idea for Christians" would not be used to undermine progressive forms of Christianity in America. But, for Stout, this critique of justice and his broader criticisms of figures like Rauschenbusch and Niebuhr have served to undermine the Christian left in America. Stout observes, "I see Hauerwas's relentless attack on Niebuhr and Rauschenbusch as partly responsible for the almost total disintegration of the religious left. The black church is just about all that's left of the religious left. Why is that? Because few people who actually live in black neighborhoods are tempted to behave politically as if justice were a bad idea."[47] Overall, Stout characterizes Hauerwas's approach to politics as one that fuels Christian resentment toward "secular political culture," provides a justification for Christians opting out of the struggle for justice for marginalized groups, and weakens Christian resistance to antidemocratic forces in American society.[48]

Hauerwas initially responded to Stout's criticisms in a 2004 essay titled "Postscript: A Response to Jeff Stout's *Democracy and Tradition*" and claimed that Stout had overestimated his influence on Christian America.[49] In a more recent essay that deals with the politics of Trump, Hauerwas notes that critics have long accused him of downplaying the significance of politics for Christians and "for some, this de-emphasis on Christian political participation is what got us in this mess."[50] In reality, Hauerwas has been remarkably consistent in his position that the church is a distinctive form of politics and that it is not permissible for Christians to disavow politics or turn away from the plight of the oppressed in society. His concern has

47. See West et al., "Pragmatism and Democracy," 23.
48. Stout, *Democracy and Tradition*, 140.
49. Hauerwas, *Performing the Faith*, 215–42.
50. Hauerwas, *Minding the Web*, 114.

been to ensure that when Christians enter the political field they do so as Christians and not as Rawlsians or partisans on the political left or right.[51] His legitimate concern is that when Christians have participated in the politics of the state, they have adopted the values of the state and relinquished the distinctive commitments of their particular community. In our earlier discussion of American civil religion, we noted that Hauerwas finds this tendency most problematic in terms of the willingness of American Christians to support the violence of the nation-state. As a result, he maintains that Christians must withdraw from the politics of the nation-state when it utilizes violence "in order to maintain internal order and external security." It is "at that point and that point alone Christians must withhold their involvement with the state."[52]

Hauerwas's constructive position is to advocate for a politics that withdraws from the violence of the nation-state but still enters the field of political struggle to transform society through nonviolent means. Christians should move away from the view that the only significant site of political action is the nation-state, because "once Christians zero in on the state as the locus of political activity, they become blind to those myriad other ways the church might politically act in the broad horizon of democratic possibility."[53] This dimension of Hauerwas's approach has confused his critics, a confusion to which Hauerwas has contributed by not being as clear as he could have been about the distinction he eventually comes to draw between liberalism and democracy. It is only in response to Stout's critique of his work in *Democracy and Tradition* that he offers this distinction in a way that avoids rhetorically collapsing democracy into liberalism.[54]

In his response to Stout, Hauerwas turns to Wolin as a resource for disentangling democracy from liberalism and acknowledges that he is likely persuaded by Wolin because his "analysis seems to suggest my kind of Christianity and church are politically significant."[55] In the second chapter,

51. Hauerwas observes, "I have never sought to justify Christian withdrawal from social and political involvement; I have just wanted us to be involved as Christians." Hauerwas, *Better Hope*, 24.

52. Hauerwas, "Why the 'Sectarian Temptation' Is a Misrepresentation," in *Hauerwas Reader*, 105. While it is "the responsibility of Christians to work to make their societies less prone to resort to violence," there exist diverse ways to approach this task and, under certain circumstances, withdrawal is the proper Christian response to the violence of the state.

53. Hauerwas, *Minding the Web*, 116.

54. Hauerwas observes that this recent engagement represents a "continuation of my attempt to find a way to talk about forms of democratic life that were not shaped by liberal presuppositions." Hauerwas, *Work of Theology*, 182.

55. Hauerwas, *State of the University*, 164. "Sheldon Wolin is right to interpret

we described Wolin's approach as a form of politics that withdraws from the state as the primary site of political activity and instead advocates for a local form of democratic politics that is "inclined toward anarchy" and "identified with revolution." According to Hauerwas, Wolin's insurgent approach to radical democratic politics cultivates the patience "to tend to one another" and to "foster cooperative action with others" beyond "current forms of state power." Furthermore, Hauerwas characterizes Wolin's approach as one that seeks to generate the skills and habits that are "required if things that matter to us are to be taken care of." He concludes that "if that is 'radical democracy,' then I think I can claim to be a radical democrat."[56]

Hauerwas argues that Wolin's postliberal description of democracy makes Christianity not only relevant to radical democratic politics, but at times an exemplification of it. Hauerwas invokes Christians witness in the Roman Empire as an example of the type of radical democratic politics Wolin describes in his work. Hauerwas observes, "I think it is not unreasonable to suggest that radical democracy is Wolin's name for the kind of interruption he thinks the church represented in the Roman Empire."[57] Of course, it makes sense that Hauerwas would be attracted to Wolin's approach to democracy as a local form of politics that serves as an alternative to the politics of centralized state power because it is similar to Yoder's localist vision for the church, which itself serves as an alternative to Constantinianism. Recall that for Hauerwas the task of the church is not to be anti-Constantinian but "to develop local forms of life that can sustain the necessary visibility of the church as an alternative to the world."[58] It follows that just as Wolin claims that democracy is fugitive or inescapably temporal and doomed to failure, Hauerwas argues that an authentic ekklesial witness has emerged only episodically in history amid various forms of Constantinianism.[59]

From an ecclesiological perspective, Hauerwas draws from Yoder's reflections on the church as a political body and, following Coles's analysis in *Beyond Gated Politics*, views Yoder's reflections on the church as generative for a Christian approach to radical democratic politics. Coles describes a number of elements of church practice that resonate with radical democracy: the practice of binding and loosing as a process of communal discernment;

---

liberalism as the attempt to avoid the challenge of democratic politics, but it is nevertheless the case that liberal presuppositions have dominated accounts as well as justifications of democracy in recent theory" (*State of the University*, 148).

56. Hauerwas, *State of the University*, 163.

57. Hauerwas, *State of the University*, 163.

58. Hauerwas, *State of the University*, 4.

59. Peter Dula presses this point on the fugitive character of the church in Dula, *Cavell, Companionship, and Christian Theology*, 95–116.

the inclusion of each member of the community in decision-making; participation in the Eucharist, which serves as a model for "every other mode of inviting the outsider and the underdog to the table"; and a commitment to nonviolence that entails extending "the processes of reconciliatory dialogue beyond the church even in the most agonistic relations."[60] Hauerwas extends Coles's analysis from a theological perspective, noting that Coles is attracted to Yoder's ecclesiological vision as a politics because of its openness and receptivity to those who do not participate in this tradition.[61] This vulnerable receptivity constitutes a form of patience that rejects any attempt to coerce or control the other by taking the time to enter into dialogue and learn from the other. Coles refers to this as Yoder's "wild patience," which, as with Hauerwas, is linked to his commitment to nonviolence.

Yoder's reflections on the political implications of the church's witness provide an occasion for Coles and Hauerwas to debate the challenges involved in viewing the church as a site of radical democratic politics. Coles expresses concern regarding pluralism. In particular, he worries that the christological confession that Jesus is Lord and the Christian commitment to orthodoxy generates a politics of exclusion. We should recall here that this is one of the reasons that Cornel West prioritizes orthopraxis over orthodoxy because he views a preoccupation with orthodoxy as a source of division. Hauerwas, however, defends the compatibility between orthodoxy and radical democratic politics by arguing that orthodoxy is the process by which the Christian tradition has sought to understand the implications of Jesus's life and death for how members of the church should live their own lives. Hauerwas observes that "rather than being the denial of radical democracy, orthodoxy is the exemplification of the training necessary for the formation of a people who are not only capable of working for justice, but who are themselves just."[62] Hauerwas largely sidesteps Coles's question concerning the capacity of the church to learn from non-Christian "others" and instead responds to Coles by arguing that orthodoxy enables the formation of a people who, in their response to the life of Jesus of Nazareth, cultivate the virtues needed to contribute to the politics of radical democracy. We will return to this point momentarily, but here we see that Hauerwas is less inclined to affirm the more radical commitment to pluralism advocated for by proponents of radical democracy, and remains primarily concerned with the church's capacity to cultivate virtues among its members.

60. Coles, *Beyond Gated Politics*, 120.

61. Hauerwas and Coles, *Christianity, Democracy, and the Radical Ordinary*, 20.

62. Hauerwas and Coles, *Christianity, Democracy, and the Radical Ordinary*, 30.

Hauerwas supplements this Yoderian approach to the church as a site of radical democracy with his engagement with the radical politics of L'Arche communities.[63] Hauerwas's reflections on L'Arche are significant not only because he has coauthored a book with Jean Vanier (*Living Gently in a Violent World: The Prophetic Witness of Weakness*) but also because he devoted two (of three total) chapters in *Christianity, Democracy, and the Radical Ordinary* to Vanier and the politics of L'Arche. Coles suggests that Hauerwas's encounter with Vanier has been as impactful on Hauerwas's approach to politics as his encounter with Yoder. And Hauerwas himself observes, "I should like to think that the attention and reflection I have developed concerning the place of those called the mentally handicapped represents my most determinative political reflections."[64] Hauerwas views these reflections as significant from a political perspective because his interest in a Christian approach to politics "is less grand than most of what is identified as work in political theology" and focuses instead on what he characterizes as the small politics of patience and gentleness embodied in intentional communities like L'Arche.[65] In particular, Hauerwas finds exemplary the fact that, as a community, L'Arche takes the time "to be constituted by practices represented by those 'slower' than most of us," noting that this form of patient attention to others is the precondition for any form of life in common.[66] In particular, the patience embodied in a community that attends to the needs of another without concern for the time it takes—it might take two hours to bathe or have a meal in L'Arche communities—serves as an important witness to a politics that differs from the politics of speed that dominates our world today. L'Arche serves as a microcosm of the type of political virtues needed to build a radical democratic politics that seeks to deliberate over and be in service of "goods held in common."[67] Furthermore, Hauerwas views L'Arche communities as serving as an important witness to a politics of peace precisely because these communities approach time and place differently than the broader society. In an extraordinary remark, Hauerwas argues that "any movement for peace not determined by L'Arche-like politics will only threaten to become

---

63. Hauerwas mentions Dorothy Day as representative of the type of Christian political witness that he characterizes as a politics of care at a local level in both *With the Grain of the Universe*, 230, and *Christianity, Democracy, and the Radical Ordinary*, 4.

64. Hauerwas, *State of the University*, 163. For Coles's comment, see Hauerwas and Coles, *Christianity, Democracy, and the Radical Ordinary*, 208.

65. Hauerwas, *Work of Theology*, 185.

66. Hauerwas, *State of the University*, 163.

67. Hauerwas and Vanier, *Living Gently in a Violent World*, 92.

a form of violence."[68] Communities like L'Arche do not go out to the world in order to eradicate violence but demonstrate through their witness that a peaceable alternative exists to the world's violence.

Overall, Hauerwas detects a remarkable resonance between the politics of Yoder's church and Vanier's L'Arche communities. Just as Yoder's church is obliged to take "the time to care for and listen to the 'weakest' members," so L'Arche is a community that is constituted by its encounter and engagement with those viewed as "'slower' than most of us."[69] And, furthermore, just as Yoder's church cultivates the virtues of patience and hope as a means of supporting a politics of peace, "at the heart of L'Arche is patience, which turns out to be but another name for peace."[70] In both instances, Hauerwas describes a Christian contribution to radical democratic politics in terms of the capacity of these communities to cultivate the virtues needed to work patiently and nonviolently together for goods held in common. The virtue of patience is the lynchpin that draws together Yoder's vision for the church, the practices of the L'Arche community, and radical democracy as theorized by Hauerwas. This is the case because he maintains that "democracy in its fundamental form is also patience. It requires that you listen, in the Pauline sense, to the lesser member, and sometimes, if the lesser member isn't convinced, you have to wait."[71]

Hauerwas describes these ordinary forms of engagement with others witnessed to in both Yoder's vision for the church and L'Arche communities as a revolutionary form of politics. As with Wolin, the form of revolution supported by Hauerwas is not one that seeks to seize state power, but rather occurs through "the fine grains of the politics of micro-relationships and small achievements."[72] Again, we recall here that Wolin defends the need for revolution in "What Revolutionary Action Means Today," but he describes revolution in terms of the capacity to cultivate new forms of life and for communities to reinvent themselves. Wolin's approach is entirely consistent with the approach to revolution adopted by Yoder (and, ultimately, by Hauerwas himself). Yoder maintains that the most significant revolutions that "change the nature of an entire civilization" take place "in secret" and involve "shifts in moral assumptions and in the availability of quality people which

---

68. Hauerwas and Coles, *Christianity, Democracy, and the Radical Ordinary*, 316.

69. Hauerwas, *State of the University*, 163.

70. Hauerwas and Coles, *Christianity, Democracy, and the Radical Ordinary*, 316–17.

71. Hauerwas, "Why Community Is Dangerous."

72. Hauerwas and Coles, *Christianity, Democracy, and the Radical Ordinary*, 4.

can take place only patiently and without notice."[73] For Yoder, one of the most effective ways to generate change in society is to "create a small group of people who are deeply committed to what you are doing and provide infrastructure for living differently from the larger society rather than just waiting for the whole society to change."[74] This model of countercultural witness serves as a more powerful impetus for social change than reformist attempts to work through the institutional mechanisms of the dominant political order. According to Yoder,

> An alternative community contributes powerfully to social change through its conscientious refusal at certain border points to participate in continuing wrong. The boycott, conscientious objection, and other patterns of respectful obstruction contribute proportionately more to a redefinition of social goals than the continuing conscientious support of established patterns by the majority of the pursuit of change through the more routine patterns of evolution provided by bureaucracies and elections. This is not to deprecate the more routine forms, but only to observe that they are not the strongest, and that patterns of minority witness are often stronger, rather than weaker, when compared to mainstream methods.[75]

Yoder describes "ekklesia" as the specific form of political community founded by Jesus that favors the underdog, shares power among its members, loves the enemy, and resists empire.[76] In essence, Yoder claims that the church's most significant resistance is the formation of communities that engage in a distinctive set of practices and thereby offer the world an alternative to a politics of violence. In this regard, Yoder argues against the Constantinian assumption that it is necessary to align with dominant powers in order to guide the world toward less problematic results. He maintains instead that "the Christian church has been more successful in contributing to the development of society and to human well-being precisely when it has avoided alliances with the dominant political or cultural powers."[77] This view resonates with the aim of Hauerwas's approach to a democratic social order in which he approvingly notes that "from Yoder's perspective, the church best serves the social orders that claim to be democratic by taking seriously the internal calling of the church rather than

73. Yoder, *For the Nations*, 118.
74. Yoder, *Revolutionary Christian Citizenship*, 28–29.
75. Yoder, *Karl Barth and the Problem of War*, 158.
76. Yoder, *Revolutionary Christian Citizenship*, 31, and Yoder, *War of the Lamb*, 174.
77. Yoder, *Royal Priesthood*, 202.

'becoming tributary to whatever secular consensus seems strong at the time.' That is the strategy I have tried to adopt in my work."[78] The church's call is to serve as a prophetic alternative to the prevailing secular consensus. Paradoxically, it is this form of witness that most effectively contributes to processes of democratization in society.

Hauerwas's recent engagement with the work of James C. Scott clarifies his position on social transformation. Scott's contention is that proponents of liberal democracy have failed to recognize the crucial role that "crisis" and "institutional failure" play in political transformation. Scott contends that more often than not democratic renewal occurs because of "extra-institutional disorder" and not because of incremental reforms made by the legislative bodies in the government. Scott observes, "In the 20th century every major episode of structural change in the United States has come from extra-parliamentary disturbances outside of the normal circuits of legislative politics. It's a kind of tragedy that all these democratic institutions, that are supposed to be vehicles of translation and change for popular wishes, actually have not worked in my country since the turn of the century, unless they were accompanied by large and massive outpourings of disorder that could not be contained."[79] Scott offers his readers an "anarchist squint" that permits them to see the political significance of small acts of disobedience, protest, lawbreaking, and local resistance. Hauerwas views Scott's approach as consonant with his own in that it represents a defense of a "small politics" that contributes to social change by witnessing to an alternative to liberalism. Accordingly, Hauerwas calls for Christians to adopt an "ecclesial squint" so that they view their own political witness—often seen as insignificant by the proponents of liberal democracy—as an attempt to offer the world an alternative to a politics rooted in fear, violence, and death. As with Scott and Yoder, Hauerwas advocates for boycott, conscientious objection, and insubordination as a means of creating the space for the emergence of political alternatives to liberalism. For instance, in *The Peaceable Kingdom* he observes that "resistance may appear to the world as foolish and ineffective for it may involve something so small as refusing to pay a telephone tax to support a war, but that does not mean that it is not resistance. Such resistance at least makes it clear that Christian social witness can never take place in a manner that excludes the possibility of miracles."[80] Similarly, in "September 11, 2001: A Pacifist Response," Hauerwas notes that he no longer sings "The Star-Spangled Banner" and views this refusal as a "small

78. Hauerwas, *Work of Theology*, 185.
79. Scott, "Interview with James Scott," 456.
80. Hauerwas, *Peaceable Kingdom*, 106.

thing that reminds me that my first loyalty is not to the United States but to God and God's church."[81] In a more recent essay, Hauerwas (with Jonathan Tran) invokes the tactic of "foot-dragging" in response to current immigration policy in the United States by arguing that if the Trump administration begins to register Muslims forcibly, then Christians should register and identify as Muslims in order to disrupt the process.[82] To refuse to pay taxes, to abstain from offering one's loyalty to the nation-state, or to register as a Muslim in an atmosphere of anti-Muslim sentiment serve as concrete ways for Christians to participate in a small politics of resistance. Hauerwas is convinced that when Christians participate in this small politics they help their neighbors by demonstrating that "it did not have to be."[83]

Whether through political acts of insubordination and disruption (Scott and Wolin), the practices of the church as a political body (Yoder's ecclesiological vision), or the witness to Christ's mercy and peace in intentional communities (L'Arche), Christians offer the world a small politics that contributes to social change in ways unrecognized by dominant approaches to social transformation. Thus, in contrast to the arguments made by his critics, it is clear that Hauerwas does offer a politics of Christian engagement with the democratic social order. But Hauerwas's politics refuses the terms that liberalism sets for engagement: namely, that the state is the locus of politics and that violence is necessary to sustain the social order. In this sense, Hauerwas's politics stands at a distance from radical democratic theorists who advocate for political engagement with the state (Laclau, Mouffe, Stout) in that he advocates for only *ad hoc* engagements with the state and, generally, devotes his time to endorsing the significance of political action that takes place beyond the official political mechanisms of the nation-state.

Here we return to the issue of whether Hauerwas's response to Stout's criticisms might allay concerns raised by Stout about the political implications of Hauerwas's theology. The answer here depends on how one defines success in these matters and even more basically how one defines democracy. Hauerwas has clarified the scope of his criticism by noting that political liberalism and not democracy is the central focus of his critique. Furthermore, he claims that on a certain reading the church's politics can be viewed as a

81. Hauerwas, *Performing the Faith*, 203.

82. Hauerwas, *Minding the Web*, 123.

83. Hauerwas, *Work of Theology*, 190. This approach is similar to the one advocated by Yoder when he insists that "there are times when a society is so totally controlled by an ideology that the greatest need is that someone simply identify a point where he or she can say a clear no in the name of loyalty to a higher authority . . . The imperative of . . . denouncing idolatry is not conditioned by our immediate capacity to bring about an alternate world." Yoder, *Royal Priesthood*, 205.

form of radical democracy. However, this defense of ekklesial politics as a form of radical democracy is predicated on the acceptance of Wolin's approach to radical democracy as a fugitive affair "inclined toward anarchy" and "identified with revolution." Hauerwas and Stout diverge in their assessment of the legitimacy of Wolin's approach to radical democracy, and so it is unclear whether Hauerwas's turn to a Wolinian form of radical democracy would convince Stout. As we discussed in the second chapter, Stout is a sympathetic critic of Wolin in that he praises Wolin's prescient diagnosis of current challenges to democracy but criticizes his failure to offer an institutional challenge to the antidemocratic elements of capitalism and empire. Stout views a "strictly" fugitive approach to democracy as one that delivers the institutional structures of government over to the antidemocratic forces of capital and empire.[84] In "Democratic Time" Hauerwas acknowledges that Stout would likely be unconvinced by his turn to Wolin because Wolin's approach to democracy differs from Stout's own. But, again, it bears noting here that Hauerwas could respond to Stout's criticisms by invoking the significance historically of insurgent politics to social transformation and democratic renewal. For instance, if Scott's reading of twentieth-century American political history is accurate—and Wolin makes similar claims in his work—then it could be argued (if Hauerwas responded in the pragmatic terms Stout sets for the debate) that insurgent politics has been more important for social transformation than the reformist politics that have been pursued via the official institutions of American liberal democracy.

At one level, the debate between Stout and Hauerwas reached an impasse because they seem to have adopted divergent positions with regard to the withdrawal-engagement debate. But since Stout's initial criticism in 2004 in *Democracy and Tradition*, he and Hauerwas have clarified the nature of their democratic commitments. Thus, as we discussed in the second chapter, Stout published *Blessed Are the Organized* in 2012 and argued that faith-based community organizations like the Industrial Areas Foundation (IAF) function as exemplary models of radical democratic politics by serving as essential intermediaries between local forms of grassroots organizing and the centralized institutions of American democracy. Stout argues that if the churches did not support the work of IAF and other forms of organizing "then grassroots democracy in the United States would come to very little."[85]

84. Stout, "Spirit of Democracy," 18.

85. Stout, *Blessed Are the Organized*, 5. On this point see also Hauerwas and Coles, *Christianity, Democracy, and the Radical Ordinary*, 227ff. Coles agrees with Stout and argues that in contrast to the episodic power of the politics of disruption of protest movements and the waning power of progressive organizations, the Industrial Areas Foundation organizations have been extraordinarily successful at mobilizing democratic power and achieving significant reforms at the local level.

Stout's affirmation of the critical importance of Christianity for grassroots democracy in America actually overlaps with Hauerwas's recent reflections. At an event focused on the grassroots democracy of the IAF, Hauerwas observed that "what I've been trying to do all along is to make the church worthy of participating in the kind of political relationships sought by IAF."[86] Furthermore, in the introduction to *Christianity, Democracy, and the Radical Ordinary*, Coles and Hauerwas point to IAF and L'Arche as exemplary forms of political witness that embody the radical democratic ethos of generous receptivity to others.[87] Thus, while Stout and Hauerwas disagree concerning any number of issues at a theoretical level—including the proper relationship between Christianity and democracy as well as the relationship between liberalism and democracy—they actually converge in their mutual support for faith-based community organizations like IAF, which serve an intermediary role between the fugitive and the institutional.[88]

Stout's engagement with Hauerwas's work challenged Hauerwas to clarify his approach to democracy. But even before this engagement there is a constancy to Hauerwas's approach insofar as he offers a Christian approach to politics that is peaceable *and* postliberal. These two features of his work are interrelated insofar as the primary critique that Hauerwas offers of political liberalism is that it represents a form of governance that is linked inextricably to violence. Here we treat them separately to clarify the distinctiveness of Hauerwas's approach to radical democratic politics and to bring his approach into conversation with the other Christian thinkers examined in this book.

First, the focus of peaceable theology departs from the mainline of theological engagement with radical democratic theory—as well as radical democratic theory itself—in its focus on American militarism rather than neoliberalism as the primary object of critique. Even though Hauerwas enumerates multiple reasons for resisting political liberalism, among them that capitalism is a problematic system of moral formation and that it tends to engender plutocratic forms of political rule, the focus of his critique remains liberalism's use of violence and sacrifice to sustain itself. He deems the violence of American empire unacceptable from a Christian perspective and, furthermore, views the failure of Christians to voice opposition to it as evidence that Christianity has been reduced to a civil

---

86. Quoted in Coles, "Democracy, Theology, and the Question of Excess," 312.

87. Hauerwas and Coles, *Christianity, Democracy, and the Radical Ordinary*, 2.

88. Yet, even as we see an area of potential rapprochement emerging between them, it remains the case that Stout views Cornel West's Christian pragmatist approach to radical democratic politics as more compelling than the insurgent and fugitive approach advocated for by Hauerwas. See Stout, *Democracy and Tradition*, 57–58, 302.

religion in the United States. As a christological pacifist, Hauerwas rejects the mainstream of Christian political theology in the United States insofar as it adopts a realist justification for violence either by viewing it as the lesser of two evils or by employing a just war defense of it as necessary in order to secure the *tranquillitas ordinis*.

Hauerwas's position is consonant with those articulated by West, Schüssler Fiorenza, Ellacuría, and Sobrino in that it rejects the bipartisan consensus on the left and the right that supports American hegemony as an unambiguous good for the world. But Hauerwas's position is distinct from that of West, Ellacuría, and Sobrino in its thoroughgoing commitment to a pacifist Christian politics. West, Ellacuría, and Sobrino reject the violence of empire but argue that under extreme conditions, insurrectionary violence is permissible as a form of self-defense in response to sustained forms of structural violence.[89] The divergence between Hauerwas and West, Ellacuría, and Sobrino concerning the relative priority given to justice in relation to peace is the decisive issue. For Hauerwas, Christian discipleship is not a political strategy for limiting violence or realizing a more just social order, but a form of life that Christians must adopt if they are to be disciples of Jesus Christ. As a result, for Hauerwas, nonviolence serves as the only permissible method in the pursuit of justice.

Second, because Hauerwas offers a postliberal approach to Christian politics, he views the primary arena of political engagement as the realm of civil society and not the state. We already have commented extensively on this feature of his thought in terms of his engagement with Wolin, and, along with Schüssler Fiorenza (and to a lesser extent West), this commitment leads Hauerwas to develop a transnational or postnational approach to Christian politics. Because the boundaries of the nation-state are socially constructed and have led Christians to subordinate their loyalty to God to the nation, the task of the church is to serve "as a political alternative to every nation"[90] and to be a "holy nation" that finds that it is "at home in no nation."[91] In defense of his politics of withdrawal from the nation, which critics often characterize as a form of sectarian tribalism, Hauerwas maintains that the mainstream of Christian theology in the United States legitimates its own form of political tribalism through its support of American liberal democracy. He observes,

> We reject the charge of tribalism, particularly from those
> whose theologies serve to buttress the most nefarious brand

89. Sobrino, *Archbishop Romero*, 96, and Sobrino, *Jesus the Liberator*, 215ff.
90. Hauerwas, *Community of Character*, 12.
91. Hauerwas, "The Servant Community," in *Hauerwas Reader*, 378.

of tribalism of all—the omnipotent state. The church is the one political entity in our culture that is global, transnational, transcultural. Tribalism is not the church determined to serve God rather than Caesar. Tribalism is the United States of America, which sets up artificial boundaries and defends them with murderous intensity. And the tribalism of nations occurs most viciously in the absence of a church able to say and to show, in its life together, that God, not nations, rules the world. We must never forget that it was modern, liberal democracy, in fighting to preserve itself, that resorted to the bomb in Hiroshima and the firebombing of Dresden, not to mention Vietnam. This is the political system that must be preserved in order for Christians to be politically responsible?[92]

This rebuttal to his critics is a succinct summary of the essence of his approach to politics. Critics contend that his politics of withdrawal from the nation-state leads to a sectarian and tribal approach that generates division among citizens and leads Christians to disavow responsibility for the government. Against his critics, Hauerwas maintains that this interpretation has the situation precisely backward. It is the mainstream of Christian theology in the United States that legitimates political tribalism by providing support for a liberal democratic order that breeds division and conflict among nations and has committed unparalleled forms of violence around the world in the name of "freedom" and "democracy." In this sense, Hauerwas contends that American liberal democracy is a much more dangerous and destructive form of tribalism than the politics of the peaceable church. He therefore concludes that a central imperative of Christian politics is to move beyond the politics of the nation-state and to develop a transnational politics.

A commitment to some form of transnational politics follows necessarily from Hauerwas's critique of idolatry and his commitment to nonviolence. But the critical question is what form of transnational politics Hauerwas's approach supports. On this point he is unclear. Hauerwas's embrace of a Wolinian-style approach to localist forms of radical democratic politics offers few resources for developing a transnational politics. Notably, however, the withdrawal model of Hardt and Negri is convergent with elements of his approach, a fact recognized by some of Hauerwas's most prominent students, who have brought elements of his approach into conversation with Hardt and Negri.[93] Of course, Hauerwas himself has never fleshed out what this means and often has limited himself to the "small" and "local" features of a politics

92. Hauerwas and Willimon, *Resident Aliens*, 33.

93. See, for instance, Bell, *Economy of Desire*; Tran, *Foucault and Theology*; and Dula, *Cavell, Companionship, and Christian Theology*.

that occurs at a level outside or beneath the politics of the nation-state. In Hauerwas's dialogue with Romand Coles in *Christianity, Democracy, and the Radical Ordinary*, Coles pushes him to articulate his politics at "larger" scales and points to the example of Mennonite missionary work as a Christian example of this type of work. But Hauerwas has yet to elaborate what a transnational Christian politics looks like.[94]

The other model for transnational politics that we have engaged in this book is the feminist approach of Schüssler Fiorenza, which offers an approach to radical democratic politics rooted in local communities around the world that seek to build transnational coalitions. Schüssler Fiorenza shares with Hauerwas a fierce opposition to nationalism, but as with the other thinkers examined in this work, she views neoliberalism as the fundamental object of critique. As we noted in the fourth chapter, for Schüssler Fiorenza inclusion within ekklesia of wo/men is determined not by creedal affiliation, the commitment to orthodoxy, or liturgical practice, but rather by resistance to structures of disempowerment and oppression. Schüssler Fiorenza adopts a pluralist position and views the ekklesia of wo/men as a community that resists kyriarchal oppression (quite similar to Hardt and Negri's "multitude"). For this reason, it is likely that Hauerwas would view Schüssler Fiorenza's approach as an example of Constantinianism on the left that utilizes a standard exterior to the gospel to judge the authenticity of Christian witness.[95] Hauerwas has observed, "Constantinianism has taken many different forms throughout history, but the common thread that constitutes the family resemblance between its various forms is that the validity of the church, of Jesus Christ, and of the New Testament is to be judged by standards derived from the world."[96] We should recall here that for Schüssler Fiorenza the Bible must be interpreted by the standard of liberation because if it is interpreted by any other standard it legitimates various forms of kyriarchal oppression. She observes, "The revelatory canon for theological evaluation of biblical androcentric traditions and their subsequent interpretations cannot be derived from the Bible itself but can only be formulated in and through women's struggle for liberation from all patriarchal oppression."[97] Thus, Schüssler Fiorenza's approach to a Christian transnational politics would be identified by Hauerwas as a

94. Hauerwas and Coles, *Christianity, Democracy, and the Radical Ordinary*, 341.

95. Generally, Hauerwas is critical of feminist theology as a problematic species of theological liberalism and of pluralism as a cultural manifestation of political liberalism. Hauerwas, "Failure of Communication *or* a Case of Uncompromising Feminism," and Hauerwas, "The End of 'Religious Pluralism,'" in *State of the University*, 58–75.

96. Hauerwas, *With the Grain of the Universe*, 221.

97. Schüssler Fiorenza, *In Memory of Her*, 30.

species of Constantinianism similar to West's generalized propheticism (and consistent with Yoder's criticism of Latin American liberation theology as a form of neo-Constantinianism).[98]

As is evident from our analysis of Hauerwas's engagement with West and our discussion of Schüssler Fiorenza, Hauerwas's approach offers the greatest obstacle to building a pluralist theo-political assemblage because he adopts an antagonistic approach to many of the theological and political commitments of the Christian left. But it is here that Yoder's reflections on "non-religious equivalents" and "tactical alliances" could offer a corrective by providing the resources needed to engage in *ad hoc* alliances with progressive forms of Christianity as well as secular allies. For instance, in *Body Politics*, Yoder maintains that the church's liturgical worship embodies an alternative form of politics and this politics offers "a paradigm for ways in which other social groups might operate" insofar as the church's witness is a public reality. As a result, Yoder observes that "people who do not share the faith or join the community can learn from them." The church's practice of sharing bread serves as a paradigm "not only for soup kitchens and hospitality houses, but social security and negative income tax."[99] These nonreligious equivalents, therefore, point to the manner in which the church can support secular political initiatives. More importantly, in *The Priestly Kingdom* Yoder offers an alternative approach in which he argues that it is necessary to establish "tactical alliances" with groups that do not share the same theological convictions as members of the church. Yoder observes that "we will share tactical use of liberation language to dismantle the alliance of the church with privilege, without letting the promises made by some in the name of revolution become a new opiate."[100] Yoder also approvingly points to Martin Luther King Jr.'s tactical alliance "with the Gandhian vision" of nonviolence.[101]

Yoder's approach to tactical alliances is consonant with the politics of radical democracy in that it is an approach animated by the attempt to build pluralist assemblages that generate a broader base of resistance than would be possible on the basis of monolithic political movements. Clearly,

---

98. In "Democratic Time: Lessons Learned from Yoder and Wolin," Hauerwas observes, "In a very important chapter, 'Christ the Hope of the World' in *The Original Revolution*, Yoder develops an account of neo, neo-neo, neo-not[sic]-neo-Constantinianism that helps us see how Constantinianism can emigrate into diverse forms from some developments in Latin American liberation theology to outright secular formations (132–154)." Hauerwas, *State of the University*, 152n25.

99. These quotes are found in Hovey, *Speak Thus*, 28ff.

100. Yoder, *Pacifist Way of Knowing*, 38.

101. Yoder, *Priestly Kingdom*, 61–62.

building coalitions is not Yoder's primary concern, but, at the same time, there are resources within his theology to support that project. Indeed, the openness and receptivity to outsiders that Coles emphasizes as a hallmark of Yoder's approach is an important example of an ekklesial approach to radical democracy.

Hauerwas has been less supportive of these efforts at engagement with secular and religious "others" and has expressed skepticism about the project of "translating" Christian convictions into a secular idiom. In *Wilderness Wanderings* Hauerwas observes that he "has little sympathy with attempts to translate Christian speech into terms that are assumed to be generally available."[102] He offers both philosophical and theological reasons for rejecting the attempt to translate Christian convictions into a "neutral" idiom and notes that the aim of such attempts is to place "the church on the side of what are assumed to be the most progressive aspects of our civilization. Such a politics and ethics appear quite prophetic insofar as they call, for example, for greater economic justice in the interest of egalitarian ideals. Unfortunately, the extent to which such a politics and ethics accommodate themselves to the presumptions of modernity is effectively concealed."[103] Hauerwas objects here to the accommodationist tendencies of Constantinian approaches to Christian engagement. Notably, however, what Hauerwas rejects here is the tendency among liberal or progressive forms of Christianity to relinquish the distinctiveness of the church's language and its practices in order to gain access to cultural or political power. By way of contrast, Yoder advocates for *ad hoc* alliances between the Christian church and non-Christian traditions insofar as they seek to defend and preserve goods held in common. Yoder never calls for the church to "translate" its convictions into a secular idiom, but for the church to open itself to commonalities among groups that differ in their theological convictions.

In this regard, despite his expressed reservations about elements of a pluralist radical democratic politics, Hauerwas's more recent engagement with radical democratic theorists can be read as an attempt to establish tactical alliances with groups that seek to build communities that tend to "common goods and differences."[104] Hauerwas's affirmation of the work of IAF as well as the Student Nonviolent Coordinating Committee (SNCC) is representative of this practice of generous receptivity to others.[105] Furthermore, the type of receptivity and openness encouraged by radical

102. Hauerwas, *Wilderness Wanderings*, 3.

103. Hauerwas, *Wilderness Wanderings*, 2.

104. Hauerwas and Coles, *Christianity, Democracy, and the Radical Ordinary*, 3n4.

105. Hauerwas and Coles, *Christianity, Democracy, and the Radical Ordinary*, 30.

democratic theorists like Coles is consonant with the implications of his nonviolent commitments. As Hauerwas notes, "All genuine politics—that is, politics in the sense of conversation necessary for a people to discover the goods they have in common—are nonviolent. Rather than denying the political, nonviolence requires that we become political by forcing us to listen to the other rather than destroy them."[106] While there could never be an easy alliance between Hauerwas and West, Schüssler Fiorenza, and Ellacuría/Sobrino, Hauerwas's commitment to nonviolence and his turn to radical democracy open lines of dialogue that resonate with Yoder's own attempt to establish tactical alliances with diverse groups in society. Furthermore, Hauerwas's call for Christians to develop the virtues and habits of receptivity necessary to participate in the efforts of IAF and SNCC demonstrates the fact that an alliance with black, feminist, and liberationist Christians on the left is not only desirable but possible.

106. Hauerwas, "On Being a Church Capable of Addressing a World at War," in *Hauerwas Reader*, 454. For a discussion of the significance of this passage, see Herdt, "Truthfulness and Continual Discomfort," 41.

Conclusion: Ekklesial Resistance
and Radical Democracy

ROSA LUXEMBURG FRAMED THE options available to the left in her pamphlet *Reform or Revolution* in 1900, observing that "between social reforms and revolution there exists for social democracy an indissoluble tie. The struggle for reforms is its means: the social revolution, its aim."[1] Although Luxemburg sought to displace the reform-revolution binary it persists as the dominant framework for leftist politics. Later in the twentieth century a third "R" was added to the political lexicon on the left: resistance.[2] Resistance differs from reform and revolution in that it stands against something but often remains agnostic about what it aims to realize. It seeks to contest oppressive political formations and acts of domination but "is neutral with regard to possible political direction."[3]

We have focused on resistance in this work because it is a form of action that enables both reform as well as revolution. Specifically, we have examined Christian thinkers who describe diverse political forms as acts of resistance to empire. Among Christian theologians it is relatively commonplace to advocate for this form of politics of resistance. But this work is novel in that it traces the arguments of Christian thinkers who either directly endorse radical democracy (West, Schüssler Fiorenza, and Hauerwas) or affirm its basic orientation in their political commitments (Ellacuría and Sobrino). And while these thinkers differ in how they describe radical democracy, with some more closely aligned with reformist approaches (West) and others drawing closer to revolutionary approaches (Schüssler Fiorenza, Ellacuría, Sobrino, and Hauerwas), a radical vision of democracy represents the common horizon for their politics.

1. Luxemburg, *Reform or Revolution*, 3.

2. Caygill, *On Resistance*; Douzinas, *Philosophy and Resistance in the Crisis*; Hoy, *Critical Resistance*.

3. Brown, *States of Injury*, 22.

This turn toward radical democracy by a number of prominent North American political theologians is significant in a context in which democracy is under sustained assault from diverse perspectives. For our purposes, we can identify three positions that have emerged in response to this political moment: (1) a centrist defense of liberal democracy, (3) the emergence of the illiberal religious right, and (3) the attempt to radicalize democracy on the left.

The center-left and the center-right have adopted the position that Trump is an aberration in American history and that his disregard for the norms and institutions of liberal democracy represents a singular threat to the stability of the American political experiment. According to this diagnosis, if Trump is defeated in 2020 the course will have been corrected and the promise of American democracy will have been restored. Those who advocate for this position—a position well represented in the crisis of democracy literature in response to the election of Trump—invariably describe populism as the most dangerous challenge to liberal democracy. This has been the position adopted by the political establishment and we find proponents of this view on both the center-left as well as the center-right. The relationship between Yascha Mounk on the center-left and David French on the center-right is representative of the broad-based establishment critique of populism. Where Mounk often serves as the centrist foil for advocates of radical democracy on the left, French has become the *bête noire* of the illiberal right. Unsurprisingly, Mounk has praised French, observing in an article on his participation in a centrist think tank after the election of Trump that if he met French in 2010 or 2015 "we would almost certainly have clashed; to my shame, I suspect that I would have left our encounter writing him off as a bigot or an idiot." But, as both Mounk and French put it, they now share more in common than divides them as a result of their shared concern to defend liberal democracy against its populist adversaries.[4]

The critical question in this context is what it means to defend American liberal democracy against populist political formations on both the left and the right. Mounk's diagnosis is that in the midst of dramatic economic and social upheaval, mainstream "politicians have found it increasingly difficult to sell the message that things are complicated." As a result, an opening has emerged for populists to inveigh against the established political order, to propose simplistic solutions to complex problems, and to mobilize citizens against political elites. Where populists on the left mobilize the people against Wall Street oligarchs, populists on the right utilize a rhetoric of racialized exclusion to assemble whites against

4. Mounk, "The Conversations We Need to Have."

persons of color and foreigners.[5] In response to this situation, Mounk endorses a renewed nationalism—"an inclusive nationalism"—that aims to resist xenophobic nationalism while restoring civic faith among American citizens in the institutions of liberal democracy.[6] This, alongside a few distributive economic policies, serves as the blueprint Mounk offers to those who wish to defend the existing political order and ward off the populist threat to liberal democracy.

Mounk's analysis has been criticized extensively as a defense of elite democracy that fails to acknowledge the very real contradictions of American democracy. For instance, Sam Adler-Bell observes that Mounk's diagnosis comforts elites because it largely exonerates them from any responsibility for the inequality that has played a central role in creating this populist moment.[7] Similarly, Jedediah Britton-Purdy argues that Mounk elides difficult questions about whether the United States has "ever been democratic, and whether the versions of capitalism that have emerged in the last forty years are compatible with democracy." Furthermore, he argues that by focusing on a comparative analysis of populisms around the world (Brexit, Erdoğan, Orban, Bolsonaro, and Trump), Mounk fails to confront the "long-running illiberal, anti-democratic, racist, nativist, and plutocratic strands in American politics."[8] The core complaint voiced by his critics is that Mounk fails to reckon with the structural dynamics that have generated the current political crisis and so responds by offering little more than a slightly reconfigured return to neoliberal-neoconservative hegemony. This approach praises democracy in public but discounts any vision of democracy that demands that the people rather than elites rule. To be sure, proponents of this approach offer a modified form of this hegemony, but their politics serves to extend the fundamental orientation of a politics of bipartisan centrism controlled by elites.

In the first chapter, we traced the ascendency of authoritarian populism in the United States as a revolt against central features of this paradigm. Obviously, a critique of non-elite forms of democracy has been a constant feature of politics on the right (recall here the criticisms of an "excess in democracy" by Samuel Huntington and James Buchanan), but the emergence of

5. Mounk, *People vs. Democracy*, 7.

6. Mounk, *People vs. Democracy*, 214.

7. Adler-Bell, "Yascha Mounk Tells People What They Want to Hear." See also Denvir and Riofrancos, "Zombie Liberalism."

8. Britton-Purdy, "Normcore."

authoritarian populism has led intellectuals on the Christian right to generate sophisticated defenses of an illiberal *and* antidemocratic politics.[9]

In an incisive essay titled "How the Intellectual Right Is Talking Itself into Tearing Down American Democracy," Damon Linker argues that the position adopted by *First Things* magazine is instructive of the transformation of the religious right in the United States over the past forty years.[10] When *First Things* was founded, the editor, Richard John Neuhaus, adopted the rhetoric of Christian conservatives, who argued that a "moral majority" existed in the United States and that this majority had been disempowered by the ruling class of liberal elites. They sought to restore religion to its rightful place in the public sphere by taking back the major institutions of government and implementing a socially conservative vision of American democracy. Neuhaus, as well as other Christian conservatives, argued that the democratic levers of electoral politics were the most effective means to achieve this end. Because Christian conservatives were a majority in the United States, they viewed their task as mobilizing religious communities to vote politicians into office who would reflect their values and implement their vision for American society. Importantly, this position, which largely dominated Christian conservative circles until the election of Obama in 2008, viewed democracy as central to its approach because it represented a means for the majority to realize their vision for society by defeating a liberal minority at the ballot box.

But with Obama's victory as well as a number of cultural and political shifts (most notably shifts concerning LGBTQ rights) over the past decade, Christian conservatives have reassessed their strategy in view of the fact that they no longer possess a majoritarian position in the American electorate. As Linker observes, in this context some Christians have started to talk of their status as a "moral minority," while others have devised strategies for coping with progressive victories by calling for a retreat to countercultural communities (see Rod Dreher's *Benedict Option* as well as Patrick Deneen's *Why Liberalism Failed*).[11] Other religious conservatives who initially offered criticism of Trump's populism have shifted their assessment of his presidency in response to his political victories and their own intensified cultural grievances against the elite liberal order. These thinkers maintain that it is

9. It is not even clear what this new political formation should be named: populist, authoritarian, or fascist. For a discussion of this, see Brown, Gordon, and Pensky, "Introduction: Critical Theory in an Authoritarian Age."

10. Linker, "How the Intellectual Right Is Talking Itself into Tearing Down American Democracy."

11. Dreher, *The Benedict Option*, and Deneen, *Why Liberalism Failed*.

necessary to reject the rules set by the liberal democratic order in order to fight without restraint to defeat secular liberals.

This position has been expressed most forcefully by Sohrab Ahmari in a *First Things* essay, "Against David French-ism," in which he argues that Christian conservatives should reject the reformist conservative project that works within the parameters of liberal democracy and instead fight "the culture war with the aim of defeating the enemy and enjoying the spoils in the form of a public square re-ordered to the common good and ultimately the Highest Good."[12] Ahmari's critique is directed at political liberalism, which he views as an individualistic political project corrosive to attempts to create a social order committed to the highest good and transcendent principles. He observes, "The movement we are up against prizes autonomy above all, too; indeed, its ultimate aim is to give the individual will the widest possible berth to define what is true and good and beautiful, against the authority of tradition." Of particular concern for Ahmari is that within the liberal political order traditional religious communities must accommodate to progressive positions on gay marriage, transgender rights, and a more inclusive immigration policy.[13] For Ahmari, as well as other religious defenders of the illiberal right, reordering the public square to the "Highest Good" seems to function as a euphemism for rolling back women's and LGBTQ rights and limiting immigration in the name of national unity. Because Ahmari and other proponents of this position reject the procedures of liberalism, they argue that Christian conservatives should pursue their project by any means necessary. This shift in tactics is significant because Ahmari effectively advocates for reordering society through illiberal means.[14] In particular, if Christian conservatives wish to defeat feminism, the LGBTQ movement, and multiculturalism, it may be necessary to do so through nondemocratic means because they no longer have the demographic base to achieve victories through electoral means. While still in its formative stages, the intellectual vanguard of the religious right is offering a defense of the illiberal and authoritarian turn on the right.

Each of these options poses obvious problems from the perspective of the analysis in the preceding chapters. The first option, supported by

12. Ahmari, "Against David French-ism."

13. Ahmari, "Against David French-ism." See also Ahmari, "The New American Right." On immigration, see the *First Things* essay entitled "Against the Dead Consensus," which was signed by Ahmari, Deneen, Dreher, and others.

14. While Ahmari provides the intellectual justification for this project of illiberal politics, it is pursued in terms of citizenship restriction, voter disenfranchisement, and immigration restriction. See, for instance, Serwer, "The Illiberal Right Throws a Tantrum."

centrists, seeks to restore normalcy by returning to a slightly modified or reconfigured neoliberal-neoconservative hegemony. The paradox is that this option seeks to restore a political order that generated the political forms that proponents now identify as a grave threat to the American political system. The second option is a sophisticated attempt to defend the illiberal and antidemocratic turn on the right. The illiberal right—particularly in its religious form—provides the legitimating discourse for the implementation of policies without the cultivation of popular support.

The book has reflected on a third possibility: a radical democratic future. Notably, while radical democrats share a common critique of liberal democracy with the illiberal right, they diverge with respect to the alternative they aim to realize. Matthew Sitman puts this point succinctly: "While the right wants to go behind liberalism, the left wants to go *beyond* it."[15] More specifically, where the right seeks to contest the rampant individualism and secularism of the liberal order to return to a premodern cultural framework that restores communal bonds, reaffirms traditional hierarchies, and seeks to order society toward its "Highest Good" (Ahmari), the left seeks to radicalize liberal democracy and to realize more fully liberal democracy's formal aspiration to equality, inclusion, and justice by offering a vision of democracy beyond capitalism, militarism, as well as racial and gendered hierarchies.

It is commonly (and quite accurately) observed that the left devours its own through internecine battles. This book has attempted to militate against this tendency by arguing that the aim of a radical democratic conception of ekklesial politics is to recognize differences between groups and forms of theology *and* to build coalitions or assemblages based upon commitments held in common.[16] In the preceding chapters, we have been careful to examine the very real differences—even disagreements—that exist between distinct trajectories in Christian political theology that advocate for pragmatic (West), transnational (Schüssler Fiorenza), populist (Ellacuría/Sobrino), and postliberal (Hauerwas) forms of radical democracy. For instance, where those on the identity axis of Christian political engagement (Ellacuría, Sobrino, and Hauerwas) challenge the pluralists (West and Schüssler Fiorenza) to offer a more robust theological account of their politics, the pluralists challenge the christologically and ecclesiologically aspirated approaches to engage more fully with theological and secular interlocutors with whom they disagree. As we have argued, the common ground among these diverse

15. Quoted in Adler-Bell, "What's Left of Liberalism?" Emphasis original.

16. Recall that this is Hauerwas's definition of radical democracy as the political act "of tending to common goods and differences." Hauerwas and Coles, *Christianity, Democracy, and the Radical Ordinary*, 3n4.

forms of Christian political engagement is their shared opposition to the politics of empire and their commitment to radical democratic politics.

Christians are rightfully suspicious of endorsing any political form as ultimate and this suspicion is applicable to democracy as well. At the same time, because democracy has served historically as a means for people to rule themselves rather than being ruled by various authoritarian structures—elites (oligarchy), the wealthy (plutocracy), or markets (neoliberalism)—it is preferable to existing alternatives from a Christian perspective. This remains true even in view of the fact that democracy is a political form that is not without ambiguity in that it can be used either to reinforce structures of domination or to support structures of liberation. But when democracy is qualified as "radical" it connotes more than self-rule. It entails a commitment to the values of egalitarianism, peace, and justice. Christians possess both pragmatic as well as substantive reasons for supporting the politics of democracy with this "radical" supplement.

We live in an "interregnum" or a period in which an old order is dying and a new one has yet to be born. There is no guarantee that democracy will emerge victorious from this period of upheaval. The possibility of a democratic future depends on the capacity of diverse groups to come together and demonstrate that alternatives to authoritarianism and right-wing populism exist by helping citizens to imagine an "alternative way of making life with other people."[17] In this book, we have described this alternative as radical democracy, and we have argued that a radical democratic vision for society is consonant with the aims of multiple forms of political theology in North America. It is not necessary to accept the maximalist position articulated by Cornel West—namely, that the future of democracy in America is dependent on the future direction of Christianity in America—to recognize that Christians have a critical role to play in the struggle over the future of democracy. This has been the case historically—Christians have aligned with political movements in order to create a more inclusive and egalitarian society (from abolitionism and the suffragist movement to the civil rights movement)—and it remains true in the present.[18] Our hope in the face of the neoliberal-neoconservative hegemony of the recent past and its mutation into authoritarian populism in the present is that a pluralist assemblage of contemporary Christians will enter the field of democratic struggle and reimagine Christian witness as a politics of resistance to empire.

17. Hall, *Road to Renewal*, 183.

18. Bretherton and Steinmetz-Jenkins, "What Progressives Need to Defeat Trump."

Bibliography

Adler-Bell, Samuel. "What's Left of Liberalism." *The Outline*, July 15, 2019, https://theoutline.com/post/7687/what-is-left-of-liberalism-ahmari-french?zd=1&zi=jn2irpor.

———. "Yascha Mounk Tells People What They Want to Hear." *The Outline*, March 11, 2019, https://theoutline.com/post/7123/yascha-mounk-tells-people-what-they-want-to-hear?zd=1&zi=jvku2t44.

Ahmari, Sohrab. "Against David French-ism." *First Things*, May 2019, https://www.firstthings.com/web-exclusives/2019/05/against-david-french-ism.

———. "The New American Right." *First Things*, October 2019, https://www.firstthings.com/article/2019/10/the-new-american-right.

Alexander, M. Jacqui, and Chandra Talpade Mohanty, eds. *Feminist Genealogies, Colonial Legacies, Democratic Futures*. New York: Routledge, 1996.

Alexander, Michelle. *The New Jim Crow: Mass Incarceration in the Age of Colorblindness*. New York: New Press, 2012.

Anderson, Victor. "The Wrestle of Christ and Culture in Pragmatic Public Theology." *American Journal of Theology & Philosophy* 19 (1998) 135–50.

Arruzza, Cinzia, Tithi Bhattacharya, and Nancy Fraser. *Feminism for the 99%: A Manifesto*. New York: Verso, 2019.

Bacevich, Andrew J. *American Empire: The Realities and Consequences of U.S. Diplomacy*. Cambridge: Harvard University Press, 2002.

———. *The Limits of Power: The End of American Exceptionalism*. New York: Metropolitan, 2008.

———. *The New American Militarism: How Americans Are Seduced by War*. New York: Oxford University Press, 2013.

Barkan, Ross. "The Fascism to Come." *Medium.com*, December 1, 2019, https://medium.com/@RossBarkan/the-fascism-to-come-59933094cb9d.

Bell, Daniel, Jr. *Economy of Desire: Christianity and Capitalism in a Postmodern World*. Grand Rapids: Baker Academic, 2012.

Bessner, Daniel, and Matthew Sparke. "Don't Let His Trade Policy Fool You: Trump Is a Neoliberal." *The Washington Post*, March 22, 2017, https://www.washingtonpost.com/posteverything/wp/2017/03/22/dont-let-his-trade-policy-fool-you-trump-is-a-neoliberal/?utm_term=.53b265foe842.

Botwinick, Aryeh, and William Connolly, eds. *Democracy and Vision: Sheldon Wolin and the Vicissitudes of the Political*. Princeton: Princeton University Press, 2001.

Bretherton, Luke. *Resurrecting Democracy: Faith, Citizenship, and the Politics of a Common Life*. New York: Cambridge University Press, 2014.

Bretherton, Luke, and Daniel Steinmetz-Jenkins. "What Progressives Need to Defeat Trump: Populism and Religion." *The Guardian*, November 24, 2016, https://www.theguardian.com/commentisfree/2018/nov/24/religion-populism-progressives-trump.

Britton-Purdy, Jedediah. "Normcore." *Dissent Magazine*, Summer 2018, https://www.dissentmagazine.org/article/normcore-trump-resistance-books-crisis-of-democracy.

Brown, Wendy. "American Nightmare: Neoliberalism, Neoconservatism, and De-Democratization." *Political Theory* 34 (2006) 690–714.

———. "Apocalyptic Populism." *Eurozine*, August 30, 2017, https://www.eurozine.com/apocalyptic-populism/.

———. "Democracy and Bad Dreams." *Theory & Event* 10 (2007) doi 10.1353/tae.2007.0036.

———. *In the Ruins of Neoliberalism: The Rise of Antidemocratic Politics in the West*. New York: Columbia University Press, 2019.

———. "Interview: Where the Fires Are." Interviewed by Jo Littler. *Soundings* 68 (Spring 2018).

———. "Learning to Love Again: An Interview with Wendy Brown." *Contretemps*, January 6, 2006, http://sydney.edu.au/contretemps/6January2006/brown.pdf.

———. "Neoliberalism's Frankenstein: Authoritarian Freedom in Twenty-First-Century 'Democracies.'" *Critical Times* 1 (2018) 60–79.

———. "Resisting Left Melancholy." *boundary 2* 26 (1999) 19–27.

———. "Sacrificial Citizenship: Neoliberalism, Human Capital, and Austerity Politics." *Constellations* 23 (2016) 3–14.

———. *States of Injury: Power and Freedom in Late Modernity*. Princeton: Princeton University Press, 1995.

———. *Undoing the Demos: Neoliberalism's Stealth Revolution*. New York: Zone Books, 2015.

———. "We're All Democrats Now." In Giorgio Agamben et al., *Democracy in What State?*, 44–58. New York: Columbia University Press, 2011.

Brown, Wendy, Peter E. Gordon, and Max Pensky. "Introduction: Critical Theory in an Authoritarian Age." In *Authoritarianism: Three Inquiries in Critical Theory*, 1–5. Chicago: University of Chicago Press, 2018.

Butler, Judith. *Notes Toward a Performative Theory of Assembly*. Cambridge: Harvard University Press, 2015.

Camp, Jordan T. *Incarcerating the Crisis: Freedom Struggles and the Rise of the Neoliberal State*. Oakland: University of California Press, 2017.

Castelli, Elizabeth A. "The *Ekklesia* of Women and/as Utopian Space: Locating the Work of Elisabeth Schüssler Fiorenza in Feminist Utopian Thought." In *On the Cutting Edge: The Study of Women in Biblical Worlds*, edited by Jane Schaberg, Alice Bach, and Esther Fuchs, 36–52. New York: Continuum, 2004.

Caygill, Howard. *On Resistance: A Philosophy of Defiance*. New York: Bloomsbury Academic, 2015.

Chomsky, Noam. *Hegemony or Survival: America's Quest for Global Dominance*. New York: Holt, 2004.

Clarke, Michael, and Anthony Ricketts. "Donald Trump and American Foreign Policy: The Return of the Jacksonian Tradition." *Comparative Strategy* 36 (2017) 366–79.

Coates, Ta Nehisi. "My President Was Black." *The Atlantic*, January/February 2017, https://www.theatlantic.com/magazine/archive/2017/01/my-president-was-black/508793/

Coles, Romand. *Beyond Gated Politics: Reflections for the Possibility of Democracy.* Minneapolis: University of Minnesota Press, 2005.

———. "Democracy, Theology, and the Question of Excess: A Review of Jeffrey Stout's *Democracy and Tradition.*" *Modern Theology* 21 (2005) 301–21.

———. "Of Tensions and Tricksters: Grassroots Democracy between Theory and Practice." *Perspectives on Politics* 4 (2006) 547–61.

———. *Visionary Pragmatism: Radical and Ecological Democracy in Neoliberal Times.* Durham: Duke University Press, 2016.

Connolly, William E. *Aspirational Fascism: The Struggle for Multifaceted Democracy under Trumpism.* Minneapolis: University of Minnesota Press, 2017.

———. *Christianity and Capitalism: American Style.* Durham: Duke University Press, 2008.

———. "Confronting the Anthropocene and Contesting Neoliberalism: An Interview with William E. Connolly." *New Political Science* 37 (2015) 259–75.

———. "The Ethos of Democratization." In *Laclau: A Critical Reader*, edited by Simon Critchley and Oliver Marchart, 167–81. New York: Routledge, 2004.

———. *The Ethos of Pluralization.* Minneapolis: University of Minnesota Press, 1995.

———. "The Evangelical-Capitalist Resonance Machine." *Political Theory* 33 (2005) 869–86.

———. *Facing the Planetary: Entangled Humanism and the Politics of Swarming.* Durham: Duke University Press, 2017.

———. *The Fragility of Things: Self-Organizing Processes, Neoliberal Fantasies, and Democratic Activism.* Durham: Duke University Press, 2013.

———. *Identity/Difference: Democratic Negotiations of Political Paradox.* Expanded ed. Minneapolis: University of Minnesota Press, 2002.

———. "An Interview with William Connolly." Interviewed by Morton Schoolman and David Campbell. In *The New Pluralism: William Connolly and the Contemporary Global Condition*, edited by David Campbell and Morton Schoolman, 305–37. Durham: Duke University Press, 2008.

———. *Pluralism.* Durham: Duke University Press, 2005.

———. "Trump, the Working Class, and Fascist Rhetoric." *Theory & Event* 20 (January 2017 Supplement) 23–37.

———. *Why I Am Not a Secularist.* Minneapolis: University of Minnesota, 1999.

———. "Wolin, Superpower, and Christianity." *Theory & Event* 10 (2007) doi 10.1353/tae.2007.0038.

———. "A World of Becoming." In *Democracy and Pluralism: The Political Thought of William E. Connolly*, edited by Alan Finlayson, 222–35. New York: Routledge, 2010.

Cooper, Frederick. "Decolonizing Situations: The Rise, Fall, and Rise of Colonial Studies, 1951–2001." *French Politics, Culture & Society* 20 (2002) 47–76.

Cooper, Melinda. *Family Values: Between Neoliberalism and the New Social Conservatism.* New York: Zone Books, 2017.

Crozier, Michael, Samuel Huntington, and Joji Watanuki. *The Crisis of Democracy: Report on the Governability of Democracies to the Trilateral Commission*. New York: New York University Press, 1975.

Davis, Angela Y. *Are Prisons Obsolete?* New York: Seven Stories, 2003.

De La Torre, Miguel. "Stanley Hauerwas on Church." In *Beyond the Pale: Reading Ethics from the Margins*, edited by Stacey M. Floyd-Thomas and Miguel A. De La Torre, 217–24. Louisville: Westminster John Knox, 2011.

Dean, Jodi. *The Communist Horizon*. New York: Verso, 2012.

Deneen, Patrick. *Why Liberalism Failed*. New Haven: Yale University Press, 2019.

Denvir, Daniel, and Thea Riofrancos. "Zombie Liberalism." *N + 1*, August 11, 2018, https://nplusonemag.com/online-only/online-only/zombie-liberalism/.

Dorrien, Gary. *Social Ethics in the Making: Interpreting an American Tradition*. Malden, MA: Wiley-Blackwell, 2011.

Douzinas, Costas. *Philosophy and Resistance in the Crisis: Greece and the Future of Europe*. New York: Polity, 2013.

Dreher, Rod. *The Benedict Option: A Strategy for Christians in a Post-Christian Nation*. New York: Sentinel, 2017.

Drolet, Jean-François. *American Neoconservatism: The Politics and Culture of Reactionary Idealism*. New York: Oxford University Press, 2014.

Dula, Peter. *Cavell, Companionship, and Christian Theology*. New York: Oxford University Press, 2011.

Dussel, Enrique. "The Philosophy of Liberation: An Interview with Enrique Dussel (Part II)." Interviewed by Mahvish Ahmed. *Naked Punch*, May 12, 2013, http://www.nakedpunch.com/articles/193.

———. *Twenty Theses on Politics*. Translated by George Ciccariello-Maher. Durham: Duke University Press, 2008.

Eggemeier, Matthew, and Peter Joseph Fritz. *Send Lazarus: Catholicism and the Crises of Neoliberalism*. New York: Fordham University Press, 2020.

Ellacuría, Ignacio. *Ignacio Ellacuría: Essays on History, Liberation, and Salvation*. Edited by Michael E. Lee. Maryknoll, NY: Orbis, 2013.

———. "The Latin American Quincentenary: Discovery or Cover-Up?" Translated by Margaret D. Wilde. In *Ignacio Ellacuría: Essays on History, Liberation, and Salvation*, edited by Michael E. Lee, 27–38. Maryknoll, NY: Orbis, 2013.

———. "Utopia and Propheticism from Latin America: A Concrete Essay in Historical Soteriology." In *A Grammar of Justice: The Legacy of Ignacio Ellacuría*, edited by J. Matthew Ashley, Kevin F. Burke, and Rodolfo Cardenal, 7–56. Maryknoll, NY: Orbis, 2014.

Errejón, Iñigo, and Chantal Mouffe. *Podemos: In the Name of the People; Iñigo Eerjón in Conversation with Chantal Mouffe*. New York: Lawrence & Wishart, 2016.

Ferguson, Niall. *Colossus: The Rise and Fall of the American Empire*. New York: Penguin, 2005.

Foucault, Michel. *The Birth of Biopolitics: Lectures at the Collège de France, 1978–79*. Edited by Michael Senellart. Translated by Graham Burchell. New York: Picador, 2008.

Fraser, Nancy. "The End of Progressive Neoliberalism." *Dissent* 64 (2017) 130–40.

———. "Feminism, Capitalism, and the Cunning of History." *New Left Review* 56 (2009) 97–117.

————. *Fortunes of Feminism: From State-Managed Capitalism to Neoliberal Crisis.* New York: Verso, 2013.

————. "From Progressive Neoliberalism to Trump—and Beyond." *American Affairs* 1 (2017) 46–64.

————. "How Feminism Became Capitalism's Handmaiden—and How to Reclaim It." *The Guardian*, October 14, 2013, https://www.theguardian.com/commentisfree/2013/oct/14/feminism-capitalist-handmaiden-neoliberal.

————. "Mapping the Feminist Imagination: From Redistribution to Recognition to Representation." *Constellations* 12 (2005) 295–307.

————. *The Old Is Dying and the New Cannot Be Born.* New York: Verso, 2019.

————. *Scales of Justice: Reimagining Political Space in a Globalizing World.* New York: Columbia University Press, 2009.

Friedman, Milton. *Capitalism and Freedom.* 40th anniversary ed. Chicago: University of Chicago Press, 2002.

Fukuyama, Francis. "The End of History." In *The Geopolitics Reader*, edited by Gearóid Ó Tuathail, Simon Dalby, and Paul Routledge, 114–24. New York: Routledge Press, 1998.

Gilmore, Ruth Wilson. *Golden Gulag: Prisons, Surplus, Crisis, and Opposition in Globalizing California.* Berkeley: University of California Press, 2007.

Gonzalez, Mike. *The Ebb of the Pink Tide: The Decline of the Left in Latin America.* Chicago: Pluto, 2018.

Gottschalk, Marie. *Caught: The Prison State and the Lockdown of American Politics.* Princeton: Princeton University Press, 2016.

Gould, Jeffrey L. "Ignacio Ellacuría and the Salvaodorean Revolution." *Journal of Latin American Studies* 47 (2015) 285–315.

Grandin, Greg. *Empire's Workshop: Latin America, the United States, and the Rise of the New Imperialism.* New York: Holt, 2007.

————. *Kissinger's Shadow: The Long Reach of America's Most Controversial Statesman.* New York: Metropolitan/Henry Holt, 2015.

Grewal, Inderpal, and Caren Kaplan, eds. *Scattered Hegemonies: Postmodernity and Transnational Feminist Practices.* Minneapolis: University of Minnesota Press, 1994.

Habermas, Jürgen. *Between Naturalism and Religion: Philosophical Essays.* Translated by Ciaran Cronin. Malden, MA: Polity, 2008.

————. *Religion and Rationality: Essays on Reason, God, and Modernity.* Edited by Eduardo Mendieta. Cambridge: MIT Press, 2002.

Hall, Stuart. *The Hard Road to Renewal: Thatcherism and the New Left.* New York: Verso, 1988.

Hampson, Daphne. *Theology and Feminism.* Oxford: Blackwell, 1990.

Hardt, Michael. "Managing Up: Assembly and the New Activism." *Artforum*, October 2017, https://www.artforum.com/print/201708/managing-up-assembly-and-the-new-activism-71249.

Hardt, Michael, and Antonio Negri. *Assembly.* New York: Oxford University Press, 2017.

————. *Commonwealth.* Cambridge: Belknap Press of Harvard University Press, 2009.

————. *Declaration.* New York: Argo-Navis, 2012.

————. *Empire.* Cambridge: Harvard University Press, 2001.

————. "The Fight for 'Real Democracy' at the Heart of Occupy Wall Street." *Foreign Affairs*, October 11, 2011. https://www.foreignaffairs.com/articles/north-america/2011-10-11/fight-real-democracy-heart-occupy-wall-street.

————. "Globalization and Democracy." In *Implicating Empire*, edited by Stanley Aronowitz and Heather Gautney, 109–21. New York: Basic Books, 2003.

————. *Multitude: War and Democracy in the Age of Empire*. New York: Penguin, 2005.

Harvey, David. *A Brief History of Neoliberalism*. New York: Oxford University Press, 2005.

————. *The Enigma of Capital: And the Crises of Capitalism*. New York: Oxford University Press, 2011.

————. "Neoliberalism Is a Political Project." Interview by Bjarke Skærlund Risager. *Jacobin*, July 26, 2016, https://www.jacobinmag.com/2016/07/david-harvey-neoliberalism-capitalism-labor-crisis-resistance/.

————. *Seventeen Contradictions and the End of Capitalism*. London: Profile Books, 2015.

————. *Spaces of Global Capitalism*. New York: Verso, 2006.

Hauerwas, Stanley. *After Christendom? How the Church Is to Behave if Freedom, Justice, and a Christian Nation Are Bad Ideas*. Nashville: Abingdon, 1991.

————. *A Better Hope: Resources for a Church Confronting Capitalism, Democracy, and Postmodernity*. Grand Rapids: Brazos, 2000.

————. *Christian Existence Today: Essays on Church, World, and Living in Between*. Durham: Labyrinth, 1988.

————. "Church Matters." In *Christian Political Witness*, edited by George Kalantzis and Gregory W. Lee, 17–34. Downers Grove, IL: InterVarsity, 2014.

————. *A Community of Character: Toward a Constructive Christian Ethic*. Notre Dame, IN: University of Notre Dame Press, 1981.

————. "The Dilemma of Martin Luther King Jr." *ABC Religion & Ethics*, December 10, 2010, https://www.abc.net.au/religion/the-dilemma-of-martinluther-king-jr/10101804.

————. *Dispatches from the Front: Theological Engagements with the Secular*. Durham: Duke University Press, 1994.

————. "Failure of Communication *or* a Case of Uncompromising Feminism." *Scottish Journal of Theology* 50 (1997) 228–39.

————. "An Interview with Stanley Hauerwas." Interview by Dan Rhodes. *The Other Journal*, October 10, 2004, https://theotherjournal.com/2004/10/10/an-interview-with-stanley-hauerwas/.

————. *Living Gently in a Violent World: The Prophetic Witness of Weakness*. Downers Grove, IL: InterVarsity, 2008.

————. *Matthew*. Brazos Theological Commentary on the Bible. Grand Rapids: Brazos, 2006.

————. "Pacifism: Some Philosophical Considerations." *Faith and Philosophy* 2 (1985) 99–104.

————. *The Peaceable Kingdom: A Primer in Christian Ethics*. Notre Dame: University of Notre Dame Press, 1983.

————. *Performing the Faith: Bonhoeffer and the Practice of Nonviolence*. Grand Rapids: Brazos, 2004.

————. "Remembering Martin Luther King Jr. Remembering: A Response to Christopher Beem." *Journal of Religious Ethics* 23 (1995) 135–48.

———. "Stanley Hauewas on John Howard Yoder [excerpted from "Messianic Pacifism"]." In *Radical Christian Writings: A Reader*, edited by Andrew Bradstock and Christopher Rowland, 250–54. Malden, MA: Blackwell, 2002.

———. *The State of the University: Academic Knowledge and the Knowledge of God.* Malden, MA: Blackwell, 2007.

———. "Why Community Is Dangerous: An Interview." *Plough Quarterly Magazine*, No. 9 (Summer 2016), https://www.plough.com/en/topics/community/church-community/why-community-is-dangerous.

———. *Wilderness Wanderings: Probing Twentieth-Century Theology and Philosophy.* Boulder, CO: Westview, 1997.

———. "Will the Real Sectarian Please Stand Up?" *Theology Today* 44 (1987) 87–94.

———. *With the Grain of the Universe: The Church's Witness and Natural Theology.* Grand Rapids: Baker Academic, 2001.

———. *The Work of Theology.* Grand Rapids: Eerdmans, 2015.

Hauerwas, Stanley, and Romand Coles. *Christianity, Democracy, and the Radical Ordinary: Conversations between a Radical Democrat and a Christian.* Eugene, OR: Cascade, 2008.

Hauerwas, Stanley, with Robert J. Dean. *Minding the Web: Making Theological Connections.* Eugene, OR: Cascade, 2018.

Hauerwas, Stanley, and Richard John Neuhaus. "Pacifism, Just War & the Gulf: An Exchange." *First Things*, May 1991, https://www.firstthings.com/article/1991/05/pacifism-just-war-the-gulf-an-exchange.

Hauerwas, Stanley, and Jean Vanier. *Living Gently in a Violent World: The Prophetic Witness of Weakness.* Downers Grove, IL: IVP, 2008.

Hauerwas, Stanley, and Samuel Wells. "How the Church Managed before There Was Ethics." In *The Blackwell Companion to Christian Ethics*, edited by Stanley Hauerwas and Samuel Wells, 39–50. Malden, MA: Blackwell, 2004.

Hauerwas, Stanley, and William H. Willimon. *Resident Aliens: Life in the Christian Colony.* Nashville: Abingdon, 1989.

Heer, Jeet. "The Populist Realignment That Never Came." *The New Republic*, February 13, 2018, https://newrepublic.com/article/147050/populist-realignment-never-came.

Heilbrunn, Jacob. "Neocons Paved the Way for Trump: Finally, One Admits It." *Washington Monthly*, November/December 2018, https://washingtonmonthly.com/magazine/november-december-2018/neocons-paved-the-way-for-trump-at-least-max-boot-admits-it/.

Herdt, Jennifer. "Truthfulness and Continual Discomfort." In *The Difference Christ Makes: Celebrating the Life, Work, and Friendship of Stanley Hauerwas*, edited by Charles M. Collier, 25–42. Eugene, OR: Cascade, 2015.

Hinton, Elizabeth. *From the War on Poverty to the War on Crime: The Making of Mass Incarceration in America.* Cambridge: Harvard University Press, 2017.

Hovey, Craig. *Speak Thus: Christian Language in Church and World.* Eugene, OR: Cascade, 2008.

Hoy, David Couzens. *Critical Resistance: From Poststructuralism to Post-Critique.* Cambridge: MIT Press, 2005.

Irigaray, Luce. "Equal to Whom?" In *The Essential Difference*, edited by Naomi Schor and Elizabeth Weed, 63–81. Bloomington: Indiana University Press, 1994.

John Paul II, Pope. *Laborem Exercens.* http://w2.vatican.va/content/john-paul-ii/en/encyclicals/documents/hf_jp-ii_enc_14091981_laborem-exercens.html.

Jones, Daniel Stedman. *Masters of the Universe: Hayek, Friedman, and the Birth of Neoliberalism*. Princeton: Princeton University Press, 2014.

Jones, Paul Dafydd. "Liberation Theology and 'Democratic Futures' (By Way of Karl Barth and Friedrich Schleiermacher)." *Political Theology* 10 (2009) 261–85.

Kagan, Robert. "Neocon Nation: Neoconservatism, c. 1776." *World Affairs* 170 (2008) 13–35.

———. *Of Paradise and Power: America and Europe in the New World Order*. New York: Knopf, 2003.

Kelley, Robin D. G. "What Did Cedric Robinson Mean by Racial Capitalism?" *Boston Review*, January 12, 2017, http://bostonreview.net/race/robin-d-g-kelley-what-did-cedric-robinson-mean-racial-capitalism.

Kinzer, Stephen. *Overthrow: America's Century of Regime Change from Hawaii to Iraq*. New York: Times Books, 2006.

Kirkpatrick, Jeane. "Neoconservatism as a Response to the Counter-Culture." In *The Neocon Reader*, edited by Irwin Stelzer, 233–40. New York: Grove, 2004.

Klein, Naomi. *The Shock Doctrine: The Rise of Disaster Capitalism*. New York: Metropolitan, 2007.

Kotz, David. *The Rise and Fall of Neoliberal Capitalism*. Cambridge: Harvard University Press, 2015.

Kramer, Paul A. "Power and Connection: Imperial Histories of the United States in the World." *The American Historical Review* 116 (2011) 1348–91.

Kriner, Douglas L., and Francis X. Shen. "Battlefield Causalities and Ballot Box Defeat: Did the Bush-Obama Wars Cost Clinton the White House?" June 19, 2017, http://www.forschungsnetzwerk.at/downloadpub/2017_SSRN-id2989040_usa.pdf.

Laclau, Ernesto. "Can Immanence Explain Social Struggles?" *Diacritics* 31 (2001) 2–10.

———. "The Future of Radical Democracy." In *Radical Democracy: Politics between Abundance and Lack*, edited by Lars Tønder and Lasse Thomassen, 256–62. Manchester: Manchester University Press, 2006.

———. "Glimpsing the Future." In *Laclau: A Critical Reader*, edited by Simon Critchley and Oliver Marchart, 279–328. New York: Routledge, 2004.

———. *On Populist Reason*. New York: Verso, 2005.

———. "Populism: What's in a Name?" In *Populism and the Mirror of Democracy*, edited by Francisco Panizza, 32–49. London: Verso, 2005.

———. "Structure, History, and the Political." In *Contingency, Hegemony, and Universality: Contemporary Dialogues on the Left*, edited by Judith Butler, Ernesto Laclau, and Slavoj Žižek, 182–213. New York: Verso, 2000.

Laclau, Ernesto, and Chantal Mouffe. *Hegemony and Socialist Strategy: Toward a Radical Democratic Politics*. New York: Verso, 2014.

Lemke, Thomas. *Biopolitics: An Advanced Introduction*. New York: New York University Press, 2011.

Levitsky, Steven, and Daniel Ziblatt. *How Democracies Die*. New York: Crown, 2018.

Linker, Damon. "How the Intellectual Right Is Talking Itself into Tearing Down American Democracy." *The Week*, June 4, 2019, https://theweek.com/articles/844957/how-intellectual-right-talking-itself-into-tearing-down-american-democracy.

Loewenstein, Antony. *Disaster Capitalism: Making a Killing Out of Catastrophe*. New York: Verso, 2015.

Lopez, German. "Trump Won Because of Racial Resentment." *Vox*, December 5, 2017, https://www.vox.com/identities/2017/12/15/16781222/trump-racism-economic-anxiety-study.

López, Ian Haney. *Dog Whistle Politics: How Coded Racial Appeals Have Reinvented Racism & Wrecked the Middle Class*. New York: Oxford University Press, 2015.

Lowe, Lisa. *The Intimacies of Four Continents*. Durham: Duke University Press, 2015.

Luce, Edward. *The Retreat of Western Liberalism*. New York: Atlantic Monthly Press, 2018.

Luxemburg, Rosa. *Reform or Revolution, and Other Writings*. Introduction by Paul Buhle. Mineola, NY: Dover, 2006.

MacDonald, Michael. *Overreach: Delusions of Regime Change in Iraq*. Cambridge: Harvard University Press, 2014.

MacLean, Nancy. *Democracy in Chains: The Deep History of the Radical Right's Stealth Plan for America*. New York: Viking, 2017.

Mahmood, Saba. "Feminism, Democracy, and Empire: Islam and the War of Terror." In *Women's Studies on the Edge*, edited by Joan Wallach Scott, 81–114. Durham: Duke University Press, 2008.

McElwee, Sean, and Jason McDaniel. "Economic Anxiety Didn't Make People Vote Trump, Racism Did." *The Nation*, May 8, 2017, https://www.thenation.com/article/economic-anxiety-didnt-make-people-vote-trump-racism-did/.

McGill, Andrew. "The Trump Bloc." *The Atlantic*, September 14, 2016, https://www.theatlantic.com/politics/archive/2016/09/dissecting-donald-trumps-support/499739/.

Mead, Walter Russell. "The Jacksonian Revolt: American Populism and the Liberal Order." *Foreign Affairs* 96.2 (March/April 2017).

———. "Trump's Jacksonian Revolt." *The Wall Street Journal*, November 11, 2016.

Milanovic, Branko. *Global Inequality: A New Approach for the Age of Globalization*. Cambridge: Belknap Press of Harvard University Press, 2016.

Milbank, John, and Adrian Pabst. *The Politics of Virtue: Post-Liberalism and the Human Future*. London: Rowman and Littlefield, 2016.

Mirowski, Philip. *Never Let a Serious Crisis Go to Waste: How Neoliberalism Survived the Financial Meltdown*. New York: Verso, 2013.

Mouffe, Chantal. "America in Populist Times: An Interview with Chantal Mouffe." *The Nation*, December 15, 2016, https://www.thenation.com/article/america-in-populist-times-an-interview-with-chantal-mouffe/.

———. *Chantal Mouffe: Hegemony, Radical Democracy, and the Political*. Edited by James Martin. New York: Routledge, 2013.

———. "Democracy Revisited (In Conversation with Chantal Mouffe)." In *The Nightmare of Participation*, edited by Markus Miessen, 105–59. Berlin: Sternberg, 2010.

———. *For a Left Populism*. New York: Verso, 2018.

———. "The Importance of Engaging the State." In *What Is Radical Politics?*, edited by Jonathan Pugh, 230–38. New York: Palgrave Macmillan, 2009.

———. *On the Political*. London: Routledge, 2005.

———. "Radical Democracy or Liberal Democracy?" In *Radical Democracy: Identity, Citizenship, and the State*, edited by David Trend, 19–26. New York: Routledge, 1996.

————. "Religion, Liberal Democracy, and Citizenship." In *Political Theologies: Public Religions in a Post-Secular World*, edited by Hent de Vries and Lawrence Sullivan, 318–26. New York: Fordham University Press, 2006.

————. *Return of the Political*. New York: Verso, 1993.

Mounk, Yascha. "The Conversations We Need to Have." *Slate*, May 23, 2018, https://slate.com/news-and-politics/2018/05/anti-trumpers-on-the-left-and-right-cant-afford-to-shun-one-another-now.html.

————. *The People vs. Democracy: Why Our Freedom Is in Danger & How to Save It*. Cambridge: Harvard University Press, 2018.

Moyn, Samuel. "Beyond Liberal Internationalism." *Dissent*, Winter 2017, 108–14.

Moyn, Samuel, and Stephen Wertheim. "The Infinity War." *The Washington Post*, December 15, 2019, B1–2.

Murakawa, Naomi. *The First Civil Right: How Liberals Built Prison America*. New York: Oxford University Press, 2014.

Muro, Mark, and Sifan Liu. "Another Clinton-Trump Divide: High Output America vs. Low Output America." *The Avenue* (blog), November 29, 2016, https://www.brookings.edu/blog/the-avenue/2016/11/29/another-clinton-trump-divide-high-output-america-vs-low-output-america/.

Newman, Saul. *Postanarchism*. New York: Polity, 2016.

Niebuhr, Reinhold. *The Irony of American History*. Chicago: University of Chicago Press, 2010.

Peck, Jamie. *Constructions of Neoliberal Reason*. New York: Oxford University Press, 2013.

Piketty, Thomas. *Capital in the Twenty-First Century*. Cambridge: Harvard University Press, 2017.

Piven, Frances Fox, and Richard A. Cloward. *Regulating the Poor: The Functions of Public Welfare*. New York: Pantheon, 1971.

Podhoretz, Norman. *The Present Danger*. New York: Simon & Schuster, 1980.

Purcell, Mark. *Recapturing Democracy: Neoliberalization and the Struggle for Alternative Urban Futures*. New York: Routledge, 2008.

Ratzinger, Joseph, and Jürgen Habermas. *The Dialectics of Secularization: On Reason and Religion*. Edited by Florian Schuller. Translated by Brian McNeil. San Francisco: Ignatius, 2006.

Rieger, Joerg, and Kwok Pui-lan. *Occupy Religion: A Theology of the Multitude*. Lanham, MD: Rowman & Littlefield, 2012.

Roberts, David. "Are Trump Supporters Driven by Economic Anxiety and Racial Resentment? Yes." *Vox*, December 30, 2015.

Robinson, Cedric. *Marxism and the Black Radical Tradition*. Chapel Hill: University of North Carolina Press, 2000.

Rosen, Fred. "Introduction." In *Empire and Dissent: The United States and Latin America*, edited by Fred Rosen, 1–20. Durham: Duke University Press, 2008.

Rottenberg, Catherine. *The Rise of Neoliberal Feminism*. New York: Oxford University Press, 2018.

Ruether, Rosemary Radford. "Feminist Theology: Where Is It Going?" *International Journal of Public Theology* 4 (2010) 5–20.

Ryan, Maria. *Neoconservatism and the New American Century*. New York: Palgrave Macmillan, 2010.

Schüssler Fiorenza, Elisabeth. "Articulating a Different Future: An Interview with Elisabeth Schüssler Fiorenza." Interviewed by Caroline Matas. *Harvard Divinity*

School Bulletin, Spring/Summer 2017, https://bulletin.hds.harvard.edu/articles/springsummer2017/articulating-different-future.

———. "The Bible, the Global Context, and the Discipleship of Equals." In *Reconstructing Christian Theology*, edited by Rebecca S. Chopp and Mark Lewis Taylor, 79–98. Minneapolis: Fortress, 1994.

———. *Bread Not Stone: The Challenge of Feminist Biblical Interpretation.* Boston: Beacon, 1984.

———. *But She Said: Feminist Practices of Biblical Interpretation.* Boston: Beacon, 1992.

———. *Changing Horizons: Exploring Feminist Interpretation.* Minneapolis: Fortress, 2013.

———. *Congress of Wo/men: Religion, Gender, and Kyriarchal Power.* Cambridge: Feminist Studies in Religion, 2016.

———. "Critical Feminist The*logy of Liberation: A Decolonizing Political The*logy." In *Political Theology: Contemporary Challenges and Future Directions*, edited by Francis Schüssler Fiorenza, Klaus Tanner, and Michael Welker, 23–35. Louisville: Westminster John Knox, 2013.

———. *Democratizing Biblical Studies: Toward an Emancipatory Educational Space.* Louisville: Westminster John Knox, 2009.

———. *Discipleship of Equals: A Critical Ekklesia-logy of Liberation.* New York: Crossroad, 1998.

———. *Empowering Memory and Movement: Thinking and Working across Borders.* Minneapolis: Fortress, 2014.

———. "Feminist Studies in Religion and the The*logy In-Between Nationalism and Globalization." *Journal of Feminist Studies in Religion* 21 (2005) 111–19.

———. *In Memory of Her: A Feminist Theological Reconstruction of Christian Origins.* New York: Crossroad, 1994.

———. "Introduction: Exploring the Intersections of Race, Gender, Status, and Ethnicity in Early Christian Studies." In *Prejudice and Christian Beginnings: Investigating Race, Gender, and Ethnicity in Early Christian Studies*, edited by Laura Nasrallah and Elisabeth Schüssler Fiorenza, 1–23. Minneapolis: Fortress, 2009.

———. *Jesus and the Politics of Interpretation.* New York: Bloomsbury Academic, 2001.

———. *Jesus: Miriam's Child, Sophia's Prophet.* New York: Continuum, 2004.

———. "The Power of the Word: Charting Critical Global Feminist Biblical Studies." In *Feminist New Testament Studies: Global and Future Perspectives*, edited by Kathleen O'Brien Wicker, Althea Spencer Miller, and Musa W. Dube, 43–62. New York: Palgrave Macmillan, 2005.

———. *The Power of the Word: Scripture and the Rhetoric of Empire.* Minneapolis: Fortress, 2007.

———. "Reading Scripture in the Context of Empire." In *The Bible in the Public Square*, edited by Cynthia Briggs Kittredge, Ellen Bradshaw Aitken, and Jonathan A. Draper, 157–71. Minneapolis: Fortress, 2008.

———. *Rhetoric and Ethic: The Politics of Biblical Studies.* Minneapolis: Fortress, 1999.

———. *Sharing Her Word: Feminist Biblical Interpretation in Context.* Boston: Beacon Press, 1998.

———. *Transforming Vision: Explorations in Feminist Theology.* Minneapolis: Fortress, 2011.

———. "The Will to Choose or to Reject: Continuing Our Critical Work." In *Feminist Interpretation of the Bible*, edited by Letty M. Russell, 125–36. Louisville: Westminster John Knox, 1985.

————. *Wisdom Ways: Introducing Feminist Biblical Interpretation.* Maryknoll, NY: 2001.

Scott, James C. "An Interview with James Scott." *Análise Social,* 207, xlviii (2013), http://analisesocial.ics.ul.pt/documentos/AS_207_f01.pdf.

Serwer, Adam. "The Illiberal Right Throws a Tantrum." *The Atlantic,* June 14, 2019, https://www.theatlantic.com/ideas/archive/2019/06/ahmari-french-orban/591697/.

Singh, Nikhil Pal. *Race and America's Long War.* Oakland: University of California Press, 2017.

Slobodian, Quinn. *Globalists: The End of Empire and the Birth of Neoliberalism.* Cambridge: Harvard University Press, 2018.

Smith, Tony. *A Pact with the Devil: Washington's Bid for World Supremacy and the Betrayal of the American Promise.* New York: Routledge, 2007.

Sobrino, Jon. *Archbishop Romero: Memories and Reflections.* Translated by Robert R. Barr. Maryknoll, NY: Orbis, 1990.

————. *Christ the Liberator: A View from the Victims.* Maryknoll, NY: Orbis, 2001.

————. "Ignacio Ellacuría, the Human Being and the Christian: 'Taking the Crucified People Down from the Cross.'" In *Love That Produces Hope: The Thought of Ignacio Ellacuría,* edited by Kevin F. Burke and Robert Lassalle Klein, 1–66. Collegeville, MN: Liturgical, 2006.

————. *Jesus the Liberator: A Historical-Theological Reading of Jesus of Nazareth.* New York: Burns & Oates, 1994.

————. *No Salvation Outside the Poor: Prophetic-Utopian Essays.* Maryknoll, NY: Orbis, 2008.

————. "On the Way to Healing: Humanizing a 'Gravely Ill World.'" *America Magazine,* November 10, 2014, https://www.americamagazine.org/issue/way-healing.

————. *The Principle of Mercy: Taking the Crucified Down from the Cross.* Maryknoll, NY: Orbis, 1994.

————. *The True Church and the Poor.* Translated by Matthew J. O'Connell. 1984. Reprint, Eugene, OR: Wipf & Stock, 2004.

————. *Where Is God? Earthquake, Terrorism, Barbarity, and Hope.* Translated by Margaret Wilde. Maryknoll, NY: Orbis, 2004.

Springs, Jason A. "The Prophet and the President: Prophetic Rage in the Age of Obama." In *Healthy Conflict in Contemporary American Society: From Enemy to Adversary,* 99–127. Cambridge: Cambridge University Press, 2018.

Springs, Jason, et al. "Pragmatism and Democracy: Assessing Jeffrey Stout's *Democracy and Tradition.*" Edited by Jason Springs. *Journal of the American Academy of Religion* 78 (2010) 1–36. http://citeseerx.ist.psu.edu/viewdoc/download?doi=10.1.1.833.690&rep=rep1&type=pdf.

Stears, Marc. *Demanding Democracy: American Radicals in Search of a New Politics.* Princeton: Princeton University Press, 2010.

Stout, Jeffrey. *Blessed Are the Organized: Grassroots Democracy in America.* Princeton: Princeton University Press, 2010.

————. *Democracy and Tradition.* Princeton: Princeton University Press, 2005.

————. "A Prophetic Church in a Post-Constantinian Age: The Implicit Theology of Cornel West." *Contemporary Pragmatism* 4 (2007) 39–45.

————. "The Spirit of Democracy." *Journal of Religious Ethics* 35 (2007) 3–21.

Streeck, Wolfgang. "The Returned of the Repressed." In *The Great Regression,* edited by Heinrich Geiselberger, 157–72. Malden, MA: Polity, 2017.

Strube, Miriam, and Cornel West. "Pragmatism's Tragicomic Jazzman: A Talk with Cornel West." *Amerikastudien/American Studies* 58 (2013) 291–301.

Tanner, Kathryn. *Theories of Culture: A New Agenda for Theology.* Minneapolis: Fortress, 1997.

Tran, Jonathan. *Foucault and Theology.* New York: T&T Clark, 2011.

Unger, Roberto Mangabeira. *Democracy Realized: The Progressive Alternative.* New York: Verso, 1998.

Unger, Roberto Mangabeira, and Cornel West. *The Future of American Progressivism: An Initiative for Political and Economic Reform.* Boston: Beacon, 2005.

Vaïsse, Justin. *Neoconservatism: The Biography of a Movement.* Translated by Arthur Goldhammer. Cambridge: Harvard University Press, 2010.

Van Houtan, Kyle, and Michael Northcott. "Nature and the Nation-State: Ambivalence, Evil, and American Environmentalism." In *Diversity and Dominion: Dialogues in Ecology, Ethics, and Theology,* edited by Kyle S. Van Houtan and Michael Northcott, 138–56. Eugene, OR: Cascade, 2010.

Wacquant, Loïc. "Class, Race, and Hyperincarceration in Revanchist America." *Daedalus* 139 (2010) 74–90.

———. *Prisons of Poverty.* Expanded ed. Minneapolis: University of Minnesota Press, 2009.

———. *Punishing the Poor: The Neoliberal Government of Social Insecurity.* Durham: Duke University Press, 2009.

Wertheim, Stephen. "Return of the Neocons." *The New York Review of Books,* January 2, 2019, https://www.nybooks.com/daily/2019/01/02/return-of-the-neocons/.

West, Cornel. "Afterword." *Theory & Event* 10 (2007) doi 10.1353/tae.2007.0051.

———. *The American Evasion of Philosophy: A Genealogy of Pragmatism.* Madison: University of Wisconsin Press, 2009.

———. "Black Lives Matter Is an Indictment of Neoliberal Power." Interviewed by George Souvlis. *Truthout,* June 20, 2016, https://truthout.org/articles/cornel-west-black-americans-neoliberal-sleepwalking-is-coming-to-an-end/.

———. *Black Prophetic Fire.* In dialogue with and edited by Christa Buschendorf. Boston: Beacon, 2014.

———. "Black Theology and Marxist Thought." In *Black Theology: A Documentary History,* edited by James H. Cone and Gayraud S. Wilmore, 1:552–67. Maryknoll, NY: Orbis, 1979.

———. "Black Theology of Liberation as Critique of Capitalist Civilization." In *Black Theology: A Documentary History,* edited by James H. Cone and Gayraud S. Wilmore, 2:410–26. 2nd ed. Maryknoll, NY: Orbis, 1993.

———. *The Cornel West Reader.* New York: BasicCivitas Books, 2005.

———. *Democracy Matters: Winning the Fight against Imperialism.* New York: Penguin, 2005.

———. *The Ethical Dimensions of Marxist Thought.* New York: Monthly Review Press, 1991.

———. *Hope on a Tightrope.* New York: Smiley Books, 2008.

———. "An Interview with Cornel West: Empire, Pragmatism, and War." In *Communicative Action: The Logos Interviews,* edited by Amy L. Buzby, 49–64. Lanham, MD: Lexington, 2010.

———. "Introduction: The Radical King We Don't Know." In *The Radical King,* edited by Cornel West, ix–xvi. Boston: Beacon, 2015.

———. *Keeping Faith: Philosophy and Race in America.* New York: Routledge, 1993.

———. "Left Matters: An Interview with Cornel West." Interviewed by John Ehrenberg. *New Political Science* 33 (2011) 357–69.

———. "On Elisabeth Schüssler Fiorenza's *In Memory of Her.*" In *Prophetic Fragments: Illuminations of the Crisis in American Religion and Culture,* 250–56. Grand Rapids: Eerdmans, 1993.

———. "Politics, Virtue, and Struggle: An Interview with Cornel West." *The Other Journal,* August 21, 2009, https://theotherjournal.com/2009/08/21/politics-virtues-and-struggle-an-interview-with-cornel-west/.

———. "Prisoner of Hope in the Night of American Empire: Dialogue with Gabriel Rockhill." In *Politics of Culture and the Spirit of Critique: Dialogues,* edited by Gabriel Rockhill and Alfredo Gómez-Muller, 113–27. New York: Columbia University Press, 2011.

———. *Prophesy Deliverance! An Afro-American Revolutionary Christianity.* Louisville: Westminster John Knox, 2002.

———. *Prophetic Fragments: Illuminations of the Crisis in American Religion and Culture.* Grand Rapids: Eerdmans, 1993.

———. "Prophetic Religion and the Future of Capitalist Civilization." In *The Power of Religion in the Public Sphere,* edited by Eduardo Mendieta and Jonathan VanAntwerpen, 92–100. New York: Columbia University Press, 2011.

———. "Prophetic Theology." In *Prophetic Thought in Postmodern Times.* Monroe, ME: Common Courage, 1993.

———. *Race Matters.* Boston: Beacon, 2001.

———. "Religion and the Left." In *Prophetic Fragments: Illuminations of the Crisis in American Religion and Culture,* 13–21. Grand Rapids: Eerdmans, 1993.

———. "Ta-Nehisi Coates Is the Neoliberal Face of the Black Freedom Struggle." *The Guardian,* December 17, 2017.

———. "Why Brother Bernie Is Better for Black People than Sister Hillary." *Politico Magazine,* February 13, 2016, http://www.politico.com/magazine/story/2016/02/bernie-sanders-african-americans-cornel-west-hillary-clinton-213627.

West, Cornel, with Mehdi Hasan. "Cornel West on Bernie, Trump, and Racism." *The Intercept,* March 7 2019, https://theintercept.com/2019/03/07/cornel-west-on-bernie-trump-and-racism/.

Williams, Marc Eric. *Understanding U.S.-Latin America Relations: Theory and History.* New York: Routledge, 2012.

Wolfe, Patrick. "History and Imperialism: A Century of Theory, from Marx to Postcolonialism." *The American Historical Review* 102 (1997) 388–420.

Wolin, Sheldon. "Democracy: Electoral and Athenian." *Political Science and Politics* 26 (1993) 475–77.

———. *Democracy Incorporated: Managed Democracy and the Specter of Inverted Totalitarianism.* Princeton: University of Princeton Press, 2008.

———. "Fugitive Democracy." In *Fugitive Democracy and Other Essays,* edited by Nicholas Xenos, 100–13. Princeton: Princeton University Press, 2016.

———. *The Presence of the Past: Essays on the State and the Constitution.* Baltimore: Johns Hopkins University Press, 1989.

———. *Politics and Vision: Continuity and Innovation in Western Political Thought.* Princeton: Princeton University Press, 2008.

————. *The Presence of the Past: Essays on the State and the Constitution*. Baltimore: Johns Hopkins University Press, 1990.

————. "What Revolutionary Action Means Today." In *Dimensions of Radical Democracy: Pluralism, Citizenship, Community*, edited by Chantal Mouffe, 240–53. London: Verso, 1992.

Yoder, John Howard. *Christian Attitudes to War, Peace, and Revolution*. Edited by Ted Koontz and Andy Alexis-Baker. Grand Rapids: Brazos, 2009.

————. *For the Nations: Essays Evangelical and Public*. Grand Rapids: Eerdmans, 1997.

————. *Karl Barth and the Problem of War, and Other Essays on Barth*. Edited with a foreword by Mark Thiessen Nation. Eugene, OR: Cascade, 2003.

————. *The Original Revolution: Essays on Christian Pacifism*. 1971. Reprint, Eugene, OR: Wipf & Stock, 1998.

————. *A Pacifist Way of Knowing: John Howard Yoder's Nonviolent Epistemology*. Edited by Christian E. Early and Ted Grimsrud. Eugene, OR: Cascade, 2010.

————. *The Priestly Kingdom: Social Ethics as Gospel*. Notre Dame: University of Notre Dame Press, 1984.

————. *Revolutionary Christian Citizenship*. Harrisonburg, VA: Herald, 2013.

————. *The War of the Lamb: The Ethics of Nonviolence and Peacemaking*. Edited by Glen Stassen, Mark Thiessen Nation, and Matt Hamsher. Grand Rapids: Brazos, 2009.

Žižek, Slavoj. "Holding the Place." In Judith Butler, Ernesto Laclau, and Slavoj Žižek, *Contingency, Hegemony, Universality: Contemporary Dialogues on the Left*, 308–26. New York: Verso, 2011.

————. *Living in the End Times*. New York: Verso, 2011.

————. *The Parallax View*. Cambridge: MIT Press, 2006.

Index